# WISCONSIN'S DOOR COUNTY

THOMAS HUHTI

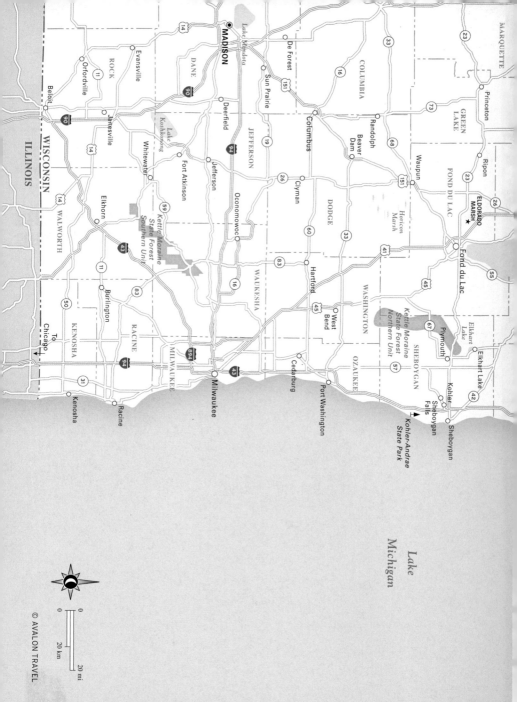

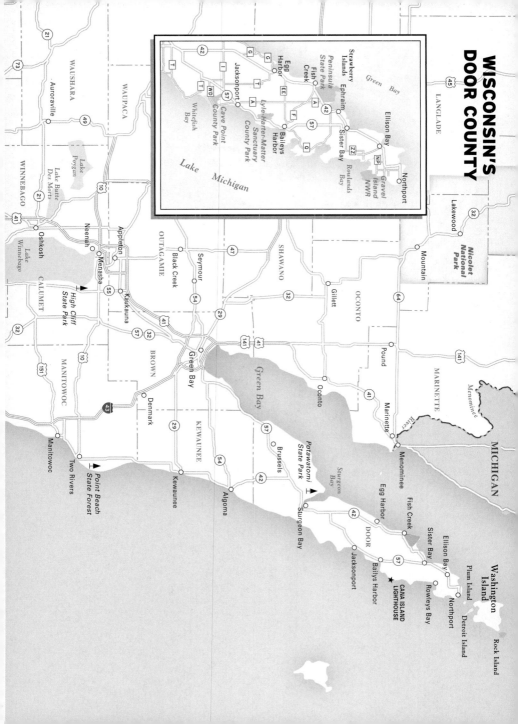

# Contents

DISCOVER

# Wisconsin's Door County

**T**he first Europeans who arrived in Door County viewed this landscape with awe and fear. Calling it "Death's Door" due to the variable weather conditions on Lake Michigan, they didn't realize its touristic magnificence.

Flash-forward a couple of centuries and new immigrants began to appreciate Door County's bounty: rich fish harvests, an equable climate perfect for agriculture, and timber ready-made for shipbuilding.

The secret eventually got out. Today, Door County is a perfectly realized Midwestern escape. You'll find epic seascapes and sculpted sand dunes; vast tracts of cherry blossoms and daffodils; artists colonies and round-the-fire chautauquas; lighthouses and isolated island camping; extraordinary fine dining in villages of less than 500 people; and yes, even one of your greatest chances to land a lunker.

Yet despite its popularity—with tourist numbers rivaling popular national parks—Door County never loses its charm. Farmers atop John Deeres raise a hand in greeting as you pedal past, locals are always willing to offer advice on anything from cherry pie to fishing holes, and quaint hasn't been forsaken for upscale.

Open the door and you'll find endless opportunities for adventure, fellowship, and even solitude. Step outside.

**Clockwise from top left:** Ice Age National Scenic Trail; Foxglove Inn in Sturgeon Bay; Cana Island Lighthouse; Sherwood Point Lighthouse; Norwegian church on Washington Island; Door County's shoreline.

# Planning Your Trip

## Where to Go

### Door County

Door County's most popular draw is the magnificent scenery along its nearly 300 miles of Great Lakes coastline, and the big three beautiful state parks—**Potawatomi, Peninsula,** and **Newport.** Bike, hike, boat, or fish, and visit the country's largest concentration of **lighthouses.** Several of the Door's villages are delightfully quaint. Find a historic hotel, a plush B&B, or a rustic cabin, and for sustenance, organic locally grown beef or, for traditionalists, a fish boil. For the more intrepid, off the northern tip of the county is time-locked **Washington Island,** and beyond that, another jewel in **Rock Island State Park,** the most superb camping spot in Wisconsin.

### East-Central Waters

These waters truly made the state, welcoming legions of immigrants and floating timber for paper mills of the **Fox Cities,** dominated by **Lake Winnebago.** To the west are picturesque resort lands as well as the wild and wonderful **Wolf River.** The heart and soul of the region is the football mecca Green Bay and **Lambeau Field,** home of the Packers football team.

### Wisconsin Gateways

This gateway region welcomes many travelers coming from Chicago. **Milwaukee** has a fabulous **art museum, Miller Beer, Harley-Davidson,** and one of the best summer festivals in the country, **Summerfest.** Extraordinary museums and parks await in **Kenosha** and **Racine,** the latter also home to architecture by Badger State native **Frank Lloyd Wright.**

# Know Before You Go

## When to Go

The droves of travelers begin arriving in **early-mid-May** to see the blossoms; then from **Memorial Day to Labor Day** there are so many visitors here that the bedrock likely sinks an inch or two. Another friendly invasion takes place at the end of **September** through the middle of **October**—leaf peepers love the Door. Remember that prices rise dramatically during these peak seasons. A nice time to visit is in September, just after Labor Day. The weather is beautiful, there are few other visitors, and prices as well as insect numbers are lower. Some find winter lovely and enjoy skiing or snowshoeing in the empty parks; others find it too cold and annoying that half the county's businesses have closed for the season. The least desirable season is **March,** when a visit is ill advised. It's cold, windy, cloudy, and muddy.

## What to Pack

You can buy almost anything you need in Door County, even in the village outposts. This does not include technology; the availability of tech supplies is severely limited. Don't get caught without **mosquito repellent** in the warmer months.

Heels, ties, and skirts are fine for a few places in Door County, but you'll stand out in all but the most chichi restaurants, so feel free to dress **casual.** Sweatshirts are perfectly fine in supper clubs. Dress appropriately for the weather at all times—that includes wearing a hat. Do not come in winter without a good pair of **gloves or mittens.** Arctic-grade mittens are something you'll be grateful for on a sleigh ride or while you wait for a tow truck. A good pair of **boots** is also a necessity in winter; some people carry a heavy-duty pair in the car at all times in case of emergency.

Given the state's somewhat iffy weather, it's paramount to prepare your car for any possibility by **winterizing your vehicle.** Carry an emergency kit with booster cables, sand, or gravel (in a pinch, try sandpaper strips), flares, candles, matches, a shovel and scraper, a flashlight and extra batteries, blankets (space blankets are excellent), extra heavy clothing, high-calorie nonperishable food, and anything else you might need if you have to spend the night in a snow bank. I cannot emphasize enough how important it is.

Flowers bloom throughout Wisconsin in spring.

Ephraim

# The Best of Door County

At only 45 miles from one end to the other, Door County is misleadingly runty if you're looking at a map. While you could hit all of the highlights in a weekend, a week-long trip would allow for more relaxed exploring.

## Day 1
Start in **Sturgeon Bay,** learning about the history of shipping and shipbuilding at the **Maritime Museum.** Head to **Potawatomi State Park** to get outdoors and get the blood moving after the drive up the day before.

## Day 2
It's time for the bay side. Avoid the congested state highway and head northward to walk along the harbor side or browse the shops in **Egg Harbor** before strolling through the historic downtown of **Fish Creek** and sampling a trail in **Peninsula State Park.** Head to **Ephraim** and secure your lodging. A great way to relax is to watch the sun go down on **South Shore Pier.**

## Day 3
Head to **Washington Island** for a lovely day trip without your car. Park it in Gills Rock in the morning and take a bicycle over (or rent one there). You can take in virtually all of the sights in a day before hopping the ferry back and over-nighting in **Baileys Harbor.**

## Day 4
Take a casual drive down the lake side to **The Ridges Sanctuary** and **Cana Island Lighthouse** near Baileys Harbor. Afterward, jump in the car for a short drive south to sit atop the dunes and take pictures of sea caves at **Whitefish Dunes State Park.**

## With More Time
There are many other sightseeing and recreational options to extend your trip by two or three days.

### IN DOOR COUNTY

Try the hiking or bicycling at **Newport State Park,** the last vestige of untouched wilderness in the county. At some point you may want to get on the water; top picks are either kayaking around **Peninsula State Park,** taking a tugboat cruise of the county out of **Sturgeon Bay,** or hiring a fishing charter out of **Baileys Harbor.** Isolated **Rock Island State Park** is as far from anywhere as you can get in the county and offers some of the best camping in the state.

### FARTHER AFIELD

To understand the region's dominant religion, visit **Green Bay** to learn everything there is to know about the Green Bay Packers professional football team and take in a game.

The **Fox Cities** are worth a day for the region's history of paper-making along with Harry Houdini at the **History Museum at the Castle,** which includes the fabulous A.KA. Houdini exhibit, and **Oshkosh** for the nation's premier aircraft museum, the **EAA AirVenture Museum.**

Another day could be spent snapping pictures of **Point Beach State Forest's lighthouse** before learning about the crucial part that **Manitowoc** has played in shipbuilding at the **Wisconsin Maritime Museum.**

# Outdoor Adventures

## Fishing

- **Guided trips:** Travelers to the county who want to wet a line generally head to **Sturgeon Bay** and **Baileys Harbor** to take a guided fishing trip onto Lake Michigan for some salmon or lake trout fishing. You can't beat charter operators here, which rival even Milwaukee for fish taken.

- **On your own:** Head to the **Sturgeon Bay Ship Canal** to try tossing your own line. You can also land salmon and trout along here starting in May.

- **Smallmouth bass fishing:** Sturgeon Bay and **Detroit Harbor on Washington Island** have some of the country's best smallmouth bass fishing, no exaggeration, and these are two great places to catch a trophy.

- **On a budget:** Travelers on a budget or leery of Lake Michigan swells have an excellent opportunity for a middle ground of fishing at **Baileys Harbor.** Guided kayak fishing tours are available.

- **Ice fishing:** You can't really say you've experienced all of Wisconsin until you've stamped your feet for hours inside a shanty fishing for whitefish, northern pike, or walleye. Head to **Green Bay or Sturgeon Bay** for the best ice

fishing around and check http://icefishdoorcounty.com for shack rental opportunities and fully-guided trips.

## Hiking

- **Potawatomi State Park:** The 3.6-mile **Tower Trail** has great lakeside scenery and a commanding view of the sunset from its fire lookout tower, but you may want to hike along the bay on the first three miles of the **Ice Age National Scenic Trail.**

- **Whitefish Dunes State Park:** The 2.8-mile **Red Trail** has outstanding dune-scape topography; alternately, take the 2.5-mile **Black Trail** to extraordinary sea caves.

- **Peninsula State Park:** The aptly named 10-mile **Sunset Trail** is a mixed-use trail with commanding views.

- **Baileys Harbor:** The **Ridges Sanctuary** has myriad nature trails through 1,000 acres of what the U.S. Department of the Interior has described as one of the most ecologically precious in the nation.

- **Newport State Park:** The seven-mile **Europe Bay/Hotz Trail** leads into the last remaining true wilderness in the county at the

## FISH

### Fish Boils

The fish boil is the requisite Door County culinary experience—revered by some with religious devotion. For more on fish boils, see page 58.

- **The Viking Grill** in Ellison Bay is credited with being the first to hit on the idea, and it's still an awesome experience.

- **Pelletier's** in Fish Creek is a larger venue appropriate for large groups or families.

### Lake Perch, Walleye, and Lawyers

Perch, the perennial fish fry favorite, has a mild, sweet flavor. Walleye, the most common fish in Wisconsin's waters, has slightly dry flesh and it can taste like chicken. A lawyer, more properly known as a burbot, is a freshwater cod-like fish that you'll find only in Door County.

- Try fresh lake perch and walleye broiled or pan-fried at the **Bluefront Café** in Sturgeon Bay.

- Head to Washington Island and order a lawyer at **KK Fiske.**

- For a fine dining experience, everyone will tell you to get the fish at **Chop** in Sister Bay.

- If you're looking for casual fare, however, try the **Cornerstone Pub** or **Harbor Fish Market and Grille** in Baileys Harbor.

## CHERRIES

There will be cherries no matter where you go in Door County, but Fish Creek is the cherry on top, so to speak. For more on cherries, see page 47.

- *Good Morning America* dubbed the cherry-stuffed french toast at Fish Creek's **White Gull Inn** the best breakfast in America.

- Pick-your-own cherries during harvest season at **Lautenbach's Orchard Country Winery & Market** in Fish Creek.

- Fish Creek's **Wild Tomato** may be famous for pizza, but its cherry walnut salad is simply divine.

Door County cherries

- The cherry glazed roast duck at **Alexander's** in Fish Creek is the perfect pairing of sweet and savory.

## CHEESE

- In Egg Harbor, one of the best uses of Wisconsin cheese is the Spanish mac and cheese at **Parador.**

- In Sister Bay, **Door County Creamery** specializes in organic goat cheese, but they also make organic, locally-sourced cow's milk cheese.

## FINE DINING

- Try **The Whistling Swan** in Fish Creek for gorgeous, seasonal entrees with local game, fish, and produce.

- Locavores will also adore the harvest dinners at **Wickman House** in Ellison Bay.

Rock Island State Park

kayaking along Door County's shoreline

only designated wilderness park in the state, and for a reward, you get magnificent lake views.

- **Rock Island State Park:** The effort of taking two ferries to get here is balanced by the reward of sublime isolation and a five-mile loop trail passing lighthouses and innumerable commanding views of Lake Michigan.

## Biking

- **Peninsula State Park:** The 10-mile **Sunset Trail** is a favorite Door County trail; it's aptly named, with lovely sunset views.
- **Newport State Park:** Off-roading is best here; it's isolated and challenging but not death-defying. The top choice is the **Europe Bay/Hotz Trail,** which leads to a promontory overlooking Lake Michigan.
- **Potawatomi State Park:** Eight miles on its bicycle-only trail takes you through woods and meadows and along ridges as well as a rocky shoreline before rewarding you with views of Green Bay from high atop a bluff.

- **Highway B:** On this road in Door County, pretty much everything is lovely, but the stretch of county road from Sturgeon Bay to Egg Harbor is unbeatable, running right above the water.
- **Highway T:** This county road departs Sturgeon Bay and leads to Whitefish Bay along a Wisconsin Rustic Road. Enjoy tunnels of trees, a lighthouse, and epic dunes.

## Kayaking and Canoeing

- **Baileys Harbor:** At **Kangaroo Lake** you'll find the easiest and most stress-free paddling; in fact, most use a canoe to explore the Nature Conservancy-protected lake, a crucial waterfowl area home to rare ecosystems. Should you wish to go out on **Lake Michigan,** do it with a guided tour to be safe. A great option is a glass-bottomed kayak tour out of Baileys Harbor.
- **Peninsula State Park:** Virtually anyone can kayak to **Horseshoe Island** and hop out to scramble along its short trail.
- **Potawatomi State Park:** Island-hop the protected bay, which is dotted with islands.

## Camping

- **Newport State Park:** It's hike-in, cycle-in, or canoe-in camping only here at the state's only designated wilderness park; you can't beat it.

- **Rock Island State Park:** Second to Newport State Park, Rock Island is as far as you can go on the Door Peninsula. There's always a refreshing breeze at the beach-side campground.

- **Peninsula State Park:** It gets more visitors than Yellowstone National Park, yet you can find your own solitude. Go for North Nicolet Bay, which is smaller and has no electricity.

- **Potawatomi State Park:** The sites are close to each other, but go for even numbered sites (against a cliff for some solitude) and you'll be all right. There's even a camping cabin.

- **Rowleys Bay:** There are many sites and top-notch facilities in a lovely setting along the bay at **Rowleys Bay Resort.** A separate tent area features three isolated tent sites. There is an excellent private campground, and you can even rent a yurt.

## Wreck Diving

- The icy waters of **Green Bay** and **Lake Michigan,** particularly near Potawatomi State Park and Baileys Harbor, have preserved numerous wrecks. Lakeshore Adventures or Dark Side Charters will take you to the best diving sites.

an aerial view of Potawatomi State Park

# Sunrises and Sunsets

Visit the Lake Michigan side of Door County for the best sunrises and the Green Bay side for the best sunsets. The northern tips of **Washington Island** and **Rock Island State Park** have the best of both.

## SUNRISES

- A favorite sunrise is along the shoreline at **Newport State Park** on the **Europe Bay/ Hotz Trail.**

- A close second is at **Whitefish Dunes State Park** because of its reflections off the mocha dunes on the beach.

## SUNSETS

- The **Sunset Trail** at **Peninsula State Park** rarely disappoints for a favorite Door County sunset.

- South of **Ellison Bay,** a couple of turnoffs for a county park offer superb sunsets too.

a sunset on Washington Island

# The Best Places to Stay

Door County, like the rest of Wisconsin, is a place where you generally deal directly with the proprietors of your lodging rather than with a centralized agency. Showing up unannounced on a summer Friday and hoping to get a room may be possible, although the options will be very limited, and you may have to drive around to find a vacancy. Each city or village has a visitors information kiosk, a few of which even have computerized lists with up-to-the-minute details on room availability.

## Cabins and Cottages

Most of the cabins and cottages in Door County are much more comfortable than typical rustic lodgings, with private baths, heat, cooking facilities, and other standard amenities. These are on the lower end but still cozy.

- There's a reason folks have been returning to **Robertson's Cottages** in Sturgeon Bay: It's quaint, offers friendly service, and has the perfect location on a peninsula near Potawatomi State Park.

- The rustic and cheery **Sunset Motel and Cottages** in Baileys Harbor have the plus of being dog-friendly.

- The traditional **Fish Creek Motel and Cottages** are also charmingly traditional and very clean.

- **Gibson's West Harbor Resort and Cottages** on Washington Island features top-notch but very rustic traditional cottages.

## Motels

Even though Door County is a relaxing getaway, it has also been a fishing and hunting ground for three centuries. For every antiques shopper there is an angler or a hunter. Remember that in the more basic motels you will hear these folks loading their gear and heading out before sunrise.

- The quaint boutique motel **Holiday Music Motel** in Sturgeon Bay is also a music studio, owned in part by musician Jackson Browne.
- The **Beachfront Inn** in Baileys Harbor offers pet-friendly accommodations, nice grounds to build fires and mingle with other guests, and helpful management.
- The **Lullabi Inn** in Egg Harbor is one of the friendliest lodgings around.
- **Julie's** in Fish Creek has great guest rooms and friendly staff, welcomes pets, and is one of the best places to eat on a budget in the county.

## Bed-and-Breakfasts and Historic Inns

If there's a Door County specialty, this is it: B&Bs have been established in every type of habitable dwelling, including lighthouses, sheep farms, and gingerbread Victorian homes. A couple of historic structures were even skidded over the ice to relocate them here.

- Top-notch for a balance of old and new and with extraordinarily gracious owners are **Black Walnut Guest House** and **Foxglove Inn** in Sturgeon Bay.

- **Lodgings at Pioneer Lane** in Ephraim also balance the past and present with the tastefully redone accommodations with a nod to its historical roots.
- Fish Creek takes the top prize for historic structures turned lush guest lodgings at both the **White Gull Inn**, welcoming guests since 1897, and **The Whistling Swan**, so precious it was relocated here in 1907, as its stately presence perfectly matched the picture-postcard quality of Fish Creek.

## Resorts

The word "resort" is used loosely in Door County. It could mean simply extra-large hotel grounds with a pool, or it could be a hotel with its own golf course. It may have guest rooms only, or it may have guest rooms, suites, or cabins. Egg Harbor and Sister Bay have the most resorts.

- The large but still cozy and impeccably well-run **Newport Resort** in Egg Harbor is good for families or couples.
- The **Country House Resort,** on more than 16 acres in Sister Bay, has 1,000 feet of its own shoreline and guest rooms with ocean views.
- One of the granddaddies of the old-style resort days is the 1920s **Gordon Lodge,** near Baileys Harbor, which has the most superb location in the county, jutting out on a promontory and offering villas right atop the water.
- The venerable **Glidden Lodge** is recommended for its absolute isolation, excellent dining, and amazing sunrises.

# Door County

Look for ★ to find recommended
sights, activities, dining, and lodging.

# Highlights

★ **Potawatomi State Park:** Hike the first miles of Wisconsin's epic 1,200-mile Ice Age Trail and overlook the historic waterways of the Door—all from a high perch atop the Niagara Escarpment (page 31).

★ **Whitefish Dunes State Park and Cave Point County Park:** Trek to the beach to check out the dunes and wildlife and then visit Cave Point's eponymous caves (page 33).

★ **Scenic Boat Tours:** See Door County's incredible coastline from offshore (page 38).

★ **The Ridges Sanctuary and Cana Island Lighthouse:** This beloved sanctuary is a must for birders and wildlife lovers. It also contains the grand, brilliantly white lighthouse (page 39).

★ **Newport State Park:** Outdoor aficionados make pilgrimages to this preserved wilderness for its pack-in campsites and off-road biking (page 41).

★ **Fish Creek:** Experience the "soul of Door County" by strolling through the village's historic buildings, taking a tour of a local winery, or seeing a play at the Northern Sky Theater (page 46).

★ **Door County's Cherries:** Whether you pick-your-own or taste them in a slice of warm pie, Door County's cherries are not to be missed, especially during harvest season in mid-July to early August (page 47).

★ **Peninsula State Park:** Bike the Sunset Trail or kayak to Horseshoe Island in this picturesque park, which has visitor numbers rivaling Yellowstone (page 50).

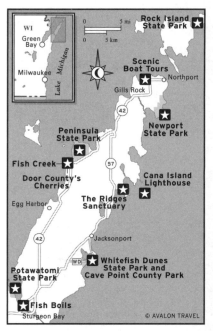

★ **Fish Boils:** You haven't experienced Door County until you've attended a fish boil, preferably on a chilly fall evening (page 58).

★ **Rock Island State Park:** This unparalleled getaway spot is as far as you can get from anywhere else in Door County. The beachside campsites make this park one of the best escapes in the state (page 67).

**H**old your left hand up for a moment, palm out. The thumb is, as the Depression-era WPA Wisconsin guidebook put it, "the spout...of the Wisconsin teakettle." That's the Door Peninsula. Today, Door County is being called the "Cape Cod of the Midwest," the "California of the North," and other silly likenings. Comparisons to Yankee seaside villages don't wholly miss the mark, although in spots the area seems just as much like chilled, stony Norwegian fjords.

Bays in all the colors of an artist's palette are surrounded by variegated shoreline: 250 miles (more than any other U.S. county) of alternately rocky beaches, craggy bluffs, blossom-choked orchards, bucolic heath, and meadows. Door County's established parkland acreage (state, county, and municipal) is staggering, considering its size. Generation upon generation of shipbuilders, fishers, and farmers have benefited from the magical microclimate here, and there's a predisposition within the populace not to get worked up about much.

## HISTORY

Human habitation at what is today Whitefish Dunes State Park dates back to 100 BC, based on traces of the North Bay people, who spread from the mouth of the bay all the way to Rock Island. Woodland Indians arrived in the mid-1600s, when hostile large-scale Iroquois expansion in Acadia forced the Hurons to flee. They likely arrived on Rock Island, which had been populated by Potawatomi, who would later return only to be displaced by the Europeans. With the aid of Winnebago and Ottawa people, one of the largest ramparts in the New World was constructed on Rock Island to repel Iroquois invaders. The U.S. government would later forcibly evict the Potawatomi from Rock Island so lumber workers could enter.

In the late 17th century on Washington

---

**Previous:** Potawatomi State Park; Rock Island State Park. **Above:** Cave Point County Park.

# Door County

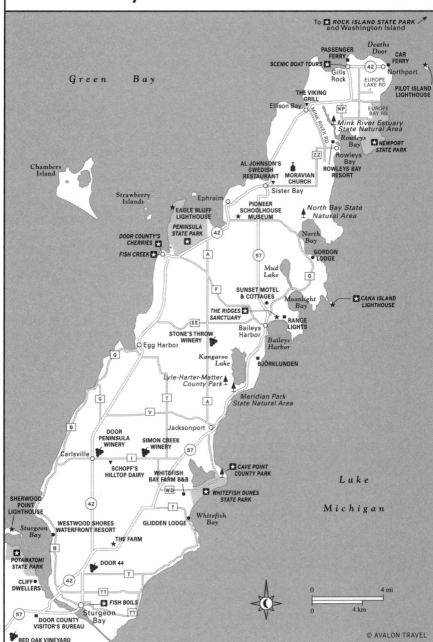

Green Bay

To ★ ROCK ISLAND STATE PARK
and Washington Island

*Deaths Door*

PASSENGER FERRY
SCENIC BOAT TOURS ★
Gills Rock

CAR FERRY
Northport
42

EUROPE LAKE RD
PILOT ISLAND LIGHTHOUSE

THE VIKING GRILL
Ellison Bay
MINK RIVER RD

NP

EUROPE BAY RD

*Mink River Estuary State Natural Area*

*Rowleys Bay*
Rowleys Bay

★ NEWPORT STATE PARK

ZZ

AL JOHNSON'S SWEDISH RESTAURANT
MORAVIAN CHURCH
Sister Bay

Rowleys Bay
ROWLEYS BAY RESORT

Chambers Island

*Strawberry Islands*

Ephraim

EAGLE BLUFF LIGHTHOUSE
PENINSULA STATE PARK

PIONEER SCHOOLHOUSE MUSEUM

*North Bay State Natural Area*

*North Bay*

DOOR COUNTY'S CHERRIES ★
FISH CREEK ★

42

A

57

*Mud Lake*

GORDON LODGE

Q

F

SUNSET MOTEL & COTTAGES

*Moonlight Bay*

★ CANA ISLAND LIGHTHOUSE

THE RIDGES ★ SANCTUARY

EE

STONE'S THROW WINERY

RANGE LIGHTS

Baileys Harbor

*Baileys Harbor*

Egg Harbor

G

*Kangaroo Lake*

BJÖRKLUNDEN

*Lyle-Harter-Matter County Park*

G

T

A

*Meridian Park State Natural Area*

B

V

Jacksonport

DOOR PENINSULA WINERY
SIMON CREEK WINERY

57

Carlsville

I

SCHOPF'S HILLTOP DAIRY

WHITEFISH BAY FARM B&B

★ CAVE POINT COUNTY PARK

*Lake Michigan*

WD

★ WHITEFISH DUNES STATE PARK

SHERWOOD POINT LIGHTHOUSE

42

WESTWOOD SHORES WATERFRONT RESORT

GLIDDEN LODGE

T

*Whitefish Bay*

★ *Sturgeon Bay*

THE FARM

B

★ POTAWATOMI STATE PARK

DOOR 44

T

CLIFF DWELLERS

42

TT

★ FISH BOILS

TT

57
DOOR COUNTY VISITOR'S BUREAU
★ RED OAK VINEYARD

Sturgeon Bay

0        4 mi
0        4 km

© AVALON TRAVEL

# Door County Driving Distances

## TO THE DOOR

- **Chicago–Sturgeon Bay:** 231 miles (4.5 hours)
- **Milwaukee–Sturgeon Bay:** 145 miles (2.75 hours)
- **Madison–Sturgeon Bay:** 184 miles (3.75 hours)

## WITHIN THE DOOR (LAKESIDE)

- **Sturgeon Bay–Jacksonport:** 15.4 miles
- **Jacksonport–Baileys Harbor:** 7 miles
- **Baileys Harbor–Rowleys Bay:** 15.5 miles
- **Rowleys Bay–Gills Rock:** 7.5 miles

## WITHIN THE DOOR (BAYSIDE)

- **Sturgeon Bay–Egg Harbor:** 19 miles
- **Egg Harbor–Fish Creek:** 6 miles
- **Fish Creek–Ephraim:** 5 miles
- **Ephraim–Sister Bay:** 4.3 miles
- **Sister Bay–Ellison Bay:** 5.6 miles
- **Ellison Bay–Gills Rock:** 3.9 miles

Island, the Potawatomi initiated commercial operations with Pierre Esprit Radisson, who considered the island one of his favorite sites in all New France.

Fishers were the first to occupy most points along the Lake Michigan coast, including Rock and Washington Islands. Some of the largest fish ever caught on Lake Michigan were landed off Rock Island. These fishing communities, which also began commercial shipping and shipbuilding, cemented the regional economy in the 1830s. Sturgeon Bay was always a smaller shipbuilding center than Manitowoc, farther south, but it was still one of the major facilities on Lake Michigan.

## GEOLOGY

Limestone bedrock rises 220 feet out of Lake Michigan; it's part of the same **Niagara Escarpment** that stretches south to Lake Winnebago and east all the way to Niagara Falls. Eons of waves have carved rough sea caves into the multihued red and smoky black cliffs. The shores on the western side of Green Bay are dramatically different—mostly low-slung topography crawling toward the shore through marsh or beach.

At the tip of the peninsula is the only major gap in the escarpment, **Porte des Mortes,** the fabled "Door of Death"—so named by early French explorers. The ferocious local climate has devoured hundreds of ships here. Accounts vary wildly regarding which tragedy gave rise to the name, but all are remarkably harrowing. Most accounts point to a band of 300 to 500 Potawatomi—some say Winnebago— who were dashed against rocks. Before the advent of modern navigation and large diesel-driven screws, most ships could not overcome the shifting currents, conflicting wind shears, and shoals.

## PLANNING YOUR TIME

The opposite of an undiscovered gem, Door County is Wisconsin tourism. It's a quintessential weekend escape that can be stretched into a battery-recharging week. If possible, try to schedule your arrival during the lovely blossom season, beginning in late April or early May, during an open-lighthouse period (generally concurrent with the blossoms), or during the fall to leaf-peep.

Choose one location as a base of operations—**Sturgeon Bay,** for less driving time when leaving, or **Fish Creek,** for its central location and because it's so darn cute. The county is also set up so that you can go up one side and return along the other. The best route is to go up the more congested bay side and to return along the more subdued lake side. And don't forgo the somewhat overlooked **Washington Island,** which itself leads to must-see **Rock Island.**

It's best to start at Sturgeon Bay, then travel to Egg Harbor/Fish Creek, Ephraim/Sister Bay, Ellison Bay/Gills Rock, Washington Island/Rock Island, and Baileys Harbor, allotting a day for each place, then return to Sturgeon Bay.

# Sturgeon Bay

The anadromous leviathans for which Door County's gateway community is named once crowded the harbor waters in such plenitude that ships would literally run aground on heaps of them.

Whether or not Sturgeon Bay is the heart and soul of the county is debated, but it lies at a most strategic location: It was used for eons by Native Americans as a portage point. When the 6,600-foot-long canal was blasted, chiseled, hacked, and dug through to link the bay with Lake Michigan in the 19th century, the town of Sturgeon Bay was set. Besides the shipbuilding, most of the county's cherries are processed here.

The genuine graciousness of the people is palpable. Sturgeon Bay was voted Wisconsin's Friendliest Small Town by those who really know—the readers of *Wisconsin Trails* magazine. The town was also the only inland town to make the top 10 Happiest Coastal Communities list of *Coastal Living* magazine in 2016.

## SIGHTS

Pick up a map for a wondrous **National Register Walking Tour** of Sturgeon Bay,

which details more than 100 neighborhood edifices. Another favorite freebie is to wander north of downtown to **Bay Shipbuilding**—a great place to see behemoth vessels as they're being launched or brought in for repair. You can't enter the grounds, but you can still get some good views from outside.

There is also lovely scenery along Lake Forest Road and Highways T and TT east of town.

## Lighthouses

Door County has more lighthouses than any other county in the United States. Starting in 1836 with Rock Island and in 1858 on Pilot Island, which can be visited only on the water, 10 lighthouses were constructed along the coasts and canals to balance Lake Michigan's stormy temperament. Almost all the lighthouses are still in recognizable condition, and tours of some are offered regularly.

One of the oldest of its kind, dating from 1899, the **Canal Station Lighthouse** originally used an experimental design in which only a latticework of guy wires supported the tower and lantern. The station was rebuilt

# Sturgeon Bay

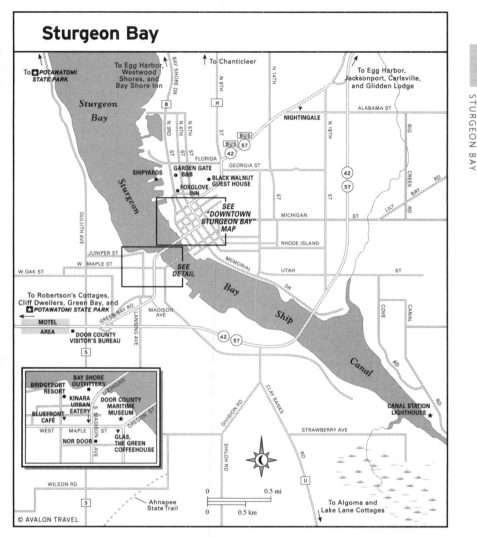

To POTAWATOMI STATE PARK

To Egg Harbor, Westwood Shores, and Bay Shore Inn

To Chanticleer

To Egg Harbor, Jacksonport, Carlsville, and Glidden Lodge

Sturgeon Bay

BAY SHORE DR

N 8TH

N 14TH

ALABAMA ST

NIGHTINGALE

N 18TH

BIG

Sturgeon

N 3RD

N 4TH

N 5TH

ST

BUS

BUS 57

42

CREEK

BAY

RD

FLORIDA

GEORGIA ST

SHIPYARDS

GARDEN GATE B&B

BLACK WALNUT GUEST HOUSE

FOXGLOVE INN

42

57

LILY

RD

SEE "DOWNTOWN STURGEON BAY" MAP

DULUTH AVE

ST

ST

MICHIGAN

ST

RHODE ISLAND

JUNIPER ST

W MAPLE ST

MEMORIAL

UTAH

ST

W OAK ST

SEE DETAIL

Bay

DR

To Robertson's Cottages, Cliff Dwellers, Green Bay, and POTAWATOMI STATE PARK

GREEN BAY RD

LANSING AVE

MADISON AVE

Ship

COVE

CANAL

MOTEL AREA

DOOR COUNTY VISITOR'S BUREAU

42 57

Canal

RD

S

BAY SHORE OUTFITTERS

BRIDGEPORT RESORT

KINARA URBAN EATERY

MICHIGAN

DOOR COUNTY MARITIME MUSEUM

CLAY BANKS

CANAL STATION LIGHTHOUSE

RD

S MADISON

BLUEFRONT CAFÉ

S MADISON AVE

OREGON ST

WEST

MAPLE

ST

GLAS, THE GREEN COFFEEHOUSE

DIVISION RD

STRAWBERRY AVE

NOR DOOR

WILSON RD

SHILOH RD

U

Ahnapee State Trail

0          0.5 mi

0       0.5 km

To Algoma and Lake Lane Cottages

© AVALON TRAVEL

---

in the early 20th century, when the skeletal steel framework was added around the 100-foot-tall light. Access to the grounds is now restricted to the annual Lighthouse Walk weekend in June, but you can also see it from Sturgeon Bay on boat tours. If you arrive on wheels, the north breakwater is accessible, but the views aren't great.

Access to the nearby **Sherwood Point Lighthouse** is similarly restricted.

## Wineries

Given the county's proclivity for fruit production, perhaps it's not surprising that wineries have sprouted up around the region. Just northeast of town, **Door 44** (4020 Hwy. 42/57, 888/932-0044, 10am-6pm daily May-Oct., shorter hours Nov.-Apr.) is a large operation featuring many grapes from the Green Bay region and virtually all from the Midwest.

**Red Oak Vineyard & Winery** (3017

## Downtown Sturgeon Bay

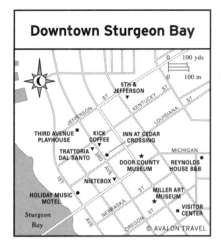

from 9am daily year-round, tours $3) is housed in an old schoolhouse. Tours take in the cellars and winemaking rooms where 40 California-style Door County fruit wines are produced; there is a new distillery, part of a $2 million renovation, and a good eatery attached.

A few more miles along Highway 42 to Highway I (turn right) brings you to **Simon Creek Winery** (5896 Bochek Rd., 920/746-9307, www.simoncreekvineyard.com, 10am-6pm Mon.-Sat. mid-May-late Oct., shorter hours Nov.-mid-May, free tours), the county's largest winery. There's an added bonus of live music on Sunday afternoon. Try the Peninsula cream sherry. Their American gewürztraminer is highly sought after.

Since you're on Highway I, you can't help but notice the enormous Holstein at nearby **Schopf's Hilltop Dairy** (920/743-9779, http://dairyview.com, 10am-6pm daily, free tours), with a viewing area where you can watch them milk the cows. You can even milk Cookie the cow yourself. Schopf's is well reviewed by people with children.

Enterprise Rd., 920/743-7729, www.redoakvineyard.com,10:30am-5:30pm Sun.-Thurs., 9:30am-6pm Fri.-Sat., tasting $6) has no official tours, but at the tasting room downtown you can sample wines made from California grapes and one local cherry wine. It's co-owned by a local Sturgeon Bayer who studied law before finally returning home to follow his passion.

Eight miles north of Sturgeon Bay, in Carlsville, **Door Peninsula Winery** (5806 Hwy. 42, 920/743-7431, www.dcwine.com,

## Door County Maritime Museum

The **Door County Maritime Museum** (120

Tour the *John Purves* at Door County Maritime Museum.

# Blooming Season

Flowers show up in **mid-May,** and you're likely to be jostled by camera-toting visitors during blooming season. Cherry trees are lovely enough, but much of the county's cutover land and agricultural pasture have been left to regrow wild. The county contains five state parks and the Ridges National Natural Landmark, a wildflower preserve with 13 species of endangered plants. Door County is also making an effort to become one of the daffodil capitals of the world, planting more than 100,000 bulbs annually. Look for the white- and peach-colored daffodil—called "doorfodil" (seriously)—that was developed locally.

Generally, blooms are peeking out by the second or third week of May. The bay side blooms first; the lake side follows a week to 10 days later. As soon as the blossoms are out, it's time for the **Season of Blossoms,** a month (or two) shindig of blossom field trips, midway rides, pageants, fish boils, shipyard tours (the only chance to see the operations up close), lighthouse tours, parades, and special cherry-centric celebrations. Check www.doorcounty.com/seasonal-promotions/season-of-blossoms/ for more information.

N. Madison Ave., 920/743-5958, www.dcmm. org, 9am-5pm daily Memorial Day-Labor Day, shorter hours Labor Day-Memorial Day, $10 adults, $13 for museum and tugboat below) is in a sparkling 20,000-square-foot complex with splendid views of the bay. It summarizes the shipbuilding industry, and kids love the periscope from a nuclear submarine; it's part of an ambitious exhibit on the crucial role that Manitowoc played in building subs during World War II. Outside, you can also tour the *John Purves* (10am-3:30pm daily, tours every 30 minutes in peak season, $6 for the boat only), a restored 1919 cherry-red tugboat.

## Door County Museum

At 4th Avenue and Michigan Street you'll find the small **Door County Museum** (18 N. 4th Ave., 920/743-5809, 10am-4:30pm daily May-Oct., free), originally built by the Works Progress Administration (WPA) during the Great Depression. The *Chicago Tribune* called it the "best small museum in the Midwest." The most popular attraction is the old-time firehouse, complete with refurbished pumper vehicles, including a horse-drawn Civil War-era model. Vehicles that you can climb aboard and get your hands on are great for the young ones.

## Miller Art Museum

The **Miller Art Museum** (107 S. 4th Ave.,

920/746-0707, www.millerartmuseum.org, 10am-8pm Mon., 10am-5pm Tues.-Sat., free) is a fine-art gallery in the Sturgeon Bay library. The top floor houses the permanent collection, with an emphasis on 20th-century Wisconsin artists. One room houses works of its namesake Gerhard Miller (1903-2003), the most famous Door County artist; he continued to paint until he was nearly 100.

## The Farm

**The Farm** (N. Hwy. 57, 920/743-6666, www. thefarmindoorcounty.com, 9am-5pm daily Memorial Day-mid-Oct., $8 adults) bills itself as a living museum of rural America, and it lives up to that. Various old-style dwellings and structures dot 40 acres of an original homestead, and pioneer implements line the walls. The primary draw for families is the menagerie of farm animals—you can never get tired of milking a goat, can you? There are also nature trails and informative displays about the diverse ecology of the peninsula.

## TOURS

A few resorts and lodges offer boat tours from their marinas; **Door County Fireboat Cruises** (120 N. Madison Ave., 920/495-6454, www.ridethefireboat.com, $25 adults) depart from the Maritime Museum and use a retired Chicago fireboat to chug along for two-hour

# Shipbuilding History

Given its welcome promontory jutting into the water, 425 miles of shoreline, the safe haven of Green Bay, innumerable bights offering linked harbors, a plethora of native oak, and most important, a channel toward the outside world, it's no surprise that Door County became so important in shipbuilding.

As early as the 1830s, Manitowoc began to turn out oak sailing ships sturdy enough for the Great Lakes on the way to the St. Lawrence River; the crowning achievement was the Great Lakes schooner, a wooden ship with tight ends front and back that met below the water, a shallow draft, and a raisable centerboard, designed specifically to tackle Lake Michigan.

Meanwhile, to the north, Door County had newer shipyards that didn't have to go through later refitting to convert facilities to turn out steamships instead of clippers. Sturgeon Bay churned out ships in amazing numbers: The first left Sturgeon Bay shipyards in the mid-1850s, but it wasn't until the prime of the schooner days, in the mid-1860s, that the town really hit the big time. In the decade following the Civil War, perhaps two dozen famed ships were manufactured in the new shipyards.

Opened in the 1880s, the first major shipbuilder in Sturgeon Bay was Leathem and Smith, predominantly a ship-repair facility. By World War I it had expanded its operations into a prosperous boat works and produced more tugboats than any other company. Now called Bay Shipbuilding, it is still the largest operator in Sturgeon Bay, comprising a number of Sturgeon Bay builders that can handle boats up to 1,100 feet long.

Many shipbuilders relocated here for the environment and the abundant resources. In 1896, Riebolt and Wolter moved an entire drydock from Sheboygan. During the past 50 years, various corporate mergers have resulted in most of Sturgeon Bay's Michigan Street Bridge area becoming an arm of one or more subsidiaries of the same company. Despite the decline in shipping brought about by the advent of railroads and autos, 40 ships were constructed between 1970 and 1986.

Peterson Builders started just after the turn of the 20th century and constructed yachts, fishing tugs, and rowboats. Business boomed during the 1930s and World War II—24-hour operations cranked out subchasers and minesweepers. Today, output includes wooden naval minesweepers, gunboats, torpedo retrievers, steel tugs, and landing craft.

cruises (10:30am and 12:30pm daily Memorial Day-Labor Day). The 10:30am tour travels through the Sturgeon Bay Ship Canal to Lake Michigan, while the 12:30pm tour travels out into Sturgeon Bay to Sherwood Point and past its lighthouse. In July-August these trips are on unless the wind is howling; in May-June and September-October, call ahead to confirm.

North of Sturgeon Bay, the **University of Wisconsin Agricultural Research Station** (4312 N. Hwy. 42, 920/743-5406, sunrise to sunset, free), a fruit and potato research center, is open for public visits. You can obtain a map for a self-guided tour of the 120-acre site.

Too tired to walk? **Door County Trolley** (920/868-1100, www.doorcountytrolley.com)

has an array of historical, themed, culinary, and other fun tours ($15-65) on an old-fashioned streetcar. It's wildly popular; check the website or phone for pickup points, which vary by tour. In Sturgeon Bay, the pickup point is the Door County Maritime Museum; for the perennially popular Lighthouse Tour ($62), which takes in the Canal Station Lighthouse outside town, the trolley leaves at 9:30am Monday-Friday.

## RECREATION
### Shore Fishing

Head for the Sturgeon Bay Ship Canal in May to fish for lake and brown trout, as many others will be doing. Chinook and steelhead salmon season starts in June.

The protected coves and harbors of the bay

have made Sturgeon Bay one of the premier places in the Midwest for smallmouth bass fishing. In fact, BASS, a bass angling society, named Sturgeon Bay all the way north to Fish Creek as the top bass spot in the country. You also have a good chance of catching the king of Wisconsin's fish, the walleye, along with northern pike, perch, and even a misplaced muskie or two.

Always be careful with fishing season dates, the allowed fishing hours, and licenses. Fishing five minutes early or late can be a mistake that costs hundreds of dollars. Contact the **Wisconsin Department of Natural Resources** (DNR, 888/936-7463, http://dnr.wi.gov) for information on regulations and obtaining a license.

## Charter Fishing

Sturgeon Bay's sportfishing charter fleet ranks high in the state in terms of the total salmon take, but that's in numbers only. When you consider the small population, the Door Peninsula is much more prolific. Around here, lunkers prevail. The Wisconsin DNR says Sturgeon Bay charters catch more fish per trip than any other north of Milwaukee, and a record 44.92-pound chinook salmon was landed by a 16-year-old off Sturgeon Bay near the legendary fishing spot called the Bank (as in bank reef); however, Algoma won't let you forget that it was from an Algoma charter boat.

You can contact the 24-hour **Fishing Hot Line** (920/746-2873) for fishing reports.

## Biking

Pick a direction, and you'll find grand bike touring. Head up the lakeside in the morning, starting from the Coast Guard Lighthouse (note that there can be lots of traffic on Highway T), and then head back along the bay in the afternoon. The **Ahnapee State Trail** (www.ahnapeetrail.org), best suited for mountain bikes, although road bikes can handle it, starts just south of Sturgeon Bay and runs to Algoma. For off-road riding, head to Potawatomi State Park south of town.

## Rentals

Outdoor recreation equipment that doesn't have an engine can be rented from several outfitters. Off the water and on wheels or skis, **Nor Door** (60 S. Madison Ave., 920/818-0803, bicycles from $25 per day) rents by the hour or day. On the water, **Bay Shore Outfitters** (27 S. Madison Ave., 920/818-0431, www.kayakdoorcounty.com) is downtown opposite the Maritime Museum and has kayak rentals (from $50 per day) as well as guided tours.

Boats, canoes, and other outdoor gear can be rented from **Door County Boat Rental** (920/746-6071, http://doorcountyboatrentals.com), with several locations in Sturgeon Bay—the most convenient at the **Maritime Museum** (120 N. Madison Ave.). Potawatomi State Park also has rentals, including kayaks. Rates run about $85 per day for a WaveRunner, $275 for a speedboat.

# ENTERTAINMENT

Sturgeon Bay is not a happening place when the sun goes down, but there are options. The **Third Avenue Playhouse** (239 N. 3rd Ave., 920/743-1760, www.thirdavenueplayhouse.com) has a year-round slate of theatrical and musical performances in a renovated movie house.

One consistently good place to catch live music is **GLAS, the Green Coffeehouse** (67 E. Maple St., 920/743-5575), with regular live music that's not on a set schedule. In addition to good coffee and a lovely view of Sturgeon Bay's waters, there are food items available as well. The name, by the way, is Gaelic for "green"—they get asked a lot.

# FOOD

A couple of old-school supper clubs beckon: Travelers adore **Nightingale** (1541 Egg Harbor Rd., 920/743-5593, dinner Mon.-Sat., $8-25), with an old-school interior and top-notch food.

The **Mill Supper Club** (4128 Hwy. 42/57 N., 920/743-5044, dinner Tues.-Sun., $9-25) is legendary for its baked chicken and prime rib, and it hosts fish boils on Tuesday and

Thursday. It's not flashy, but expect great food and chipper service.

Stop for java at **Kick Coffee** (148 N. 3rd Ave., 920/746-1122), serving coffee by Milwaukee's Colectivo Roasters. You'll also find healthful foods, such as the walnut burger. The java's great, and there is a computer to use if your laptop isn't with you. It's tiny enough to have standing room only if you bring a family (there's a small garden out back in summer), but it's cozy and friendly.

Great coffee but even better burritos—for breakfast or late lunch—are at **5th & Jefferson** (232 N. 5th Ave., 920/746-1719, 7am-5pm Mon.-Fri., 7:30am-5pm Sat., 8am-3pm Sun., from $6), where the pulled pork is sublime and served with a smile.

Tuckered travelers will adore ★ **Nistebox** (24 N. 3rd Ave., 920/495-0081, lunch Mon., Wed., Fri.-Sat., dinner Mon., Wed., Fri., from $7), a tough-to-find food truck in an alley. Run by a Door Peninsula local and a Norwegian, they describe themselves as "slow-cooked fast food on wheels." They have the best burritos in northeastern Wisconsin.

Another delicious food-on-the-fly option is the Indian cuisine at **Kinara Urban Eatery** (25 N. Madison Ave., 920/743-8772, breakfast Mon.-Fri., lunch Mon.-Sat., from $6), inside a gas station.

West of the ship canal, ★ **Bluefront Café** (86 W. Maple St., 920/743-9218, lunch and dinner Tues.-Sat., $8-18) is a casually chic and energetic place that defines eclectic. It is Sturgeon Bay's eatery of choice when you need something cheery and fresh and is often recommended by locals. You'll find locally caught panfried walleye next to a Thai vegetarian wrap; try the fish tacos.

Solid northern Italian cuisine in a cozy but contemporary setting is right downtown at **Trattoria dal Santo** (147 N. 3rd Ave., 920/743-6100, http://dalsantosrestaurant.com, 5pm-9pm daily, $17-25). This wonderful place has been honing its cuisine for nearly two decades, and they've never overlooked anything in terms of atmosphere; the wine bar is a recent addition.

An epicurean mainstay is the **Inn at Cedar Crossing** (3rd Ave. and Louisiana St., 920/743-4200, 7:30am-9pm Sun.-Thurs., 7:30am-9:30pm Fri.-Sat., $8-32), featuring original decor, including pressed-tin ceilings, ornate glasswork, and a roaring fireplace in each dining room. The menu, heavy on fresh fish and seafood, emphasizes regional ingredients.

## ACCOMMODATIONS

Expect multiple-night minimum stays during peak season, and even year-round at some venues if your stay includes a Saturday night. Unless specified, all these accommodations are open year-round.

### $50-100

A few of the cheapest motels might have high-season rates in the $75-85 range for a single in summer; these dip as low as $49 in nonpeak seasons. However, most places cost much more.

Home away from home has always been ★ **Holiday Music Motel** (30 N. 1st Ave., 920/743-5571, www.holidaymusicmotel.com, $90, weekends $139). In 2007 a group of local and national musicians, including Jackson Browne, came here to write songs for a benefit for the Michigan Street Bridge. They loved the experience, and the place was for sale, so they bought it and rejuvenated it into a budget boutique venue. You likely won't need the recording studio (don't worry, it's quiet), but the rooms have fridges and new amenities. This is truly one of the most unique choices in Door County.

Lodging generally a few bucks cheaper can be found a couple of miles north of Sturgeon Bay along Highway 42/57 at an old standby, the old-school but well-run **Chal-A Motel** (3910 Hwy. 42/57, 920/743-6788, Apr.-Nov., $90), where Wi-Fi is included and there's a fridge in every room—not to mention friendly owners.

Lots of folks come for cottage life, and all the higher-end resorts have isolated cottages strong on creature comforts. On the economical end, **Lake Lane Cottages** (5647 Lake Lane, 920/743-3463, www.lakelanecottages.com, $89, weekly $535) sleeps 2-4 people. It even has a tree house outside for the kids, and pets are welcome. It's southeast of Sturgeon Bay via Highway U (Clay Banks Rd.).

## $100-150

**Robertson's Cottages** (4481 Cabots Point Rd., 920/743-5124, http://robertsoncottages. com, from $700 per week, daily rentals in low season) north of Potawatomi State Park costs a bit more but has island cottages and gets many multiple-decade repeat customers.

A warm welcome awaits at the ★ **Garden Gate Bed & Breakfast** (434 N. 3rd Ave., 920/217-3093, http://doorcountybb.com, from $120). While the rooms may not be enormous (except the Lavender Room, which has a double whirlpool tub), they are modern and well-kept.

Right on the main drag of Sturgeon Bay, a century-old commercial building and erstwhile soda fountain, the **Inn at Cedar Crossing** (3rd Ave. at Louisiana St., 920/743-4200, www.innatcedarcrossing.com, $130-215) is best described as Victorian country; the owner's flair and passion for folk-art decoration is expressed in the guest rooms (room 6 is particularly warm and spacious). The inn also has a well-regarded (if always busy) dining room.

Ditching quotidian day jobs, the transplanted Milwaukeeans of **Whitefish Bay Farm B&B** (3831 Clark Lake Rd./Hwy. WD, 920/743-1560, www.whitefishbayfarm. com, $130), a 1908 farmhouse with four sunny rooms five miles north on Highway 57, now raise Corriedale sheep on a 75-acre farm. With all that wool, the owners, accomplished weavers, give spinning and weaving demonstrations in their barn-art gallery.

## Over $150

Given the rave reviews garnered by the **Bridgeport Resort** (50 W. Larch St., 920/746-9919, http://bridgeportresort.net, from $150), one has to wonder how they maintain their attentive service. Its one- to three-bedroom suites each have a fireplace, a kitchen, and a double whirlpool tub. I love how they thought of having extra sinks. It's a great place to bring kids, with amenities such as an indoor pool and a ball crawl area, but it's just as nice for a romantic getaway.

At the ★ **Reynolds House B&B** (111 S. 7th Ave., 920/493-1113, www.reynoldshousebandb. com, $160-200), the ersatz anachronism of spinning parasols is eschewed; it actually feels like a century ago in this antique-adorer's paradise. It emphasizes small but gorgeous guest rooms and superb service, and it was voted as having the best breakfast in the Midwest by the knowledgeable readers of *Midwest Living* magazine.

More sheep grazing in a 30-acre orchard are a highlight of the restored farmhouse **Chanticleer** (4072 Hwy. HH N./Cherry Lane Rd., 920/746-0334, www. chanticleerguesthouse.com, $180-300). Find multilevel suites with 15-foot vaulted ceilings and private terraces, lofted suites with bisque pine ceilings and rafters, and an array of amenities in each. Notable extras include a solarium, a sauna, hiking trails, and a heated pool. Guests adore this place.

You're not likely to find more welcoming proprietors than those at the splendid ★ **Black Walnut Guest House** (454 N. 7th Ave., 877/255-9568, www.blackwalnut-gh. com, $145-160). The inn's four relaxing guest rooms are entirely different from one another—choose one with a spiral staircase to a hot tub in a tower, or one with a double-sided fireplace—and all are delightfully well-conceived. This guesthouse is highly recommended.

People rave about **Westwood Shores Waterfront Resort** (4303 Bay Shore Dr., 800/440-4057, www.westwoodshores.net, from $185), with one- and two-bedroom suites with full kitchens, all of which have commanding views of the bay. The suites have every amenity you could want, and staff friendliness is as noticeable as the views.

With a lodge that was once a 1920s dairy barn, the **Bay Shore Inn** (4205 Bay Shore Dr., 920/743-4551, www.bayshoreinn.net, $199-310) has long been known as one of the most family-friendly resorts in the United States; it has three dozen luxurious apartment suites overlooking the bay as well as a private beach. Follow Highway B north from Sturgeon Bay.

The exteriors of the cottages at **Cliff Dwellers** (south of Potawatomi State Park, 920/333-0345, http://cliffdwellersresort.com, from $185) look quaint, but the one- and two-bedroom units are done up quite nicely inside (townhouse units are more expensive). Guests also have access to an indoor whirlpool tub, a sauna, and an outdoor pool, along with complimentary use of bicycles and rowboats.

Eminently gracious are the proprietors at ★ **Foxglove Inn** (344 N. 3rd Ave., 920/746-9192, www.foxglovedoorcounty.com, from $220). The inn's historically modern (no oxymoron) rooms are amazing, and the sister owners have a real knack for the trade. Guests have raved about this place, and for good reason.

The 1930s **Glidden Lodge** (4676 Glidden Dr., 920/746-3900 or 866/454-3336, www.gliddenlodge.com, $240-425) was the epitome of hedonistic delight in its time—a massive fieldstone main building offering stunning lake views. On the quiet side of the peninsula, it has a prime location. It is all suites, all with breathtaking lake views and magnificent sunrises. Follow Highway 57 north to Highway T and turn right to Glidden Drive.

## INFORMATION

The **Sturgeon Bay Visitors Center** (36 S. 3rd Ave., 800/301-6695, www.sturgeonbay.net) is downtown. The **Door County Visitors Bureau** (1015 Green Bay Rd., 920/743-4456 or 800/527-3529, www.doorcounty.com), just south of town, has all the information you're likely to need. It has a 24-hour touch-screen information and reservations service. You'll find boatloads of local newspapers and other media.

the Foxglove Inn

**DoorCounty-WI.com** (www.doorcounty-wi.com) is a good website with links to other businesses and local media. **Door County Navigator** (www.doorcountynavigator.com) is a sounding board for locals as well as travelers who've tried local attractions, lodgings, and dining; it even has listings of dog-friendly lodgings.

## GETTING THERE

Wait till you see the auto traffic on a peak weekend: Door County shares the American antipathy toward public transportation. People disembarking from a Greyhound bus evidently doesn't fit into the sunset postcard scene. There are no buses, no trains, and no ferries from points south. Entrepreneurs are constantly floating proposals to run a passenger-only ferry from here to Menominee in Michigan's Upper Peninsula or other towns, but don't count on it.

Limited air shuttles from Chicago to Sturgeon Bay have occasionally popped up, but none are operating at present. The only option to fly in is Green Bay's **Austin Straubel International Airport** (GRB, Hwy. 172, Green Bay, 920/498-4800, http://flygrb.com) and rent a car.

## ★ POTAWATOMI STATE PARK

Unfolding along the western edge of Sturgeon Bay and flanked by Sherwood and Cabot Points, **Potawatomi State Park** (920/746-2890) is known for rolling birch-lined trails atop the limestone ridges scraped off the Niagara Escarpment. Indeed, the stone from here was carted off to build ports all around the Great Lakes. Islets rimmed in hues of blue and gray pepper the outlying reaches off the park (bring a polarizing filter for your camera on a sunny day). The geology of the park is significant enough that Potawatomi marks the eastern terminus of the Ice Age National Scenic Trail. You won't need a science background or superlative designations to appreciate its inspiring vistas and solitude; it is simply one of the peninsula's magical not-to-be-missed natural retreats.

### Sights

The great **Tower Trail** quickly ascends the ridges through thicker vegetation, leading to a 75-foot-tall **observation tower** with a belvedere vantage point of Michigan's Upper Peninsula, some 16 miles away, visible on a good day; come for sunset.

Beech trees, in this region found only close to Lake Michigan, are a highlight of the nature in the park. Otherwise, expect to see some 50 types of resident songbirds, plenty of hawks riding bluff wind currents, or deer staring quizzically at you from stands of sugar maples, basswood, and white and red pines.

For a quick road trip, head back toward Highway 42/57, turn right onto Highway C, and then right onto Highway M, which takes you all the way to the **Sherwood Point Lighthouse;** it's a bit difficult to spot. Built in 1883, it took a century before it was finally automated. The 38-foot-high structure guarding the bayside entrance to Sturgeon Bay was constructed with a 10-sided cast-iron light. Closed to the public, today the lighthouse and the old keeper's house are used as a retreat by the Coast Guard. It is open during designated Lighthouse Festival times, generally in late May or early June. Check with the Door County Maritime Museum (www.dcmm.org) for official dates.

Potawatomi State Park

# Recreation

## HIKING

Almost 11 miles of trails wind through the park; you'll see hemlock, sugar maple, aspen, and birch trees in addition to the beech trees. The trails become nine miles of cross-country skiing trails in winter. Vertical gain is only around 150 feet, but the trails rise and fall a lot. Maps are available at the nature center.

The easiest trail is the 0.5-mile **Ancient Shores Trail,** which begins near the nature center; it's loaded with easy-to-understand signs pointing out geology and flora along the way.

The most popular trail is the 3.6-mile **Tower Trail,** which runs up and over ridges to the observation tower. The most popular trailheads are at the tower itself or at a nearby overlook (an old ski hill) on the main park road. In the southern half of the park, closer to the water, the 2.6-mile **Hemlock Trail** doesn't have the sweat-inducing climbing and passes the most popular recreation areas; access it at Parking Lot 2 in the picnic area.

The must-hike trail is the three-mile segment of the **Ice Age National Scenic Trail** that begins next to the observation tower and runs along the ridgeline above the water. It's only a small part of the epic trail's 1,000 miles, but this is where it starts.

## BIKING

An eight-mile **off-road bicycle trail** also meanders through mostly grassy meadows and mildly challenging terrain. If you're a novice, go slowly. Bikes can be rented in the park. The trailhead is at Parking Lot 1 at the picnic area.

## FISHING AND WATER ACTIVITIES

Fishing in the naturally protected bay is some of the best in the lower Door, especially for smallmouth bass. The chilly waters also offer some fantastic scuba diving, with wrecks visible below. The park has no scuba outfitter on-site. Contact **Lakeshore Adventures** (920/493-3474, http://lakeshore-adventures. com) in Baileys Harbor for tips. Another outfitter is **Dark Side Charters** (10302 Townline Rd., Sister Bay, 920/421-3483, http://divedoorcounty.com), farther away in Sister Bay. Canoes and kayaks are also rentable at the park.

A large caveat: There is no sand beach in Potawatomi State Park, just lots of rocky shoreline.

## CAMPING

Camping at the park's **Daisy Field Campground** (reservations 888/947-2757, www.wisconsinstateparks.reserveamerica. com, from $23 nonresidents, plus $10 reservation fee) is very popular, so reserve on the first day possible the winter before your trip. Even with 125 or more sites in two loops along the shoreline, it is always chock-full in summer. A camping cabin is available for disabled travelers in the south loop; it even has a stove, a microwave, and a fridge, along with air-conditioning. A park sticker is required in addition to the campsite fee. Showers are available in season in both loops.

The campground locations are wonderful, and you can get sites with splendid views, but they are very close to each other. Prime sites are numbers 54 or 104, as they're farthest from the madding crowd. Also consider the even-numbered sites 32-50, since they back up on the Niagara Escarpment and provide a bit of isolation.

Administrators take quiet hours seriously. Expect a ranger visit any time after 10pm if you are being too loud.

# Getting There

There is no public transportation. Drive south of Sturgeon Bay to the bridge over the canal, head west, and then head immediately north—all roads lead to the park. It's also possible to take an obscenely expensive taxi ride from Green Bay.

# Lakeside

Otherwise known as the "quiet side," this area shows less commercial development than the rest of the peninsula. The lakeshore side of the Door is a wonderland of pristine heath, healed cutover forest, rocky sea caves, some of Lake Michigan's finest beaches, biome preserves, picture-postcard lighthouses, and two of Wisconsin's best state parks.

The quick way into the area is Highway 57, branching off Highway 42 north of Sturgeon Bay. Farther off the beaten path, get right above the water along the coast starting southeast of Sturgeon Bay at the Sturgeon Bay Ship Canal North Pierhead Lighthouse. From here, an established State Rustic Road hugs the coastline all the way to Whitefish Dunes State Park, bypassing Portage and Whitefish Points and the Lilly Bay curve. Don't worry about getting lost once you find Highway T; there are no other roads.

## ★ WHITEFISH DUNES STATE PARK AND CAVE POINT COUNTY PARK

Some say **Whitefish Dunes State Park** (920/823-2400), eight miles northeast of Sturgeon Bay, is the most pleasant park in the state system. The beach is indisputably so, with miles of mocha-colored dunes sculpted into ridges by the prevailing winds. The contiguous **Cave Point County Park** is technically a separate park, but it's only a one-minute drive to the northeast from Whitefish Dunes, and there's also a trail connecting the two parks. It's best to visit them at the same time.

Archaeologists surmise that the lakeshore site's proximity to inland lakes and creeks (nearby Clark Lake is over 800 fish-rich acres) was the primary reason that Native Americans settled here. Eight temporary or permanent encampments and semipermanent villages have been excavated, dating as far

Cave Point County Park

back as 100 BC and spreading over three acres that are now within the park. The North Bay people were the earliest, occupying the shores from Green Bay north to Rock Island seasonally until AD 300. The water levels of Lake Michigan rose and flooded the site, and the Heins Creek and Late Woodland people occupied the area AD 500-900; by that time, the itinerant camps had grown into a sizable village. The Oneota people, descended from the Late Woodland people, held sway on the peninsula in two different periods beginning in 900. European settlers arrived in 1840, when a commercial fishing operation on Whitefish Bay was begun by the Clark brothers, who lent their name to the nearby lake, working side by side with the Winnebago people.

Today, visitors come for the massive dunes.

## Plants and Animals

Stay off the dunes to protect the fragile plants and microscopic critters. Staying on the trail also avoids contact with the abundant poison ivy. Many of the grasses holding together the mounds are unique to this park, and once they're gone, the dunes will disappear; just take a look at the lifeless gashes created by motorcyclists before the park was established. The park is also the home of the Lake Huron locust, which lives only in Door County. The cooler prevailing winds mean that there is about one month's delay in flowers blooming compared to the bay side of the county. Rare and threatened plant species include dune goldenrod, dune thistle, dwarf lake iris, and sand reedgrass.

Large wildlife sightings are rare, other than an occasional white-tailed deer or red fox, but there have been occasional reports of black bears.

## Recreation
### HIKING

The dunes are among the highest on Lake Michigan. They were formed by numerous advances and retreats of ancient lakes, and later Lake Michigan, as well as countless storms. Sand banks first closed off Clark Lake

in what is now the mainland, and as vegetation took hold three millennia ago, wind deposits began piling up atop the sandbar. The result is a microcosm that couldn't occur on the bay side of the peninsula—a wide beach rising to forested dunes. The tallest, Old Baldy, stands 93 feet high.

Check out the nature center, where all trails start and where you can pick up trail maps, for its exhibits on the geology and anthropology of the area. A Native American village site (10am-4pm Sat.-Sun. summer) has been recreated just outside to illustrate life during one of the eight periods of human habitation.

There are nearly 15 miles of trails; thoughtfully, the park has a plasticized trail mat on the first hundred yards of all trails to both protect the ground and make it easier for you to trudge. Until you get to the dunes themselves, the park is completely flat. Plank-and-rope boardwalks off the trail allow beach access on the 2.8-mile **Red Trail;** at the midpoint, it branches away from the water to link with longer trails through mixed hardwood, red pine, and oddball wooded dune areas. The beginning of the Red Trail is also the only place where you can ride a mountain bike. Continuing on the Red Trail to its southern end, hikers can reach the only climbable dune—Old Baldy, which offers panoramas of Lake Michigan and Clark Lake inland. From there, it's possible to connect to longer trails, including the **Yellow Trail,** which heads west for another 1.5 miles through a red pine plantation and wooded dune area that is very solitary, even for this park, and passing the 0.5-mile **Red Pine Trail** through more red pines and a 0.25-mile-long spur trail to Clark Lake.

If you want to start hiking from the other direction, starting from the nature center parking lot, the second-most popular trails after the one to Old Baldy is the 2.5-mile **Black Trail,** which heads northeast along the limestone bedrock of the Niagara Escarpment and leads to **Cave Point County Park,** likely the most photographed parkland in Door County. (If you want to visit Cave

Point County Park but don't want to hike this trail, you can reach the park by driving about a minute to the north.) Along the way the trail joins up with an interpretive trail with an anthropomorphic brachiopod (a prehistoric clam-like creature) named Byron who explains the geology of the area.

Cave Point is a must-stop. From south to north in Whitefish Bay, the geology shifts from dunes to mixed sand and stone to, at Cave Point, exposed limestone ledges thrusting up to 50 feet above the water on the Niagara Escarpment, the bedrock of the peninsula. Some 425 million years ago, the Silurian Sea covered this entire region, and you can still find fossils in exposed rock. These ledges are on a bowl, the opposite side of which is Niagara Falls. Aeons of crashing waves have hewn caves and cenotes that show up as blowholes as the surf pounds and crashes, echoing like rolling thunder. The whole effect is not unlike the crumbled parapets of a timeworn castle. Sea kayakers have a field day exploring this small promontory. Straight-faced old-timers tell of a schooner that slammed into the rocks at Cave Point in 1881 (true). Laden with corn, the ship cracked like a nut and spilled its cargo (true), and within a few days, corn had mysteriously appeared in Green Bay, on the other side of the peninsula (hmm).

## SWIMMING

Do not take swimming lightly here. The concave bend of Whitefish Bay focuses all the current, forming tough riptides. Predicting where these form is never entirely possible, and lifeguards are never on duty. If you do plan on swimming, practice extra caution and pay strict attention to all posted signs.

## CAMPING

This park is for day use only, and camping is not allowed. It is great for picnicking, which can be done right atop the limestone ledges overlooking the lake, not to mention along the beaches.

# JACKSONPORT

You can always tell those who have explored the bay side of the peninsula first and then backtracked through Sturgeon Bay to come back up this side. Generally, these are the people who race right through Jacksonport as if they didn't know it was there and then slam on the brakes to turn around to try to find what they missed.

At one time, Jacksonport rivaled Fish Creek

Jacksonport's beach

# Calmer Near the Lake

Jacksonport is on the 45th parallel, exactly halfway between the equator and the north pole, but the peninsula's climate is far more temperate than northern Wisconsin. The waters of Lake Michigan, legendary for their unpredictability, also even out the weather, keeping things cool in the summer and taking the bite out of winter's Alberta clippers.

Early weather reports from Door County show that the northern tip of the peninsula is generally a few degrees warmer than the southern end, although the difference between the bay side and the lake side is climatically more important. This partly explains why most Door residents live on the bay side: With Lake Michigan in a huff, blowing fog, spray, and mist, Green Bay, in the lee of 15 miles of limestone wind-block, remains sedate, if a bit cloudy.

Another oddity is "lake effect" snow: Much more snow falls at the lakeside than even a few miles inland, especially on the eastern shores of the Great Lakes. Green Bay is not large enough to produce the necessary conditions, so Door County receives some of the lowest amounts of precipitation in the state.

as the epicenter of economic activity on the Door. Once the local lumber was depleted, Jacksonport's docks were relegated to fishing boats.

## Sights

Somnolent Jacksonport hosts a few antiques shops and gift cottages selling crafts from dozens of Door County artists. A lazy stretch of sand acts as a beach, and top-notch fun comes in the form of the sweets at the **Town Hall Bakery** (6225 Hwy. 57, 920/823-2116).

## Festivals

The last community to be settled in the county, Jacksonport caught one of the waves of Germanic immigrants, and its annual **Maifest** (www.jacksonport.org) is among the larger shindigs held during the summer.

The Jacksonport Historical Society hosts a **Cherry Fest** (www.jacksonporthistoricalsociety.org) on the first Saturday in August every year. There are all kinds of cherry-related foods, historical displays, and arts and crafts.

## Food and Accommodations

The supper club of choice is **Mr. G's** (5890 Hwy. 57, 920/823-2112, dinner Tues.-Sat., $6-14), with a ballroom that once had live entertainment; most entertainment today is the tall

tales told at the joint's Tiki Bar, part of the local Yacht Club, which is more Jimmy Buffett than America's Cup.

Right downtown is the pinnacle of Jacksonport's developmental ambition: the **Square Rigger Lodge and Cottages** (6332 Hwy. 57, 920/823-2404, www.squareriggerlodge.com, from $170). More than a dozen basic but comfortable modern motel and condo units overlook the water (some do not), and most have private balconies or patios. One- to three-bedroom cottages also line the waterfront. They have lively fish boils here nightly in July and August, four times a week September to June.

Rooms (spartan but decent) for about half the price can be found nearby at the **Innlet Motel** (6269 Hwy. 57, 920/823-2499, www.innlet-motel.com, from $85). This is also the home of **Mike's Port Pub** (920/823-2081, 11am-10pm daily, from $6) for some pretty good food, including breakfast.

## BAILEYS HARBOR

Lake Michigan sportfishing is evident as you enter Baileys Harbor, with every inch of road chockablock with trucks and boat trailers and a glistening new marina. It's a fitting legacy: In 1844 a Captain Bailey and his crew were foundering in a sudden squall when they found this cove and took shelter. They were amazed to find a deep, well-isolated harbor and gorgeous stands of cedar backing the beach. So enthralled was the captain that he and the owner of the shipping company persuaded the U.S. government to construct a lighthouse at the harbor's entrance some years later, marking the first nonnative settlement in Door County. The harbor remains the only designated Harbor of Refuge on the peninsula's lake side.

## Sights

Before you arrive, remember that the sights are mostly south of Baileys Harbor, on the way from Cave Point County Park, just northeast of Whitefish Dunes State Park. South of town along Highway 57 at the southern end of Kangaroo Lake are two undiscovered gems—**Lyle-Harter-Matter County Park** and **Meridian Park State Natural Area,** which sandwich the highway and feature rough undeveloped trails past Niagara Escarpment rocks and one of the largest dunes in the county. As you sit here and munch your granola bar, you're halfway to the North Pole. If you're really looking to escape the crowds, even on a chaotic mid-July day, head north a few miles on Highway 57, then west two miles or so on Highway E to a trail spur leading toward **Kangaroo Lake,** a state wildlife area that's best explored on a canoe trip. It's beautiful and home to an impressive ecosystem; somehow the northern half of this lake has escaped development and is currently owned by the Nature Conservancy. The mesic open areas are rare in Wisconsin and are home to a staggering list of threatened species, particularly the Hines emerald dragonfly (this is one of only two breeding areas in the country). You'll never be disappointed by the waterfowl that call this place home, including the local black tern.

A bit south of town and along a splendid stretch of beach is a decidedly different kind of vacation, an educational seminar (from $1,000, including superb food, far less if you're staying off-site) at **Björklunden** (7590 Boynton Lane, 920/839-2216), more a relaxed soul-searching means of personal growth than a for-credit school experience, although it is the northern campus of Lawrence University in Appleton. Participants can live in a recently reconstructed Norwegian-style lodge built of local fieldstone and take courses in humanities and natural sciences. Some midweek seminars are cheaper. It's possible to stay at the lodge, which looks like a Viking ship, without taking courses if space is available. Travelers can also visit the **Boynton Chapel** (902/839-2216, tours given mid-June to late-Aug. Mon. and Wed. 1pm-4pm, $5) built in a late 12th-century Norwegian *stavkirke* (stave church) style.

During the summer, the gardens of the estate host **Door Shakespeare** (920/839-1500, www.doorshakespeare.com), with evening performances Thursday-Tuesday.

In Baileys Harbor, take a simple stroll along one of the county's longest sand beaches at **Baileys Harbor Park.** The Town Hall—you can't miss it—has the local **visitors information center** (Hwy. 57 and Hwy. F, 920/839-2366, www.baileysharbor.com, daily summer and fall).

## Recreation
### SPORTFISHING

Chinook salmon and rainbow and brown trout are the quarry for local charter boats, and the fishing in Baileys Harbor is some of the best in the county. All charters will be met at the Baileys Harbor marina/town dock. Lilliputian Baileys Harbor (pop. 780) boasts a salmon harvest half the size of Milwaukee's. Plenty of local guides are available. The captain at **Lynn's Charter Fishing** (Baileys Harbor Yacht Club, 920/854-5109, http://lynnscharterfishing.com) has a PhD in zoology, has been guiding for many years, and runs an unequaled kayak fishing tour.

Another outfit with great reviews is **Silver Strike Charters** (151 Ridges Rd., 920/854-6069, doorcountycharterfishing.com), which has slightly cheaper rates than others.

## BOAT TOURS

One of the more intriguing options is to take a guided tour (generally 8am and/or 3pm daily, $55) of the local bays, including the legendary Cana Island lighthouse, in a clear-bottomed kayak with **Lakeshore Adventures** (8113 Hwy. 57, 920/839-2055, http://lakeshore-adventures.com), which also rents virtually everything recreational.

## Food

Door County wines get all the press, but suddenly craft brewing is not far behind. Newest are the whimsical overseers of the **Door County Brewing Company** (2434 Hwy. F, 920/834-1515, www.doorcountybrewingco.com, 11am-10pm daily), housed in an erstwhile feed mill. They've got select all-season beers, the favorite being Polka King Porter. Live music and generally zany antics (mustache contests, etc.) are great fun. Tours (4:30pm Fri.-Sat., 11am Sun.) are worth it.

Newest is **Chives Door County** (8041 Hwy. 57, 920/839-2000, dinner Wed.-Mon. high season, from $8). It's a casual, but borderline fine-dining, place whose chorizo and kale soup paired with their otherworldly New York strip could be anyone's mainstay.

★ **Harbor Fish Market and Grille** (8080 Hwy. 57, 920/839-9999, breakfast, lunch, and dinner daily, from $10) is a casually fine dining place in a 120-year-old building with a wondrous atmosphere. All comers will be happy; try the lobster boil (Wed. and Fri.-Sun. summer, Fri.-Sun. off-season). There's great custard and espresso next door. You can sit outside with your pooch and order from the "doggie menu" for your best friend.

If you're old-school (or a Packers football fan), head immediately to **Cornerstone Pub** (Hwy. 57, 920/839-2790, breakfast, lunch, and dinner daily May-Oct., shorter hours off-season, $6-16), which has three squares of solid comfort food (panfried perch since 1926) and quite honestly, the best service; it's also pooch-friendly.

# ★ Scenic Boat Tours

To get one of the best views of Door County, hop on a boat! You'll see lighthouses, cliffs and caves, and islands, as well as hear about Door County's fascinating history.

## STURGEON BAY

- **Door County Fireboat Cruises** (page 25) uses a retired Chicago fireboat to chug along for two-hour cruises onto Lake Michigan or Sturgeon Bay.

## BAILEYS HARBOR

- **Lakeshore Adventures** (page 38) offers guided tours of the local bays, including the legendary Cana Island lighthouse, in a clear-bottomed kayak.

## FISH CREEK

- **Fish Creek Scenic Boat Tours** (page 46) provides the easiest way to take in the views of Chambers Island.

- **Friendly Charters** (page 46) offers quiet tours of Fish Creek on their sailboat.

## GILLS ROCK

- **Shoreline Resort** (page 60) has narrated boat tours of Death's Door as well as popular sunset cruises.

## Accommodations

Baileys Harbor has a couple of basic, modestly priced motels. The **Sunset Motel and Cottages** (8404 Hwy. 57, 920/839-2218, www.baileysunsetmotelandcottages.com, from $75) is casual and rustic but comfortable, with friendly proprietors—the way things used to be everywhere in these parts. The single room is very tiny and a bit musty. It's about 0.5 miles north of the Highway Q turnoff.

On the south side of town are above-average motel rooms and a lovely lakeshore setting at the **Beachfront Inn** (8040 Hwy. 57, 920/839-2345, www.beachfrontinn.net, from $125). In addition to a private beach, an indoor heated pool, and regular campfires, the inn gets many kudos for being so pet-friendly—they even have their own rescue dogs.

What may be the most enviably sited lodging in all of Door County is ★ **Gordon Lodge** (1420 Pine Dr., 920/839-2331, www.gordonlodge.com, $240-425). Spread across the tip of a promontory jutting into Lake Michigan's North Bay, the long-established Gordon Lodge sprouted in the 1920s as an offshoot of a popular Sturgeon Bay doctor's summer home. It has been updated just enough to be modern but not so much as to lose its rustic charm. The main lodge has a lake view, while villas with fireplaces creep out over the water. Some original cottages are set back and nestled under the pines, which also drape over fitness trails. The dining room is casually elegant, and the Top Deck lounge, originally a boathouse, is unsurpassed for after-dinner dancing. Go north out of town and follow Highway Q toward the lake to Pine Drive.

The ★ **Blacksmith Inn** (8152 Hwy. 57, 920/839-9222, www.theblacksmithinn.com, $245-305) is opulent and historic with stunning sunset views and no frilliness—and absolutely fabulous service.

## ★ THE RIDGES SANCTUARY AND CANA ISLAND LIGHTHOUSE

Baileys Harbor is sandwiched between the strategic safe harbor on Lake Michigan and Kangaroo Lake, the peninsula's largest inland body of water. Travelers are so preoccupied with these two sights that it's easy to miss the two large promontories jutting off the peninsula just north of town, forming **Moonlight Bay.** These two capes may be the state's most awesome natural landmarks and definitely have the most inspiring lighthouses.

North along Highway Q is a critical biotic reserve, **The Ridges Sanctuary** (Ridges Rd., 920/839-2802, www.ridgesanctuary.org, trails open daily, $5 adults), with 1,000 acres of boreal bog, swamp, dunes, and a complete assortment of wildflowers in their natural habitat. The eponymous series of ancient spiny sand ridges mark the advance of ancient and modern Lake Michigan. All 23 native Wisconsin orchids are found within the sanctuary, as are 13 endangered species of flora. The preserve was established in the 1930s by hard-core early ecologists, such as Jens Jensen, in one of the state's first environmental brouhahas, incited by

homesteader cabin at Toft's Point

a spat over plans for a trailer park. The U.S. Department of the Interior recognizes the site as one of the most ecologically precious in the region; it was the first National Natural Landmark in Wisconsin.

The famed **Baileys Harbor Range Lights** are a pair of small but powerful lighthouses—a shorter wooden octagonal one across the road on the beach, the other 900 feet inland—erected in 1869 by the Coast Guard. There are 20 miles of trails that are well worth the effort, including three easy trails, ranging from just under two miles to five miles, that snake through the tamarack and hardwood stands. Also on the grounds is a nature center, with some of the best educational programs in the state.

Continue on Ridges Road to additional sites deemed National Natural Landmarks by the Department of the Interior and dedicated by the Nature Conservancy. **Toft's Point** (also called Old Lighthouse Point) is along a great old dirt road that winds through barren sands with innumerable pullouts. A few trails can be found on the 600-plus acres that take up the whole of the promontory, which includes almost three miles of rocky beach shoreline.

To the north of the Ridges, the **Mud Lake Wildlife Area** is over 2,000 acres protecting the shallow lake and surrounding wetlands. In fact, its second-growth mesic ecosystem of white cedar, white spruce, and black ash is a rarity in Wisconsin. A prime waterfowl sanctuary, Mud Lake and its environs may be even more primeval and wild than the Ridges, and it is home to one of the few breeding spots of the threatened Hine's emerald dragonfly along with a lengthy list of waterfowl, including ospreys. Canoeing is also very popular, as Reibolts Creek connects the lake with Moonlight Bay.

On the southern promontory of Moonlight Bay is the one must-visit lighthouse on the peninsula that everyone photographs, the **Cana Island Lighthouse** (10am-5pm daily May-Oct., $6, plus $4 to climb the tower), accessible via Highway Q to Cana Island Drive to a narrow spit of gravel that may be under

Cana Island Lighthouse

water, depending on when you get here. Note that this is a residential area, so go slowly—blind curves are everywhere—and don't park inappropriately if the new parking area is full, which is not impossible. Impressively tall and magnificently white, the lighthouse is framed by white birch. One of the most crucial lighthouses in the county, it stands far off the coast on a wind-whipped landform. Built in 1870, it was considered a hardship station during storm season. North Bay is also the site of Marshall's Point, part of the **North Bay State Natural Area,** an isolated stretch of wildland completely surrounded by private development often touted as a potential state park for its remarkable microclimate and the fact that it's one of the last remaining stretches of undeveloped Lake Michigan coastline on the Door Peninsula. You'll find threatened and endangered species everywhere; most interesting is the fact that more than one million (of the local population estimate of up to 1.5 million) whitefish spawn in these waters.

# ROWLEYS BAY

Out of Baileys Harbor, Highway 57 swoops back toward Sister Bay to Highway 42. The next lakeside community, Rowleys Bay, is mostly a massive and well-established resort and nearby campground, **Rowleys Bay Resort** (1041 Hwy. ZZ, 920/854-2385, www. rowleysbayresort.com, May-Oct., lodge or cottages $119-319). Many people still call it "Wagon Trail," which was its name for many years when it included the nearby campground. Originally a barebones fishing camp and later a rustic lodge, the city-state has transformed into what is certainly the most comprehensive operation on the upper Door Peninsula. From rustic-looking lodge rooms to plush suites and cottages of all sorts, somehow the place does it all and does it well. Rustically upscale two- and three-bedroom vacation villas are set on wooded or waterfront sites; some can house a dozen people comfortably, and all have whirlpool tubs and fireplaces.

The adjacent but unaffiliated **campground** (920/854-4818, www. wagontrailcampground.com, from $39 tents), in fact still called the Wagon Trail, spread over 200 acres along the bay, is really quite fastidious and professionally run; cabins and even yurts are available. Reservations are advised.

Several miles of trails wend through the resort's acreage; one leads to Sand Bay Beach Park on Rowleys Bay, another to the Mink River estuary. On the bay, the resort's marina offers bicycles, canoes, kayaks, paddleboats, charter fishing boats, and scenic excursions.

The reason most people come to the resort, however, is ★ **Grandma's Swedish Bakery** (920/854-2385, daily May-Oct.), a magnet for anyone with a sweet tooth for 10 kinds of homemade bread, cardamom coffee cake, cherry pie, Old World-style bread pudding, and scads of muffins, cookies, and pastries. The specialty is Swedish sweets—*limpa* and *skorpa* (thinly sliced pecan rolls sprinkled with cinnamon sugar and dried in the oven).

## Mink River Estuary State Natural Area

Stretching southeast from Ellison Bay to the edge of Newport State Park, the Mink River Estuary State Natural Area acts, by grace of the Nature Conservancy, to protect the river system as it empties into the bay through marsh and estuary. A crucial bird migratory site, the waters also act as a conduit for spawning fish. The topography of the 1,500 acres is astonishingly diverse and untouched; two threatened plant species—the dune thistle and dwarf lake iris—are found within the site's boundaries, and more than 200 species of birds pass through.

## ★ NEWPORT STATE PARK

Not much is wild in Door County anymore, but the state's only designated wilderness park is here; the rough, isolated, backwoods **Newport State Park** (920/854-2500) constitutes half of the northern tip of the county, accessed from Highway 42 and stretching for almost 12 miles along the Lake Michigan coast through an established scientific reserve—a perfectly realized park.

A remarkable diversity of hardwoods and conifers, isolated wetlands, bogs, and even a few hidden coves along the lakeshore make the hiking appealing. Once an up-and-coming lumber village in the 1880s, the town decayed gradually as the stands of forests were depleted. Ghostly outlines of the foundations of buildings are still scattered in the underbrush.

Once wasted white pine cutover land, the inner confines of the park are now dense tracts of bog forest. The southern section of the park is an established scientific reserve on 140 acres of mixed hardwoods. The park's magnificent ecosystem draws one of the planet's highest concentrations of monarch butterflies, which make a mind-boggling trip from Mexico all the way here. Unfortunately, biologists have noted a dramatic drop-off in monarch numbers, attributed to pollution and logging.

And the best part: Even on a summer holiday weekend, few people visit the gorgeous beachfront here, probably because it requires a bit of walking. It is truly a secluded gem in a busy region.

## Hiking

The park maintains nearly 40 miles of trails, along which you'll find wilderness campsites. A "rugged" rise here means 40 or 50 feet. Basic maps are available at the contact station. By far the most popular area of the park is the northern tier and trails leaving from the picnic area, including the **Europe Bay/Hotz Trail** (over 3 miles one-way) to Europe Lake, one of the largest of the county's inland lakes and a pristine sandy gem uncluttered by development. The trail runs through sandy forests to rocky beaches with great views of Porte des Mortes and the surrounding islands.

As you stroll the Europe Bay/Hotz Trail toward the lake, consider a quick jaunt toward a promontory called Lynd Point along **Lynd Point Trail** (1 mile one-way). Gravel Island, viewable from Lynd Point, is a national wildlife refuge.

In the southern section of the park, the picnic area also has access to the **Newport Trail** (a 5-mile loop), which heads west to Duck Bay on the eastern edge of the park; Spider Island, viewable from here, is another national wildlife refuge for nesting gulls. Along its western segment, the Newport Trail connects to the **Rowleys Bay Trail** (4 miles), which heads to the southern tip of the park at Varney Point and also passes most of the campsites. Both trails alternately pass through meadows, wooded areas, and along limestone headlands on the coast, mostly along old logging roads.

## Biking

Mountain bikes are allowed on 17 miles of the park's trails; essentially, anywhere that hikers can go, bikers can also get to, but generally on a parallel trail. Basic maps are available at the park contact station. Bike camping is possible, although the park warns of porcupine damage to bikes parked overnight. Note that the trails are mostly hardpacked dirt but have regular bikers' land mines—potholes of quicksand, python-size tree roots hidden under leaves, and more than a few patches of gravel. The most conspicuous off-limits areas are the shoreline routes—it's too tempting for bikers to whip down onto the fragile sands.

Lake Michigan coastline in Newport State Park

## Camping

Here's the reason outdoor aficionados pilgrimage here regularly—there's no vehicular access to the campsites. The 16 sites (13 are reservable) are strictly walk-in—a serious hike to most, but it beats the traffic of Potawatomi and the peninsula; the shortest hike in is 0.5 miles, the longest nearly 4 miles. Two sites on Europe Lake are waterside, so canoes can land and camp. The Lake Michigan side has plenty of lakeside sites. Winter camping is outstanding here. Make your **reservations** (888/947-2757, www.wisconsinstateparks.reserveamerica.com, from $25 for nonresidents plus a $10 reservation fee) as early as possible.

# Bayside

Highways 42 and 57 have been undergoing widening and straightening for years, and the debate over the project possibly exceeds the actual amount of work done. South of Sturgeon Bay, the road has already turned into multilane madness, and Highway 42 north of Sturgeon Bay is gradually approaching interstate-highway capacity and speeds.

Highway 42 has perhaps the most intriguing history of any county road. Not your average farm-to-market remnant, it was hewn from a tundra-like wilderness in 1857 by starving millers and fishers who became desperate when winter arrived earlier than expected and froze their supply boats out of the harbor.

On the way to Egg Harbor from Sturgeon Bay, a great on-the-water side trip is along Highway B. Eventually, Highway B merges with Highway G around Horseshoe Bay and leads directly to Egg Harbor.

## EGG HARBOR

There's something of a contrived (officially, "revitalized") feel to Egg Harbor on Highway 42. A couple of 19th-century structures have been redone with fresh facades, and there's more than a little new development, including a pseudo-Victorian strip mall that could have been plunked down in any city suburb or fringe sprawl in the country.

Built on a rise overlooking one of the most

Frank E. Murphy County Park

accessible and well-protected harbors along either coast, the harbor had long been in use by the Winnebago people before military material and trade ships anchored here—it was the only safe harbor between Fish Creek and Little Sturgeon Bay. In the 1850s, Jacob and Levi Thorp, two brothers of the founder of Fish Creek, collaborated to build a pier to allow the transport of local cordwood. By the 1890s the town rivaled Fish Creek.

The name Egg Harbor isn't about an ovoid land configuration but comes from a legendary 1825 battle between vacationing rich folk. While rowing to shore in longboats, boredom apparently got the best of the well-to-do, who started throwing eggs from their picnic provisions at each other. Locals celebrate this event with occasional staged—and eminently delightful—egg throws. Thus, everything here is an "eggscape."

## Sights

As you wind off Highway 42 and down the hillside into Egg Harbor, the first sight is perhaps the most picturesque **village park** in the county, with a small strand of smooth-stone and sand beach. There are lovely free concerts Thursday and Sunday in summer. A couple of miles farther south on Horseshoe Bay Road is an even better view of Horseshoe Bay and another very sandy beach at **Frank E. Murphy County Park.**

A noteworthy sight and a landmark for denizens of the Door is the Gothic Revival **Cupola House** (7836 Hwy. 42, 920/868-3941), a massive building constructed in 1871 by Levi Thorp, a local cordwood dealer and one of the wealthiest men in the county. During the summer, resident artists at the Birch Creek Center give performances at the house; the mansion houses an assortment of shops and boutiques.

Ultrapremium wines, made through what they call microvinification, are sold at **Stone's Throw Winery** (3382 Hwy. E, http://stonesthrowwinery.com, 920/839-9660), in a cool old barn. In Egg Harbor, **Harbor Ridge** (Harbor Ridge Court, http://

harborridgewinery.com, 920/868-4321) has as many cheeses and soaps as wines, but they get kudos for their dedication to charities.

## Entertainment

Just east of Egg Harbor, a quaint old dairy barn now houses the **Birch Creek Music Center** (Hwy. E, 920/868-3763, www.birchcreek.org). The acoustics are extraordinary, considering that cows once lived here. Evening concerts by students and national names in the big barn are scheduled regularly, generally mid-July through Labor Day, and are something of a tradition in the area—the big band series is particularly popular, and percussion performances are the specialty.

## Food

All of these options are right on the main drag. A favorite for a grab-and-go meal in the state is at **Macready Artisan Bread** (7836 Hwy. 42, 920/868-2233, http://macreadyartisanbread.com, 9am-4pm Thurs.-Mon., from $5). The bread is sublime, and there are many varieties—including sweet potato bread. The proprietors are two of the nicest folks you will run into on your travels. Pair that up with cheese and dry cured meats from over 30 small-scale Wisconsin cheesemakers at **Schoolhouse Artisan Cheese** (7813 Hwy. 42, 920/868-2400, 10am-5pm Sun.-Thurs., 10am-6pm Fri.-Sat.) nearby and head out on a picnic!

The early meal and lunch of choice is at the long-standing **Village Cafe** (7918 Hwy. 42, 920/868-3342, 8am-10pm daily, entrées $14-25) at the north end of town, a from-scratch place where you can find a vegan burger or chicken-fried steak done up Door County style with cherries and pecans, or a waiter entertaining diners when things are slow (rarely).

**Shipwrecked** (7791 Egg Harbor Rd., 920/868-2767, 11am-10pm daily) has good pub grub but is better known as the county's only microbrewery; watch them brewing as you quaff, and try the cherry wheat ales. Al Capone supposedly loved to hang out with the lumberjacks here and used the subterranean caverns to hide from the law.

If you're skeptical about finding decent tapas in the Great Lakes region, rest assured that ★ **Parador** (7829 Egg Harbor Rd., 920/868-2255, from 5pm daily, from $8) has fantastic Spanish cuisine in a comfortably small setting. As you're in the land of the Cheeseheads, be sure to try the Spanish mac and cheese.

Kids may prefer the **Log Den** (6626 Hwy. 42, 920/868-3888, lunch and dinner daily, brunch Sun., $8-25), just south of Egg Harbor on Highway 42, a 10,000-square-foot place that doesn't really feel immense. The name is no misnomer, as there is wood everywhere, much of it ornately, at times cheekily, carved into a menagerie of anthropomorphisms. The menu runs from great—and moderately priced—burgers and sandwiches to ahi tuna, bluepoint oysters, and prime rib. The families that run the place have lived along these shores and in these woods for more than a century. It's also a fun place to watch a Packers football game.

Carnivores will want to head directly to **Casey's BBQ & Smokehouse** (7855 Hwy. 42, 920/868-3038, http:// caseysbbqandsmokehouse.com, 11am-9pm Sun.-Thurs., 11am-10pm Fri.-Sat., $8-24), just about the perfect place to gorge on brisket or ribs after a long day of paddling or pedaling.

## Accommodations

The cheapest accommodations to be found in Egg Harbor will usually run $90 or more. That said, the **Lullabi Inn** (7928 Egg Harbor Rd./Hwy. 42, 920/868-3135, www.lullabi-inn.com, from $90), on the north end of town, the cheapest available, sometimes has guest rooms for less than that, and you can expect a welcoming atmosphere despite the low rates. Stay in small but clean doubles, or upgrade to an array of larger guest rooms and apartments.

Similar rates and modest but clean lodgings—along with a nearby orchard—can be found at the **Cape Cod Motel** (7682 Hwy.

42, 920/868-3271, capecodmoteldoorcounty. com, from $90), where the proprietors are always helpful.

Plenty of self-contained islands of luxury surround Egg Harbor. The least expensive guest rooms at the **Landing Resort** (7741 Hwy. 42, 920/868-3282, http:// thelandingresort.com, $140-250) are cramped but clean and well-appointed. Higher rates apply to the dizzying array of condo apartments. You can't beat a place that has been recommended by people for more than a generation. Ask for a room with the woodside view.

You'll find award-winning guest rooms at **Ashbrooke Suites** (7942 Egg Harbor Rd., 920/868-3113, www.ashbrooke.net, $170-249), with one- and two-bedroom suites done up in myriad styles, such as French country and wicker. It's just up the road from the Lullabi Inn.

One of the best-run resort complexes in the county, ★ **Newport Resort** (7888 Church St., 800/468-6160, www.newportresort.com, $179-249) has various one- and two-bedroom options, all with spectacular views. There are indoor and outdoor pools, a sauna, and lots of stuff for families, including a coin laundry.

Other travelers have opined that the service is superlative and the views equally spectacular from the villas at the **Bay Point Inn** (7933 Hwy. 42, 800/707-6660, http:// baypointinn.com, from $249). The beds are amazingly soft.

Nonresort options abound in Egg Harbor. Try **Woldt's Intown Farmette** (7960 Church St., 920/559-7475, www.richwoldt. com, $125, $725 weekly). This two-story cottage is adjacent to a reconstructed Dutch colonial barn and windmill. The proprietors, locals to the core, strive to make it feel like the good old days. Turn east on Highway E, then north onto Church Street.

Coming into town on Highway 42, turn east onto Highway T for one mile to reach **Door County Cottages** (4355 Hwy. T, 920/868-2300, www.doorcountycottages. com, $170-248, $1,250-2,300 weekly). It has a reconstructed main cottage, lovingly put together from collected fieldstone. In fact, this place was green before green was in. Built into earthen berms with southern glassed exposure, two of the main retreats are very cozy. The sun-soaked two-bedroom cottage can sleep six and offers a combined kitchen-dining room-living area and a boardwalk to a Finnish wood sauna.

## Information

The local library has a small **Visitors Information Center** (920/868-3717, www.egghabordoorcounty.org).

## ★ FISH CREEK

This graceful community offers visitors the anticipated coffee-table pictorials. It may be the soul of the county, but it's also just another Door County village with a small population. The most picturesque view in the county is along Highway 42 as it winds into the village from a casual bluff. The official village history describes the town's situation succinctly— "with its back to a rock and its face to the sea." A treasured stretch of road with a few hairpin turns, a roller-coaster drop, and suddenly you're in a trim and tidy Victorian hamlet that could have come from a Currier and Ives print. Fish Creek boasts the most thoroughly maintained pre-20th-century architecture on the peninsula, with about 40 historic structures.

In 1844, trader Increase Claflin, the first nonnative permanent settler in Door County, left Sturgeon Bay after a few less-than-propitious incidents with the Potawatomi people and wound up here. About the same time, an Eastern cooper afflicted with terminal wanderlust, Asa Thorp, made his way to Door County, searching for his fortune. With his two brothers, Thorp constructed a loading pier and began a cordwood cutting business to supply the steamships plying the coast. Later, Fish Creek transformed itself into the hub of commercial fishing on the Door Peninsula. Fortuitously, growing tourism took up the slack when the steamship supply

business petered out. By the late 1890s locals were already putting out "Tourist Home" signs. Within a decade, even the home of Asa Thorp had been transformed into the Thorp Hotel.

## Sights

Most visitors to Fish Creek simply stroll around to see the 19th-century architecture. The harbor area has remnants of the earliest cabins, and the remains of an 1855 cabin built by the founding Thorp brothers stands on the grounds of the modern Founders Square mélange of shops and restaurants in the village center; after a fire, they were rebuilt as closely as possible to the original designs. Another landmark structure is the notoriously haunted 1875 Greek Revival **Noble House** (Hwy. 42 and Main St., 920/868-2091, noon-5pm Fri.-Sat. mid-May-mid-June, noon-5pm Tues.-Sun. mid-June-Labor Day, $3). The **Gibraltar Historical Association** (920/868-2091) provides **historic walking tours.**

Perhaps the most accessible winery in Door County, and one that focuses on the county, **Lautenbach's Orchard Country Winery & Market** (Hwy. 42 S., 866/946-3263, www.orchardcountry.com, 9am-5:30pm Sun.-Thurs., 9am-6pm Fri.-Sat., $4 tours) is a favorite for everyone. The winery has award-winning county fruit wines, pick-your-own fruits, sleigh rides, and more. They hold a summer cherry festival with complimentary wine and food tastings and live music at the end of July. The winery is a pickup point for the tours run by Sturgeon Bay's **Door County Trolley** (920/868-1100, www.doorcountytrolley.com).

## Recreation

Without chartering a boat or flying your own plane, the easiest way to take in (but not actually step onto) **Chambers Island,** located across the Strawberry Channel, is via **Fish Creek Scenic Boat Tours** (Clark Park, 920/421-4442, $39), which offers a variety of tours. You can take a quieter tour of Fish Creek twice daily with sailboat rides by **Friendly Charters** (920/256-9042, www.

# ★ The Cherry on Top

Home to almost 50 orchards, Door County is the fourth largest cherry producing region in the nation. Seriously, you can't leave this place without trying some cherry concoction. The cherry trees blossom in May and harvest season runs from mid-July to early August.

If you're not sure where to begin, try one of the following:

- Pick-your-own cherries during harvest season at **Lautenbach's Orchard Country Winery & Market** (page 46).

- Try the cherry-stuffed french toast at Fish Creek's **White Gull Inn** (page 48). It was good enough to take first place in *Good Morning America*'s quest for the best breakfast in America.

- Attend a **cherry festival** in late July in Fish Creek (page 46) or in early August in Jacksonport (page 36).

- Buy a cherry pie, jam, or one of many other cherry souvenirs at **The Cherry Hut** (page 48) in Fish Creek or at **Seaquist Orchards Farm Market** (page 56) in Sister Bay.

- Sample a local cherry wine at **Red Oak Vineyard & Winery** (page 23) in Sturgeon Bay.

friendlycharters.com, from $45 pp), which also has several tour options.

Boat and bicycle rentals are available in town at **Nor Door Sport and Cyclery** (4007 Hwy. 42, 920/868-2275) near the entrance to Peninsula State Park. It is the place to get a hybrid bike, a mountain bike, or a single-speed cruiser ($25 per day). Plenty of other equipment is also for rent. In winter, you can rent cross-country skis and even snowshoes and ice skates.

At **Edge of Park Bikes and Mopeds** (Park Entrance Rd., 920/868-3344), moped rental includes a state park access sticker.

## Entertainment and Events

The country's oldest summer theater, the **Peninsula Players** (Peninsula Players Rd., off Hwy. 42 south of Fish Creek, 920/868-3287, www.peninsulaplayers.com) perform Broadway plays and musicals in a gorgeous garden setting with bay-side trails late June through mid-October, a tradition in its seventh decade. Reservations are advised. Relatively recent renovations to the theater include heated floors.

Less than half as old but with boatloads of attitude, the tongue-in-cheek **Northern Sky Theater** (920/854-6117, www.

northernskytheater.com) is an acclaimed theater-and-song troupe, as likely to perform their own rollicking originals (*Cheeseheads: The Musical* and *Guys on Ice*, a paean to ice fishing) or a ghost-story series as they are the works of the Bard. Performances (May-mid-Oct.) are held in Peninsula State Park and now include an autumn Town Hall Series, performed at venues around the county. Mixed with the zaniness is an admirable amount of history.

During August, professional musicians from across the country assemble in Fish Creek for the annual **Peninsula Music Festival** (920/854-4060, www.musicfestival.com), which offers Renaissance, Reformation, baroque, and chamber ensembles, along with an array of thematic material. Nationally known folk musicians and touring troupes appear at the **Door County Auditorium** (3926 Hwy. 42, 920/868-2787, www.dcauditorium.com); theater and dance performances are also held regularly.

At the north end of town, the **Skyway Drive In** (3475 Hwy. 42, 920/854-9938, www.doorcountydrivein.com) is a throwback movie experience—it's charming to catch a flick under the stars with a wafting Green Bay breeze.

## Food

Road warriors with little time to spare: Coming into Fish Creek from the south, hit **Lautenbach's Orchard Country Winery & Market** (9197 Hwy. 42 S., 866/946-3263, www.orchardcountry.com, 9am-5:30pm Sun.-Thurs., 9am-6pm Fri.-Sat.) for some cheese, then up the road 0.5 miles to **The Cherry Hut** (8813 Hwy. 42, 920/868-3406, 9am-6pm daily) to pick up cherry pie. Then head downtown to **Fish Creek Market** (4164 Hwy. 42, 920/868-3351, 9am-8pm Mon.-Sat, 9am-6pm Sun.) for some freshly baked bread. Find a spot on Green Bay and have a picnic. It's not necessarily the cheapest option, but it's an unbeatable experience.

**The Cookery** (Hwy. 42, 920/868-3634, breakfast, lunch, and dinner daily, $7-30), a sunny café with great healthy takes on standards, is a well-thought-out and well-run place despite often being packed. A 2009 rebuild was done with sustainability in mind, and the food comes from local producers as much as possible.

Even picky foodies rave about the pizzas at ★ **Wild Tomato** (4023 Hwy. 42, 920/868-3095, 11am-10pm daily summer, 11am-10pm Thurs.-Sun. other seasons, closed Jan., $9-27). Even this author, no fan of tomato sauce and thus pizza, eats here regularly. Eat local, act local—it's all here.

Fish boils are a must, and Fish Creek's choice is the boisterous **Pelletier's** (Founder's Square, 920/868-3313, 5pm-7:30pm Sun.-Thurs., 5pm-8pm Fri.-Sat., fish boil $17). The fish boil is the best thing on the menu, but family-style meat-and-potatoes items are less expensive than at most other restaurants in town; this is also a great spot for a crowd of kids.

Resist the urge to balk at the words "fondue" and "Asian" in the same restaurant description: ★ **Mr. Helsinki** (above the Fish Creek Market, Main St., 920/868-9898, 5pm-11pm daily, $7-22) is an international fusion bistro that specializes in everything from crepes to a dash of Latin and a lot of Asian tastes, and does it well, right down to homegrown Kaffir limes and Mexican epazote. You can even get a luscious vegan squash curry. It's a bit funky, irreverent, and a whole lot of something else.

The food at the almost-historic **Alexander's** (3667 Hwy. 42., 920/868-3532, dinner daily, brunch Sun., $14-30) can best be called an upscale supper club; the 1950s easy listening music is definitely so. It is worth a visit for the cherry duck or the broiled whitefish.

**Gibraltar Grill** (3993 Main St., 920/868-4745, lunch and dinner daily May-Oct., $7-20) is an absolutely unpretentious place with above-average fare, from sandwiches to seafood risotto. Enjoy high-quality fare in shorts and a T-shirt with your pooch while sitting outside. There is often live music, and an all-electric shuttle ferries guests from any local location to and from the establishment. For a ride, just call the restaurant's phone number.

The ★ **White Gull Inn** (4225 Main St., 920/868-3517, www.whitegullinn.com, breakfast 7:30am-2:30pm daily, lunch 12pm-2:30pm daily, dinner 5pm-8pm on varying weekdays, $14-25) is legendary for its breakfast—*Good Morning America* even declared its cherry-stuffed french toast the best breakfast in the country. The restaurant has a tasty selection of sandwiches for lunch and a seasonal dinner menu with a lot of seafood options. Dinner is lower-key and definitely for early birds. Note that dinner is served Saturday through Thursday only in the winter months and Monday, Tuesday, and Thursday in the summer months. The Inn also hosts fantastic fish boils. In the summer, fish boils are offered on Wednesday and Friday-Sunday at 5:45pm, 7pm, and 8:15pm; in winter, only one fish boil is offered on Friday at 7pm.

The White Gull Inn gets much-deserved media attention for its dining, but for dinner, you may not be able to beat ★ **The Whistling Swan** (4192 Main St., 920/868-3442, www.whistlingswan.com, Tues.-Sat. 5pm-10pm, $18-36). Expect a gorgeous setting, gorgeous food impeccably done, and top-notch staff. The menu includes locally sourced, seasonal entrées with foraged produce, wild game, and local fish. This is a genuine treat.

## Accommodations

Pet-friendly **Julie's** (4020 Hwy. 42, 920/868-2999, www.juliesmotel.com, $85-120), a home-away-from-home near the state park, has basic but good-quality guest rooms and a super café, where breakfast rivals the pricier and better-known digs in town.

The nice guest rooms at **Applecreek Resort and Cottages** (Hwy. 42 and Hwy. F, 920/868-3525, www.applecreekresort.com, from $110) come in a variety of configurations.

Despite its name, the wonderful **Main Street Motel** (4209 Hwy. 42, 920/868-2201, http://mainstreetmoteldc.com, from $108) is nothing ordinary. The solicitous, friendly proprietors offer very well-maintained themed guest rooms, but don't blanch at staying in the Teddy Bear Room, as the guest rooms and service rival any resort in terms of value—and it isn't kitschy.

The **Fish Creek Motel and Cottages** (Cottage Row, 920/868-3448, www.fishcreekmotel.com, from $119), at the end of Cottage Row, a block and a half past the stop sign off Highway 42, is an amazing motel that was actually built in Ephraim and boated around the point in 1981; it has since been renovated. Complimentary use of bicycles is a nice touch.

If you're not a fan of the "old stuff crammed in an old building" school of interior decorating, the **Juniper Inn** (9432 Maple Grove Rd., 920/839-2629, http://juniperinn.com, from $140) is refreshingly modern. The rates are also decent; each of the four guest rooms offers something different, such as a gas fireplace, a private sitting room, and a deck with gorgeous views, and all share a lovely library.

Travel writers scour every inch of the peninsula annually, looking to scoop other media outlets on an undiscovered gem, but they generally rehash the same old thing: the stately grace and charm of the ★ **White Gull Inn** (4255 Main St., 920/868-3517, www.whitegullinn.com, $175-325). A proud old guesthouse since 1897, it's truly the grande dame of Door County. Guest rooms—a couple with private porches—are anachronistic but still plush; a few cottages and guest rooms in a cliff house are also available. The dining room serves a spectacular array of continental, creative regional, and seafood cuisine in a

The Whistling Swan

country-inn atmosphere that's not at all stuffy. And then there's that legendary boisterous fish boil, so popular that people swear they've made the return trip just to experience it. It's made extra special by the boil masters, who often preside over impromptu singing.

You'll find the most history of all at the **Thorp House Inn and Cottages** (4135 Bluff Rd., 920/868-2444, www.thorphouseinn.com, $125-205 rooms, $175-225 cottages), on land that once belonged to Freeman Thorp, nephew of Fish Creek's founding father. The inn is backed by the bluff overlooking the harbor. When Thorp perished in a 1903 shipwreck, his widow was forced to convert their new Victorian into a guesthouse. The B&B-style guest rooms at the inn and the great beach house feel anachronistic, and the cottages are quaint but modernized just enough that you can dock your iPod and access Wi-Fi.

A main rival to the White Gull Inn is ★ **The Whistling Swan** (4192 Main St., 920/868-3442, www.whistlingswan.com, $150-220), with the most dramatic local history—it was originally constructed across Green Bay in Marinette and skidded across the winter ice in 1907 to its present site. Five period guest rooms and two suites are available; the arched windows, fireplace, and high ceilings of the lobby are a draw for casual browsers in the shops on the main level.

The most unusual place you're likely to find in Door County is the four-floored **Silo Guest House** (3089 Evergreen Rd., 920/868-2592, $110), near the state park. It has two bedrooms and is fully furnished. The top floor is the living room, which offers a grand view of the surrounding areas. It rents by the week only ($700) in July-August; it's available by the night ($110) September to June.

Nightly rates of more than $350 may sound outrageous, but the villas at the **Little Sweden** (8984 Hwy. 42, 920/868-9950, http://little-sweden.com) timeshare property are absolutely enormous (the smallest two-bedroom is nearly 1,200 square feet). Guest rooms can sleep 4 to 10 people, the site is heavily wooded with good privacy, and you can access recreation options such as bicycles, golf, and more.

## Information

The **Fish Creek Information Center** (4097 Hwy. 42, 920/868-2316 or 800/577-1880, www.visitfishcreek.com) is fully equipped to deal with your travel queries or last-minute needs.

## ★ PENINSULA STATE PARK

The park comprises 3,800 variegated acres stretching from the northern fringe of Fish Creek, past Strawberry Channel, past Eagle Bluff, past Nicolet Bay, and finally to Eagle Harbor and Ephraim, all of it magnificent. Deeded to the state in 1909, Peninsula is the second-oldest park in the state system and the most visited—it draws more visitors per year than Yellowstone National Park.

The peninsula, rising 180 feet above the lake at Eagle Bluff, is a manifestation of the western edge of the Niagara Escarpment, here a steep and variegated series of headlands and reentrants. The ecosystem is unparalleled: Near Weborg Point in the southwest, the Peninsula White Cedar Forest Natural Area is a 53-acre stand of spruce, cedar, balsam, and hemlock along with the boggy residual tract of an ancient lake. The 80-acre Peninsula Beech Forest Natural Area is a primitive example of northern mixed hardwood; it's also a relatively uncommon stand of American beech. Within both natural areas are a few threatened species, including the vivid dwarf lake iris. Other rarities include gaywings, Indian paintbrush, blue-eyed grass, and downy gentian. Be sure to stay for the sunset.

## History

Like elsewhere, the first European in the area, Increase Claflin, was a squatter; he built his cabin high above the Strawberry Islands in 1844. Encampments of the Plano people have been examined that date to 7000-4000 BC, and the Menominee, Fox, Winnebago, Iroquois, and Potawatomi peoples have all occupied lakeside sites. The Native American presence and unusually harmonious relations with them are symbolized by the **Memorial Pole.** This 40-foot totem pole commemorates Potawatomi chief Simon Khaquados, laid to rest here in 1930 before thousands of admirers. Unfortunately, the newcomers didn't love him enough to preclude building a golf course around his grave; the pole today sits between the 1st and 9th fairways.

## Sights

A must-see is the **Eagle Bluff Lighthouse** (920/421-3636), built during the Civil War by U.S. lighthouse crewmen as the second of the peninsula's lighthouses, a square tower about 45 feet tall attached to the keeper's house. It stands atop the bluff and can be seen for 15 miles; the views from its top stretch even farther. The prize assignment for lighthouse keepers on the peninsula, it had a commanding view and the best salary, the princely sum (for 1880) of $50 per month. Public interest prompted local historical societies to peel off 80 layers of paint and set to work refurbishing the lighthouse in the late 1950s. Tours ($5 adults) are given in early summer and autumn every 30 minutes 10am-4:30pm Monday-Friday, with shorter hours the rest of year.

Two 75-foot towers were erected at the park's inception and used as fire-spotting towers; one was later removed because of dry rot. **Eagle Tower** was built because so many people wanted to view a pair of long-term nesting eagles—the two for whom the bluff, the harbor, and the peninsula were eventually named. In 2015 the tower was closed due to structural decay, and rebuilding it may not be feasible.

Before going hiking, most visitors head to the **White Cedar Nature Center** (Bluff Rd., 920/854-5976, 10am-2pm daily Memorial Day-Labor Day, shorter hours Labor Day-Memorial Day) to walk a nature trail and view a host of exhibits covering the park's natural history.

## Recreation
### GOLF

Deemed one of the gems of Midwestern courses by the golf press, this 18-holer is in the eastern part of the park. It was built by a group of Ephraim businessmen in the early 1900s as a nine-hole course with sand greens. Tee-time **reservations** (920/854-5791) are required at this busy course. Make them as early as possible.

swans at Peninsula State Park

## HIKING

More than 20 miles of hiking trails lace the park and the shores of the bays. After parking and checking out Eagle Tower in the northern section of the park, ambitious visitors can take **Minnehaha Trail** (easy, 0.5 miles) or **Sentinel Trail** (easy, 2-mile loop) for some grand hiking. Minnehaha also connects to the South Nicolet Bay campground (near site 844) and runs along the lakeshore with great bay vistas; Sentinel runs through stands of maple, birch, and red pine, and 0.5 miles is surfaced with gravel for accessibility. The moderately difficult 0.5-mile spur **Lone Pine Trail,** off Sentinel Trail, leads up a dolomite bluff and through beech and oak trees, at one point passing the trail's solitary pine tree, now fallen along the trail. The toughest trail, but also the most rewarding, is **Eagle Trail,** skirting the harbor and a couple of natural springs for two miles and affording challenging scrambles over 200-foot bluffs; it's a workout, but you'll see lots of trilliums and thimbleberries.

In the north and west sections of the park, there are a couple of must-hike trails. In the north, so many people hiked from Nicolet Bay to Eagle Bluff lighthouse through cool stands of trees that an easy 0.5-mile trail was blazed, now dubbed the **Trail Tramper's Delight Trail.** Also from Welcker's Campground at Nicolet Bay, the 2.2-mile (one-way) **Nicolet Bay Trail** is a good bet for birders; you'll likely see wild turkeys.

At its halfway point, the Nicolet Bay Trail connects with two great trails, both moderately difficult. The two-mile **Hemlock Trail** rises up a modest bluff to great views of the Strawberry Islands, and the three-mile loop **Skyline Trail** rises up minor Sven's Bluff and past the remains of old homestead farms and fences, now decaying gracefully in the grasses and meadows.

## BIKING

There are 15 miles of road and off-road bike trails; a state trail pass is required. What may be the most heavily used recreational trail—**Sunset Trail**—starts near the park entrance and roughly parallels Shore Road for nearly five miles through marsh and stands of hardwoods and conifers and along the lakeside perimeter of Nicolet Bay Beach, at which point lovely back roads lead back to the park entrance. At dusk it is definitely not misnamed. Remember that this trail is multiuse, meaning pedestrian and wheelchair traffic; wheels yield to heels.

Bicycle rentals ($25 per day) are available

Eagle Bluff Lighthouse

at **Nicolet Beach Rentals** (920/854-9220) in the northern end of the park.

## KAYAKING AND CANOEING

You won't forget a kayak or canoe trip to **Horseshoe Island,** which has its own one-mile trail. It is rugged and definitely isolated even though it's only a mile from Nicolet Bay. Kayakers and canoeists love Tennison Bay on the west side of the park due to its shallow draft. Kayak rentals ($50 per day) are available from **Nicolet Beach Rentals** (920/854-9220) in the northern end of the park.

## CAMPING

Camping was once allowed almost anywhere the ranger waved his hand and was either free or cost $0.50 per week. Today, the state's Department of Natural Resources receives up to 5,200 applications for summer reservations in January. At last count there were 469 campsites in five sectors, and even though 25 are not reservable, it's almost impossible to get a site without a **reservation** (888/947-2757, www.wisconsinstateparks.reserveamerica. com, from $25 per site, $10 reservation fee), especially on Friday and Saturday.

Only one sector is open year-round. All sectors have showers, but a couple have no electrical hookups. Many people prefer **South Nicolet Bay** (143 sites) since it's large, has electrical hookups, and is closest to the sandy beach. You have to reserve early in January to get a waterside site. **North Nicolet Bay** campground (44 sites) is also not far from the beach but is smaller and has no electricity. Early reservations are also a must to get a waterside site. The park's largest campground is **Tennison Bay** (188 sites); this is also the accessible campground. There is no beach nearby, however, and no waterside sites. **Weborg Point** (12 sites) and **Welcker's Point** (81 sites) fill up last. Given the small size, Weborg should be quieter, but the electrical hookups mean there is generator noise; it does have waterside sites. Welcker's Point, without electrical hookups, is quieter.

# EPHRAIM

As the map tells it, five miles separate Fish Creek and Ephraim (pronounced EE-frum), but you'd hardly know it. On the way north, as you pass the north entrance of Peninsula State Park, a modest jumble of development appears and then vanishes, and shortly the fringes of beautiful Ephraim appear.

Another endlessly long Door County village along a vivid harbor, Ephraim isn't the oldest community in the county, nor are its structures the most historically distinguished, but aesthetically the community is the most perfectly preserved slice of Door County. The quaintness isn't accidental—for a while the village dictated, via social pressure, that all structures were to be whitewashed in proper fashion. The town is set along gorgeous Eagle Harbor. An enclave of pious fortitude, it was settled by Norwegian Moravians and named Ephraim, which means "doubly fruitful" in Hebrew.

## Sights

The oldest church in the county, the **Moravian Church** (9970 Moravia St., 920/854-2804), built out of necessity when the village founder's living room no longer sufficed, was built in 1857 of cedar from the Upper Peninsula; local logs were too rough for such a sacred house. Tours ($5) of the church are offered at 1:30pm Thursday.

Also on Moravia Street are three other structures that operate as one museum (920/854-9688, 11am-4pm Mon.-Sat. mid-June-Aug., 11am-4pm Fri.-Sat. Sept.-Oct., $5 includes tour). The **Pioneer Schoolhouse Museum** (9998 Moravia St.) doubles as a repository of local history. Displays of local art in various media, from juried shows and chosen by local arts associations, are worth a look. The third historic structure along the street is the **Thomas Goodletson Cabin,** an 1857 original inside and out and one of the peninsula's first cabins. Down off the bluff are the **Anderson Barn and Store,** a ruddy barn built in 1870. During the summer, it's open for browsing; the prominent square silo is a rarity. Built in 1858 by Aslag Anderson, one of the original Scandinavian settlers, it sports old-time store items along with museum-like pieces.

Summertime **walking tours** of all the historic structures depart at 10:30am Tuesday-Friday (call to verify) from the Anderson Barn. Nice are the less-sweat-inducing 90-minute **tram tours** (11am Tues.-Sat., $10), a quick way to take in all the local history.

## Recreation

South Shore Pier, in the heart of Ephraim village, has a large number of water-based recreation and tour opportunities. Hour-plus catamaran cruises (from $29), including a sunset cruise, depart seven times daily aboard the *Stiletto* (920/854-7245). Or rent your own pontoon boat, kayak, WaveRunner, paddleboat, or fishing boat from the **South Shore Pier** (920/854-4324). Other operations offer kayak and windsurfing lessons and rentals, and even parasail rides.

## Festivals

The highlight of the entire year in Ephraim is the Scandinavian summer solstice celebration **Fyr Bal Festival.** Bonfires dot the shoreline and fish-boil cauldrons gurgle to commemorate the arrival of summer. A "Viking chieftain" is crowned and then blesses the ships and the harbor. The accompanying art fairs are less Norse in nature.

## Food

There are precious few restaurants in Ephraim; the lodges and resorts take most of the food business. And until 2016, Ephraim was the only municipality in Wisconsin that banned the sale of alcohol. In a state where drinking seems second only to Packer-backing, this lone dry town was something of an anomaly. However, a referendum was passed allowing the sale of beer and wine (only).

At **Good Eggs** (9820 Brookside Lane, 920/854-6621, 7am-1pm daily May-Oct., $5-9), set back along Highway 42, you can build

your own omelet, wrap it up in a tortilla (try the cilantro), and dash. Or sit at their surfboard tables and relax with a view of the water.

A tiny step up in price is the casually creative ★ **Chef's Hat** (Hwy. Q, 920/854-2034, 8am-9pm daily, $7-22), off the main highway. Pear and pumpkin soup and a sandwich pretty much sum it up, and the scones are delicious.

The **Old Post Office** (10040 Hwy. 42, 920/854-4034, breakfast and dinner daily, $5-10) in the Edgewater Resort is known mostly for one of the biggest fish boils in the county, but also for Belgian waffles.

It's nearly a Door County law that you stop at **Wilson's** (9990 Water St., 920/854-2041, from 11am daily May-Oct.), an old-fashioned ice cream parlor in the heart of the village. Opened in 1906 and serving ever since, it has ice cream cones as big as bullhorns as well as burgers and homemade soups and salads (but stick to the ice cream). Hanging out on the white-framed porch, you'll feel as if you're in a Norman Rockwell painting.

## Accommodations

Understated and good for the wallet, **Trollhaugen** (Hwy. 42, 920/854-2713, www.trollhaugenlodge.com, $88-169), just north of the action in the village, is part motel, part lodge, and even has a log cabin. It's in a quiet wooded setting with updated lodge decor.

You won't find more charming hosts than those at the **Ephraim Motel** (10407 Hwy. 42, 920/854-5959, from $104); the guest rooms are worth the rates as well.

The **Eagle Harbor Inn** (9914 Hwy. 42, 920/854-2121, www.eagleharbor.com, $115-275) is well reviewed. Some swear it's better value than anywhere else in the region. The elegant nine-room inn, with two suites, is antique-strewn and offers a sumptuous country breakfast in the garden. The one- to three-bedroom cottages on nicely wooded grounds are also very appealing.

★ **Lodgings at Pioneer Lane** (9998

Pioneer Lane, 920/854-7656 or 800/588-3565, www.lodgingsatpioneerlane.com, from $199) has themed guest rooms. This might evoke images of embarrassing tackiness, but here it is impeccably executed, with kitchenettes, fireplaces, private porches or balconies, and superb details. The owners get rave reviews as well. It's north of Wilson's ice cream parlor, then right on Church Street.

## Information

Ephraim's **Information Center** (920/854-4989, www.ephraim-doorcounty.com), is right along Highway 42. A 24-hour kiosk is there in season for last-minute motel seekers.

# SISTER BAY

Sister Bay can get congested on a typical summer Saturday—symbolic of its status as the largest community north of Sturgeon Bay, even though the population is a mere 900. It's also the only spot north on the peninsula with a small shopping mall. Named for twin islands offshore, the bay—not offering quite the windbreak of Eagle Harbor—never got much notice from southbound steamers until Scandinavian settlers discovered the dense forestland in the surrounding hills and erected cabins in 1857.

## Sights

Sister Bay's quaint **waterfront park** is the largest in the county at a third of a mile long, with one of the longest—and prettiest—stretches of beach around. Meaning: this is a good spot to get a bit of elbow room even in high season.

On the south edge of town is the **Old Anderson House Museum** (Hwy. 57 and Fieldcrest Rd., 920/854-7680, tours 10am-3pm Tues.-Sat. and holidays mid-May-mid-Oct., free), a restored house dating from 1895. The house was built in Marinette, Wisconsin, and dragged across the ice. Other area historical structures have also been relocated to this site.

## Recreation

**Bayshore Outdoors** (920/854-7598, www.kayakdoorcounty.com) has daily guided kayak tours along with rentals of cross-country skis, snowshoes, and bicycles.

Sister Bay has a local **dog park** (Woodcrest Rd., east of Hwy. 42 on Hwy. ZZ) to let the furry knuckleheads romp.

## Festivals and Events

The waterfront park hosts the huge **Fall Festival** with a 900-square-foot outdoor

Sister Bay

stage. The park is the linchpin of a fine community network of parks that offer regular doses of free big band, jazz, country, and folk concerts—there is one every Wednesday in summer.

## Food

For the "only in Wisconsin" file: The **Sister Bay Bowl and Supper Club** (504 Bay Shore Dr., 920/854-2841, daily Apr.-Jan., Sat.-Sun. Feb.-Mar., from $5), right downtown, does have bowling, and it offers one of the better fish fries around—great if you're wearying of fish boils.

The **Base Camp Coffee House** (10904 Hwy. 42, 920/854-7894, 7:30am-2pm daily) is hard to notice, as it's in the basement of an old church behind a clothing shop. Run by a transplanted Frenchman, it has a simple, special vibe. Besides coffee, you'll find ever-so-fresh sandwiches ($6), quiches, and a limited breakfast menu ($4-6).

For a great—no, otherworldly—treat, head for ★ **Door County Creamery** (601 Hwy. 42, 920/854-3388, 10:30am-9pm, from $4), opened by lifers in the county's culinary industry. Try goat's milk gelato made daily (the goat farm is mere miles away). They've also got extraordinary handcrafted cheeses and use them to create sandwiches and salads.

**Grasse's Grill** (10663 N. Hwy. 42, 920/854-1125, lunch and dinner daily, $5-16) is utterly unpretentious and friendly; it's run by a husband-and-wife team who obviously love food. Dishes include fish tacos, meatloaf, a black-bean burger, and veggie lasagna.

The most famous international eatery in the county, if not the state, is ★ **Al Johnson's Swedish Restaurant** (702 Hwy. 42, 920/854-2626, 6am-9pm daily, $8-18), where cars regularly screech to a halt when drivers see the legendary live goats munching the sod roof. The menu offers Swedish and American food. Pounds of Swedish meatballs are served nightly, and other favorites are the Swedish beefsteak sautéed in onions and lingonberry pancakes for breakfast. It's often standing room only, quite lively, and doesn't

Yes, Al Johnson's Swedish Restaurant has goats on the roof!

take reservations. Famous Al died in 2010, a great loss for the county.

Two other slightly upscale spots also warrant attention. The excellent steakhouse ★ **Chop** (10571 Country Walk Lane, 920/854-2700, dinner daily May-Oct., dinner Wed.-Sat. Nov.-Feb., from $14) has a Kobe burger that serves as a highlight for any hungry road hog. Its fish is also outstanding.

On the north end of town, the **Waterfront** (10947 N. Hwy. 42, 920/854-5491, 5pm-9pm Tues.-Sun., $24-37) is run by a couple with three decades in the Door restaurant business; it is well-known for its seafood.

Two miles north of town, **Seaquist Orchards Farm Market** (11482 Highway 42, 920/854-4199, 9am-5pm daily) sells cherry pies as well as cherry jams, pie filling, salsa, vinaigrette, and more.

## Accommodations

Getting a room for around $75 is definitely doable in Sister Bay, a rarity in Door County. One of the cheapest motels on the Door is the

Ellison Bay

920/854-2025, www.libertyparklodge.com, from $115). The main lodge has guest rooms dating back to the Door's tourism beginnings, now lovingly redone. Also available are Cape Cod-style woodland and shore cottages. Overall there is a rich balance of old and new, and for the price, you cannot beat it.

Forty-five large (up to 600 square feet) and attractive guest rooms are available at the ★ **Country House Resort** (715 N. Highland Rd., 920/854-4551 or 800/424-0041, www. country-house.com, $125-350). All feature fridges and private waterside balconies, and some have whirlpool tubs and other miscellaneous amenities. The grounds cover 16 heavily wooded acres with private nature trails and a 1,000-foot shoreline. It's just south of the main drag, off Highway 42 and then toward the bay.

Like the county "used to be," and perhaps a steal for such updated old-school charm, **Little Sister Resort** (10620 Little Sister Hill Rd., 920/854-4013, www.littlesisterresort. com, from $160) is in a cedar forest south of Sister Bay off Highway 42 near a gorgeous bay. These very comfortable surroundings also cater to families. You'll need to brew some coffee and take a seat to go through the mind-boggling array of cabins and chalets, but this place is worth the money unless you're a solo traveler.

## Information

Sister Bay has a quaint **Visitor Information Center** (416 Gateway Dr., 920/854-2812, www.cometosisterbay.com) in a refurbished log schoolhouse.

## ELLISON BAY

Plunked along the decline of a steep hill and hollow tunneling toward a yawning bay, Ellison Bay's facade isn't initially as spectacular as Ephraim's, the architecture isn't as quaint as Fish Creek's, and it's a fifth the size of Sister Bay. Nonetheless, there is something engaging about the place. It begins with what may be the best view from the highway in the whole county. Atop the 200-foot bluff on the

pleasantly anachronistic **Bluffside Motel** (10641 Bluffside Rd., 920/854-2530, from $75). Perfectly fine for the price, it's backed up off the road for quiet and has nice tables outside. Also a bargain in the same price range is **Village View** (10628 N. Bay Shore Dr., 920/854-2813, www.villageview.com, from $75).

The helpful proprietors of **Coachlite Inn** (2544 Hwy. 42, 920/854-5503, http://coachliteinn.com, from $99) provide simple, well-kept guest rooms with fridges, and there's a nice whirlpool and hot tub room.

The guest rooms and breakfast area make the **Open Hearth Lodge** (2669 S. Hwy. 42, 920/854-4890, http://openhearthlodge.com, from $108) stand out. Indeed, the guest rooms are very well appointed, and they've done a nice job on the grounds as well; there's even enough room for a bit of hiking in the woods nearby. You'll also find a playground, an indoor pool, and fridges in every room.

Also good is the rustic, century-old **Liberty Park Lodge** (Hwy. 42, north of Sister Bay,

# ★ Fish Boils

Just when travelers think they've come to understand Wisconsin's predilection for fish fries, Door County throws them a curveball with the fish boil, which is not at all the same thing.

Scandinavian immigrants came with their own recipes for fish soups and stews, but the fish boil likely came about for purely practical reasons. Door County had few cows or pigs but was rich in whitefish; the hardy potato and onion were also abundant.

The modern version is a different story. As some tell it, the proprietor of Ellison Bay's Viking Grill concocted the first modern fish boil back in the 1960s, ostensibly searching for something unique to serve at the restaurant. It was an immediate hit that snowballed into the de rigueur culinary experience of Door County. Whatever the historical genesis of the boil, it has become a cultural linchpin for the peninsula community.

A Door County fish boil requires only a couple things: a huge iron cauldron, sufficient firewood, and the ingredients—fish steaks, small potatoes, onions, and a lot of salt. Purists favor whitefish, but don't let that stop you from trying other varieties, such as trout.

Add salt to the water and bring to a boil (the salt raises the boiling temperature of the water and helps keep the fish from flaking apart in the water). Add potatoes and boil for 15 minutes. Add onions and boil another 4-5 minutes. Add the fish, which is often wrapped in cheesecloth to

south side of town, you can see clear to Gills Rock, farther up the peninsula. Founded in the early 1860s, the village originally served as a hub for lumber, courtesy of the operations in nearby Newport State Park. As recently as the 1930s, the town's commercial fishery led Wisconsin in tonnage—perhaps the reason a local restaurant is credited with creating the first fish boil.

## Sights

Its name is often misinterpreted as representing the 130 lovely acres overlooking the northern fringe of Ellison Bay, but in fact, **The Clearing** (12171 Garrett Bay Rd., 920/854-4088, www.theclearing.org) refers to the metaphysical—"clarity of thought." A contemplative retreat for the study of art, natural science, and the humanities—philosophy is ever-popular—the school was the result of a lifetime's effort by famed landscape architect Jens Jensen.

Much like his contemporary Frank Lloyd Wright, Jensen's maverick style and obdurate convictions grated against the entrenched elitism of landscape architecture in the early 20th century. His belief in the inseparability of land and humanity was considered foolish,

even heretical. A Danish immigrant, Jensen arrived in the United States in 1884 and became more enamored of the wild Midwestern landscape while simultaneously cultivating his radical notions of debt to the earth and the need to connect with it. While in Chicago creating the parks that made his name, he began buying land around Ellison Bay. By the 1930s he had a cohesive plan, and he spent the next 15 years establishing his retreat according to the folk educational traditions of northern Europe.

The grounds contain a lodge, a library, a communal dining area, and cottages and dormitories for attendees. Summer classes are held May-October and last one week, though some day seminars are also offered. Meals are included. Lots of group work, outdoor exploration, campfires, and other traditional fare are the rule. Nonparticipants can visit 1pm-4pm Saturday-Sunday mid-May-mid-October.

Ellison Bay has the grand **Bluff County Park,** three miles southwest of town along Highway 42. Nearly 100 wild acres atop 200-foot bluffs overlook the lake. Camping is not allowed here, but some rough trails wind through the area, although none go to the water. You'll find some great views.

prevent it from falling apart, and boil for another 10 minutes. Now, here's the fun part: Right before the fish is done, use kerosene to jack up the flame to rocket-launch proportions. The kerosene induces a boil-over, which forces the oily top layers of water out of the cauldron, to be burned off in the fire. Drain the rest and slather it with butter. The requisite side dishes are coleslaw, dark breads, and this being Door County, cherry pie or cobbler for dessert.

Try one of the following places for a superb fish boil:

- **Mill Supper Club** (page 27)

- **Square Rigger Lodge and Cottages** (page 36)

- **White Gull Inn** (page 48)

- **Pelletier's** (page 48)

- **Old Post Office** (page 54)

- **The Viking Grill** (page 59)

## Food

The best fish boil spot has long been **The Viking Grill** (12029 Hwy. 42, 920/854-2998, 6am-9pm daily summer, 6am-7pm in other seasons, $4-15). The Viking is credited with filling that first iron cauldron with whitefish, potatoes, and onions, and brewing up a culinary tradition.

★ **Wickman House** (11976 Mink River Rd., east of Hwy. 42, 920/854-3305, 5pm-10pm Wed.-Mon. May-Mar., $12-30) is a Door County bistro worthy of an extra nickel or two. It features as much sustainably raised local food as possible in a cheery, welcoming atmosphere. Take in one of their memorable harvest dinners.

Not at all like a Wisconsin supper club, **The Fireside Restaurant** (11934 Hwy. 42, 920/854-7999, 4pm-9pm Tues.-Sat., $13-32) serves creative but casual comfort food, like Andouille mac and cheese and chicken and waffles.

## Accommodations

The best places to stay are in the vicinity of Ellison Bay. Cheaper options haven't been panning out of late. Likely the most worthy for a splurge is the **Bayview Resort** (12030 Cedar Shore Rd., 920/854-2006, www.bayviewresortandharbor.com, from $195), with everything from simple rooms up to suites for eight people. They even have a harbor.

## Information

The smallest visitors center on the peninsula might be the closet-size **Ellison Bay Information Kiosk** (Hwy. 42, 920/854-5448, May-Oct.), across from the Viking Grill.

## GILLS ROCK AND NORTHPORT

North of Ellison Bay, Highway 42 cuts east and then bends 90 degrees north again into the tightly packed fishing village of Gills Rock (pop. about 75). High atop 150-foot Table Bluff overlooking Hedgehog Harbor and across from Deathdoor Bluff, pleasant Gills Rock is as far as the road goes on the Door. Sleepy and quaint and known as the tip or top of the thumb, Gills Rock has the feel of an old tourist camp from the 1930s. A couple of miles farther east on Highway 42 is truly the end of the line, Northport. The highway leading to the ferry at Northport offers splendid scenery in fall.

## Sights

### DOOR COUNTY MARITIME MUSEUM

Door County's other maritime museum, an offshoot of Sturgeon Bay's, is on a dusty little side road in Gills Rock—the **Door County Maritime Museum** (12724 W. Wisconsin Bay Rd., 920/854-1844, www.dcmm.org, 10am-5pm daily May-Oct., $6 adults). This museum features gill nets and plenty of other old equipment related to the commercial fishing industry. The highlight is an old fishing tug. Admission generally includes a chatty guided tour.

### DOOR BLUFF HEADLANDS

Here you'll find the most solitude and best views of the bay at the largest park in the county, **Door Bluff Headlands,** comprising almost 200 acres of wild trails and woodland. That's over 7,000 feet of shoreline! Note that this park has deliberately been underdeveloped. The trails are rough and unmarked, and there are no established or safe trails to the water from the top. Go at your own risk. From Highway 42, take Cottage Road to Garrett Bay Road.

## Recreation

### FISHING

**The Mariner** (920/421-1578) is the go-to boat in Gills Rock for a fishing charter ($90 pp). Chinook salmon and German brown trout are the specialties, and the rates are reasonable; you fish virtually the entire time.

### DIVING

Scuba divers come to Gills Rock for underwater archaeology. Beneath the surface of local waters lie more than 200 wrecks, and the Wisconsin Historical Society has ongoing "digs" on its Wisconsin Maritime Trails project. If you don't want to dive, the local visitors centers have maps of land-based information markers pointing out wreck sites from shore; visit the **Wisconsin Historical Society** (http://maritimetrails.org) for more information. The **Shoreline Resort** (920/854-2606, www.theshoreleineresort.com)

has dive charters, but you must have your own gear and already be certified. The resort also offers daily narrated scenic boat tours ($40) of Death's Door.

### FERRIES AND CRUISES TO WASHINGTON ISLAND

The most luxurious way to Washington Island is a narrated cruise aboard the *Island Clipper* (920/854-2972, www.islandclipper. com), a 65-foot cruiser specifically designed by a Sturgeon Bay boatbuilder for the Death's Door crossing. A basic crossing ($13 adults) is possible, as well as a crossing plus a Viking Train island tour ($25). In peak summer season there are five departures 10am-4pm daily.

Northport exists solely to accommodate the ferry line to Washington Island. The pier was built to escape the fierce prevailing winds on the Gills Rock side, and Northport has in fact eclipsed Gills Rock as a ferry departure point to Washington Island; it is almost always free of ice and saves precious crossing time.

Northport is the ferry to use to take a car to Washington Island. The **Washington Island Ferry** (920/847-2546 or 800/223-2094, www. wisferry.com) takes autos and passengers, and it connects with the Cherry Train tour of the island if you take the 9:45am or earlier crossing from Northport (11am from Gills Rock). The ferry runs frequently: in high season (July-late Aug.), 25 daily round-trips depart to and from the island beginning at 6:45am from the island, 7:30am from Northport (no early trip on Sun.). Fewer trips depart in other seasons. In December-January there are only four trips per day; in February-March only one or two per day, and vehicle reservations are mandatory. In the off-season, call to check departure times. A car costs $26 (passengers not included), adults are $13.50, bicycles are $4, and motorcycles are $15; all prices are round-trip.

## Food

The best food in Gills Rock is the grand smoked Lake Michigan fish at ★ **Charlie's Smokehouse** (12731 Hwy. 42, 920/854-2972,

9am-6pm daily May-Oct., 9am-4pm Sat., 12:30pm-4pm Sun. Nov.-Apr.), which has been doing it since 1932.

The **Shoreline Resort** (12747 Hwy. 42, 920/854-2900, www.theshorelineresort.com, lunch and dinner daily May-Oct., $7-22) is the other dining option, with good whitefish and basic hearty fare.

## Accommodations

Prominent in Gills Rock, the **Shoreline Resort** (12747 Hwy. 42, 920/854-2900, www.theshorelineresort.com, $119) offers waterfront guest rooms with patios and a popular rooftop sun deck; the views are grand. Charter fishing tours and assorted sightseeing cruises (the sunset cruise is perennially popular) also leave the on-site marina. Shoreline also rents out bicycles.

Unheard-of **On the Rocks Cliffside Lodge** (849 Wisconsin Bay Rd., 920/854-4907, www.cliffsidelodge.com, Apr.-Nov., from $350) is possibly the most private Door County experience; you have to see it to believe it. This jewel is a massive 3,500-square-foot A-frame lodge with a fieldstone fireplace atop a 60-foot cliff. It was overwhelming enough for *National Geographic* to feature it. Rates start at $350 for two people, but it can accommodate up to 18 people ($775).

# Washington Island and Rock Island

Rustic, time-locked Washington Island (an easy and safe ferry ride from the mainland across Death's Door) very nearly wasn't included as part of the Door, but in 1925 the U.S. Supreme Court ruled in Wisconsin's favor in a border dispute with Michigan. At issue were a number of the dozen or so islands in the Grand Traverse Chain, of which Washington and the surrounding islands are a part.

The island isn't like Michigan's candy-facade Mackinac Island, with historically garbed docents and fudge hawkers every few steps; Washington Island is populated by 650 permanent residents, and development is absolutely unobtrusive. The place has a pleasant weather-beaten seaside look to it rather than the sheen of a slick resort. Best of all, Washington Island has the feel of a small Midwestern town, right down to the well-used community ballparks. This explains the island's perfectly apt advertising slogan: "North of the Tension Line."

## History

The fierce waters around Washington and Rock Islands didn't prevent Native Americans from settling the islands, once one of the richest Native American archaeological time capsules in the Midwest before the sites were destroyed by vandals and encroaching thickets. The original island dwellers were likely the Potawatomi people and later the Hurons (the island's original name was Huron Island), among others, who arrived in flight from the bellicose Iroquois in what is now Quebec.

Island-hopping voyageurs plying the expanses of New France found a ready-made chain of havens and temporary fishing grounds stretching from Michigan to the Door Peninsula, and thus to the Fox and Wisconsin Rivers. Purportedly, famous French explorer Jean Nicolet himself was the first European to set up camp on Washington Island. Pierre-Esprit Radisson, who wintered here with the Huron in the 17th century, dubbed it the most pleasant place he had experienced in the Great Lakes. The most famous early European visitor is still the subject of murky legends. In 1679, Robert La Salle sailed the *Griffin* into Detroit Harbor, where he met and bartered fur and iron wares with the Potawatomi people and then left for Mackinac Island. The ship vanished, and ever since, mariners have told tales of a shrouded ship matching its description haunting the shoals around the Door.

Large-scale European settlement started

in the early 1830s, when immigrants to Green Bay heard of trout the size of calves being taken from the waters around the island. The first nonnative fishers were Irish, but several thousand Icelanders took readily to the isolation and set down permanent roots. Their heritage is clearly manifested in the **Washington Island** *Stavkirke* (1763 Town Line Rd., 920/847-2341), a wooded stave church gradually built by island residents, one massive white pine log at a time, and by the proud Icelandic horses that roam certain island pastures.

## Geography

Beyond Washington Island is one of the Niagara Escarpment's longest gaps as it stretches under the waters to Michigan and Ontario. Both geologically and historically, Washington is the granddaddy of the islands stretching across the lake to Michigan's Upper Peninsula. The island's rough, wave-battered circumference of just over 25 miles bounds 36 square miles of the escarpment on a consistent, gradual 2- to 5-degree descending slope, a mere 160 feet above the lake's surface. Nowhere on the Door Peninsula does nature manifest itself with more force—wind-whipped stretches of open meadow and equally wind-bent scattered hardwoods—than on this tough island.

# WASHINGTON ISLAND
## Sights
### ART AND NATURE CENTER

A mix of island natural and cultural history is displayed at the **Art and Nature Center** (1799 Main Rd., 920/847-2025, 10:30am-4:30pm Mon.-Sat., 11:30am-4:30pm Sun. mid-June-mid-Sept., 11am-3pm daily in other seasons, $1 adults), at the corner of Main Road and Jackson Harbor Road, in an unassuming building resembling an old schoolhouse. Permanent artwork displays are housed within, and nature trails start from the rear. Art classes are offered, and regular musical events are held during a summer festival (the first two weeks of August).

### MUSEUMS

The top stop for museum hoppers is the **Maritime Museum** (10am-4pm Mon.-Fri. Memorial Day-Oct., some weekends in summer, donation) at the east end of Jackson Harbor Road, opposite the ferry landing. The museum retains significant relics of the

the Washington Island *Stavkirke*

# Washington Island and Rock Island

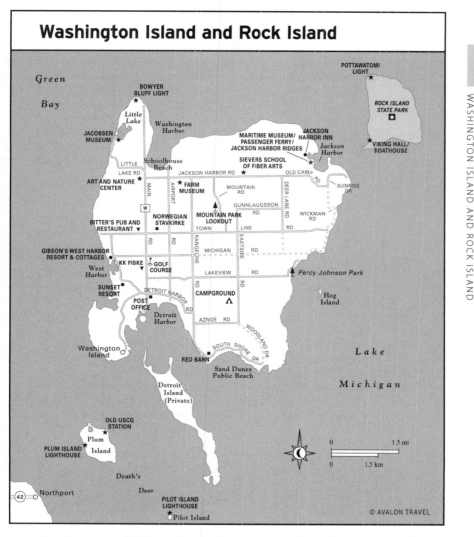

island's commercial fishing industry, which still operates out of secluded Jackson Harbor. You'll find a reconstructed fish shed, a couple of ice houses, an old fisher's house, outdoor displays that include a Kahlenberg engine, an old Coast Guard boat, and remnants of a wreck. The museum is housed inside two fishing shacks.

The **Jacobsen Museum** (920/847-2213, 10am-4pm daily Memorial Day-mid-Oct., donation) is housed in a vertical log building once owned by early settler Jens Jacobsen on the south shore of Little Lake. Jacobsen collected a huge number of natural history artifacts, mostly Native American arrowheads and beads. Also inside are Danish scrollwork, maps, models of shipwrecks, fossils, and tools. There are unusual things lying out front, such as a massive ancient rudder from the steamer *Louisiana,* which ran aground here in 1913; ice cutters; and huge capstans for raising anchors.

The smallest museum is the **Farm Museum** (920/847-2156, hours vary June-Oct., free), a set of pioneer structures off Airport Road along Jackson Harbor Road. A pioneer log home, a double log barn and shed with a collection of hand tools, 15 pieces of horse-drawn machinery, a forge and blacksmith shop, a reconstructed stone building, and a popular petting zoo are on the grounds. Regularly scheduled farm activities for kids and families (Wed. July 5-mid-Aug.) are held.

### SIEVERS SCHOOL OF FIBER ARTS

In its second decade, the **Sievers School of Fiber Arts** (Jackson Harbor Rd., 920/847-2264, www.sieversschool.com) is the most intriguing island highlight. It's less a school than a retreat into weaving, papermaking, spinning, basket weaving, batik, tapestry, drafting, Scandinavian woodcarving, and a number of other classes in vanishing folk arts. On any given day, the solitude is accentuated by the thwack of looms or the whirring of spinning wheels. Classes are offered May-October, and weekend or one-week classes are available. Fees range $200-400, plus up to $350 for dorm fees for a weeklong class. A downtown consignment shop displays and sells the works created along with cherry-wood looms.

## Recreation

With 75 miles of paved roads, Washington Island was made for cycling. A weekend here is just about enough time to spin around the main perimeter and nose off on a few side roads. Much of the eastern lakeshore roadway is gravel, as is the main artery, Michigan Road, in the center of the island. Bicycles can be rented at the ferry dock, and trails are marked by green signs.

**Field Wood Farms** (W. Harbor Rd., 0.5 miles west of Main Rd., 920/847-2490) offers trail rides on descendants of original Icelandic stock horses—a rarity anywhere—and the oldest registered herd in the United States. Pony rides, riding instruction, and horse-drawn wagon rides are also available by appointment.

Fishing for 30-pound salmon is not unheard of in the sheltered waters around the island's bays; other big takes include perch, smallmouth black bass, rock bass, and especially northern pike, right in Detroit Harbor. A number of charter operators are available, including salmon and bass charters. Check the **Washington Island website**

the Jacobsen Museum

(www.washingtonisland.com) for current charters.

## DUNES

No visit to the Maritime Museum is complete without a stroll on the nature trail through the ecosystem of the **Jackson Harbor Ridges,** a 90-acre State Scientific Reserve. The fragile mix of shore meadows, dunes, and boreal forest is not found anywhere else on the peninsula. Northern plant species such as the rare dwarf lake orchid and arctic primrose, along with white cedar, fir, and spruce, are found here. Part of the reserve was established with a Nature Conservancy tract. There is an isolated and generally underused beach adjacent to the reserve.

More great *Lawrence of Arabia* dunescapes are found across the island, southeast of Detroit Harbor along South Shore Drive at **Sand Dunes Public Beach.**

## PARKS

The generally gravelly shoreline is rimmed with parks and beaches: **Schoolhouse Beach** in Washington Harbor, with tough and chilly swimming in a secluded setting (and extraordinarily smooth stones); the **Ridges** in Jackson Harbor; and **Percy Johnson Park** on the eastern side at the tip of Lakeview Road, offering vistas of Hog Island and a nesting sanctuary. None of the parks allow camping.

Inland are two interesting parks. A small picnic area and park are adjacent to the airport, and people head out with a lunchtime sandwich to watch the odd plane arrival. To get here, take Main Road north, then Town Line Road east to Airport Road. The most commanding views of all are at the 200-foot heights of **Mountain Park Lookout,** just about the center of the island.

## Entertainment

The **Red Barn** (1474 S. Shore Dr., 920/847-3064), south of Gislason Beach along South Shore Drive, features a regular assortment of local talent—musicians or whoever else can be drummed up.

The **Art and Nature Center** (1799 Main Rd., 920/847-2025) offers a music festival during the first two weeks of August with concerts and other programs.

## Food

An island delicacy is a "lawyer"—another name for the burbot, a mud-dwelling fish with barbels on its chin. To sample lawyers, **KK Fiske** (1177 Main Rd., 920/847-2121, breakfast, lunch, and dinner daily, from $6) is the place that specializes in them.

Delicious Icelandic pancakes and Norwegian *barkram pankaka*—cherry- and cream-filled pleasures—are the house specialties at breakfast at **Sunset Resort** (Old W. Harbor Rd., 920/847-2531, 8am-11am daily July-Aug., 8am-11am Sat.-Sun. June and Sept., $2-7). This local hot spot serves morning grub, including homemade breads.

You'll hear quite a bit about the potent bitters—a freeze-proof Scandinavian tradition still served in local pubs. If you can stomach a shot, you're in the club. The landmark ★ **Bitters Pub and Restaurant** (Main Rd., 920/847-2496, lunch and dinner from 11:30am daily) is in Nelsen's Hall, a century-old structure in the center of the island. Famed for its Bitters Club, initiated in 1899, it draws about 10,000 visitors annually. Bitters is the best elbow-rubbing option on the island; the restaurant is classic Americana—steaks, seafood, and chicken.

## Accommodations

Washington Island features a patchwork of lodging options, stemming from its isolation. You'll find basic motels, intriguing and microscopic kiosk-cottages, spacious but threadbare cabins that look like deer-hunting shacks heated with oil furnaces, and even the odd resident's spare bedroom. Finding a room under $100 is generally no problem.

A really cheap sleep, **Gibson's West Harbor Resort and Cottages** (920/847-2225, http://gibsonswestharbor.com, $35 s,

# The Man of the Rock

In 1910, Milwaukee inventor Chester H. Thordarson plunked down $5,725 for 775-acre Rock Island. Over the next 55 years, Thordarson gradually tamed the wilds and carefully transformed at least part of the island into his own private retreat.

Thordarson initially restored a few squat settlers' cabins while he pondered his masterpieces—a boathouse hewn meticulously from island limestone and, later, his grand mansion (it was never built), as well as gardens and other experiments in horticulture.

This was no simple exercise in a rich man's indulgence. As prescient as he was entrepreneurial (he made his fortune inventing more than 100 patentable devices), Thordarson developed only 30 acres of the island, with the full intent of leaving the remaining 745 as an experiment in ecological preservation. With a profound knowledge of the natural world, much of it the result of self-educated sweat, he spent the rest of his days analyzing the biological minutiae of his island. Because of this, in 1929 the University of Wisconsin gave him an honorary master of arts degree. The school also purchased his entire island library, containing one of the world's greatest collections of Scandinavian literature.

$45 d, no cards), about halfway up the west shore from the ferry landing, was fire damaged in 2009 but has been rebuilt. They've got basic housekeeping cottages (about $90), but the coolest lodgings are the sleeping rooms—tiny but tidy—with shared baths above the main building, an erstwhile logging boarding house; they even have a five-person room for $65. There is absolutely nothing like it anywhere else.

A slight step up, the **Sunset Resort** (Old W. Harbor Rd., 920/847-2531, www. sunsetresortwi.com, $105) is a long-standing island getaway run by the fifth generation of the inn's original Norwegian founding family, who started the business in 1902. Cupped by spinneys of pine, the inn offers knotty pine cottages and one superb loft cabin. Guest rooms are simple but clean; impromptu campfires typify the family atmosphere. Breakfasts here are legendary.

On the far side of the island overlooking Rock Island is perhaps the nicest place on the island. **Jackson Harbor Inn** (920/847-2454, http://jacksonharborinn.com, $60-120) is meticulously kept by very friendly owners; you'll find several lovely guest rooms, all different, as well as a cottage. The inn is open Easter weekend through the end of October.

## Information

The **Washington Island Chamber of Commerce** (920/847-2179, http://washingtonisland.com, http://washingtonislandchamber.com) has all the information you might want; it often has folks to greet you on the mainland side of the ferry.

## Getting There

Ferry lines run to and from Washington Island via the "top of the thumb" (Gills Rock and Northport). Ferries have made the five-mile (30-minute) crossing somewhat ordinary, but it wasn't always so. Winter crossings used to be made by horse-drawn sleigh or—unimaginably—car, but weather conditions could change the ice or eliminate it altogether within a relatively short period. Today, the ice freezes the crossing nearly solid for more than 100 days each year, but modern ferries can get through it. When ice floes pile up during extreme cold, the ferries either "back up" and try to make an end run, or "back down" and run right at the ice. At those times, ferry crossings are few and reservations are necessary to cross with an automobile.

The **Washington Island Ferry** (920/847-2546 or 800/223-2094, www.wisferry.com) takes autos and passengers, and it connects with the Cherry Train tour of the island if you take the 9:45am or earlier crossing from Northport (11am from Gills Rock). The ferry runs frequently; in high season (July-late Aug.), 25 daily round-trips depart to and from the island beginning at 6:45am from the island, 7:30am from Northport (no early trip on Sun.). Fewer trips depart in other seasons. In December-January there are only four trips per day; in February-March only one or two per day, and vehicle reservations are mandatory. In the off-season, call to check departure times. A car costs $26 (passengers not included), adults are $13.50, bicycles are $4, and motorcycles are $15; all prices are round-trip.

You could theoretically paddle a sea kayak from Northport all the way to Washington Island—and it has been done—but the currents and winds in the Porte des Mortes are deadly.

## Getting Around

If you come without a car, bicycle and moped rentals await you at the dock. Otherwise, **Dor Cros Inn** (920/847-2126) rents bicycles ($15 for 2-4 hours, $20 per day; call before arrival). **Annie's Island Mopeds** (920/847-2790) has mopeds from $55 per day. Taxi services come and go, so you can never be sure if one is available.

The main route is Main Rd. north to Jackson Harbor Rd. to Jackson Harbor (eight or so miles). After that, it depends where you want to go. A car is not absolutely necessary given the availability of rentals; in fact, the Gills Rock parking lot is generally full of parked cars from folks who go over for the day. This author has biked the circumference of the island in one day, but it was a long, sweaty day, and it didn't leave much time to explore Rock Island State Park.

A few tours and shuttles regularly depart from the ferry dock, linking with the ferries from Northport and Gills Rock. People rave about the **Cherry Train** (920/847-2039, www.cherrytraintours.com, $15), essentially a Chevy Suburban pulling carriages, which offers four tours daily.

Head up Main Road from the ferry dock to **Bread & Water Bakery & Café** (1275 Main Rd., 920/847-2400, breadandwaterwi.com, 8am-3pm daily), where they have great food but more importantly where "kayak is spoken." The island has great kayaking, and this is the place to find a rental ($50 per day); there's even a paddling museum. They've recently opened up lodge rooms (from $90) and farm accommodations (from $75).

## ★ ROCK ISLAND STATE PARK

Less than a mile from Washington Island's Jackson Harbor is one man's feudal estate turned overgrown state park. Getting to **Rock Island State Park** (920/847-2235), the most isolated state park in Wisconsin's system, necessitates two ferry rides. When you get here, it's a magnificent retreat: a small island, yes, but with delicious solitude, icy but gorgeous beaches, and the loveliest starry skies and sunrises in Wisconsin.

Native Americans lived in sporadic encampments along the island's south shore from 600 BC until the start of the 17th century. Around 1640, the Potawatomi people migrated here from Michigan; their allies, the Ottawa, Petun, and Huron people, followed in the 1650s, fleeing the threat of extermination at the hands of the Iroquois. The Potawatomi were visited in 1679 by René-Robert Cavelier, Sieur de La Salle, whose men built two houses, the remains of which are still visible amid the weed-choked brambles off the beach. Eventually, the French and the Potawatomi returned, establishing a trading post that lasted until 1730. Until the start of the 20th century, the island was alternately a base camp for fishers and the site of a solitary sawmill. Rock Island is thus arguably the true "door" to Wisconsin, and a ready-made one at that—the first rock on the way across the temperamental lake from Mackinac Island.

Note that water is available here, but that's all; you have to bring everything you'll need and pack it all out when you leave.

## Plants and Animals

Here's why the isolated island is so great: There are no ticks, no pesky raccoons, no skunks, and no bears—no perils for backpackers. The worst thing is the rather pernicious fields of poison ivy (though these are usually well marked). There are white-tailed deer, lemmings, foxes, and a few other small mammals and amphibians. Plenty of nonpoisonous snakes can also be seen.

The northern hardwood forest is dominated by sugar maples and American beeches; the eastern hemlock is gone. The perimeters have arbor vitae (white cedar) and small varieties of red maple and red and white pine.

## Sights

Two of the most historically significant buildings in Wisconsin, according to the Department of the Interior, are Thordarson's massive limestone **Viking Hall** and **boathouse.** Patterned after historic Icelandic manors, the structures were cut, slab by slab, from Rock Island limestone by Icelandic artisans and workers and ferried over from Washington Island. Only the roof tiling isn't made from island material. That's a lot of rock, considering that the hall could hold more than 120 people. The hand-carved furniture, mullioned windows, and rosemaling detail, including runic inscriptions outlining Norse mythology, are magnificent.

The original name of Rock Island was Potawatomi Island, a name that lives on in one of the original lighthouses in Wisconsin, **Pottawatomie Light,** built in 1836. The original structure was swept from the cliffs by the surly lake soon after being built but was replaced. Unfortunately, it's not open to the public except for ranger-led tours. The area is accessible via a two-hour hike.

On the east side of the island are the remnants of a former fishing village and a historic water tower that's on the National Register of Historic Places. The village dwelling foundations lie in the midst of thickets and are tough to spot; there are also a few cemeteries not far from the campsites. These are the resting places of the children and families of lighthouse keepers and even Chief Chip-Pa-Ny, a Menominee leader.

Otherwise, the best thing to do is just skirt the shoreline and discover lake views from atop the bluffs, alternating at points with up to 0.5 miles of sandy beach or sand dunes. Near campsite 15, you'll pass some carvings etched into the bluff, made by Thordarson's bored workers.

Rock Island's historic boathouse

# Firewood Bugs Us

Wisconsin now has quite strict restrictions on firewood due to the invasive insect called the emerald ash borer, which has been found in southern Wisconsin counties and is attempting to move northward. The name says it all—it has an emerald-colored coating on its back, and ash trees are its primary food. The larvae burrow under the bark and ravage the trees, most of which die within four years. Seven percent of Wisconsin's forests are ashes; it's even worse in cities, where 20 percent of trees are ashes.

The key for travelers is never to transport wood—including firewood for camping—from one location to another. The insect can only fly a mile or two, so its primary mode of expansion is unknowing humans and their wood. Out-of-state firewood and any wood from more than 25 miles away from any campground is strictly forbidden. Local wood is always available. Yes, it's more expensive, but for a few extra dollars you can help preserve Wisconsin's forestlands.

## Recreation

With more than 5,000 feet of beach, you can find somewhere to be alone, although the waters are chilly and currents are dangerous. At one time a sawmill buzzed the logs taken from the island; the wheel-rutted paths to the mill turned into rough roads. Thordarson let them grow over during his tenure on the island, but today they are a few miles of the park's 9.5 miles of hiking trails. The island is only about 900 acres, so you'll have plenty of time to cover it all if you're spending more than an afternoon. On a day trip, you can cover the perimeter on the 5.2-mile **Thordarson Loop Trail** in just under three hours. You'll see all the major sights and a magnificent view on the northeast side—on a clear day you can see all the way to Michigan's Upper Peninsula. For those less aerobically inclined, head for the **Algonquin Nature Trail Loop,** at most a one-hour hike. The other trails on the island are essentially shortcuts to cross the island and are all approximately one mile long.

No wheeled vehicles are allowed in the park. The dock does allow private mooring for a fee of $1 per foot.

## Camping

The camping at Rock Island is absolutely splendid, with sites strung along a beachfront of sand and, closer to the pier, large stones. Many of the sites farthest from the main compound are fully isolated, almost scooped into dunes and thus fully protected from wind but with great views (site 13 is a favorite). The island has 40 primitive campsites, all reservable, with water and pit toilets: 35 to the southwest of the ferry landing, and another 5 isolated backpacker sites spread along the shore farther southeast. Two additional group campsites are also available. **Reservations** (888/947-2757, http://wisconsinstateparks.reserveamerica.com, $25 sites for nonresidents, plus $10 reservation fee) are a good idea in summer and fall, and essential on weekends during those times.

Note that the park is pack-in, pack-out, so plan wisely.

## Getting There

If you're not kayaking over, the **Karfi** (920/847-2252) has regular service; the name means "seaworthy for coastal journeys" in Icelandic, so fear not. Boats depart Jackson Harbor on Washington Island daily from late-May to mid-October, usually Columbus Day; the boat leaves hourly 10am-4:15pm daily in high season (late June-Aug.) with an extra trip at 6pm Friday. Round-trip tickets cost $11 adults and $14 for campers with gear. In the off-season you can arrange a boat, but it's expensive.

Private boats are permitted to dock at the pier, but a mooring fee ($1 per foot) is charged.

# OTHER ISLANDS
## Plum and Pilot Islands

Before the establishment of the lighthouse on Plum Island, more than 100 ships were wrecked on the shoals of the Door. In one year alone, Plum Island became the cemetery for 30 ships. Though safer than any U.S. highway today, it will never be stress-free; as recently as 1989 a ship was thrown aground by the currents. The U.S. Lighthouse Service established the **Pilot Island Lighthouse** in 1858. It stands atop what an early guidebook described as "little more than a rock in the heavy-pounding seas." Two brick structures stand on Pilot Island and are about the only things still visible. Once-dense vegetation has nearly been completely killed off, the island turned into a rocky field by the ubiquitous and odoriferous droppings of federally protected cormorants, which long ago found the island and stuck around.

Plum Island had to wait until 1897 to get its imposing 65-foot skeletal steel light, after which the number of wrecks at the Door dropped significantly. Plum Island—so-called for its plumb-center position in the straits—is home to an abandoned Coast Guard building on the northeast side, an old foghorn building on the southwest tip, and yet another decaying Cape Cod-style light keeper's residence near the range lights.

Neither island is accessible—unless your sea kayak runs into trouble—except on boat tours given during the **Festival of Blossoms** (late-Apr.-early June), usually offered three times daily from Gills Rock.

## Detroit Island

Steaming into Detroit Harbor on Washington Island, look to the starboard side. The island with the crab-claw bay is Detroit Island, one of the largest satellite islands surrounding Washington Island. Settlers built the first permanent structures on the island in the early 1830s and gradually forced the displacement of the resident Ottawa and Huron people, who had been there for generations. The island was once an archaeological gem, but thieves have looted it. Today it is privately owned and not accessible.

a campsite near the water at Rock Island State Park

# East-Central Waters

Look for ★ to find recommended
sights, activities, dining, and lodging.

# Highlights

★ **Kohler:** The state's most storied resort is located in this one-time factory town (page 80).

★ **Wisconsin Maritime Museum:** Learn about everything from wooden schooners to World War II submarines at this museum (page 86).

★ **Point Beach State Forest:** Relax along a grand lakeshore stretch of sandy beaches (page 89).

★ **The Pack:** Wisconsin's beloved Green Bay Packers hold court at Lambeau Field (page 90).

★ **History Museum at the Castle:** Learn the secrets of the famed escape artist at the **A.K.A. Houdini** exhibit (page 102).

★ **High Cliff State Park:** It's worth a stop for its magnificent perch above Lake Winnebago (page 107).

★ **EAA AirVenture Museum:** The museum is worthwhile and its airshows are even more incredible; try to attend the annual **EAA AirVenture Oshkosh** fly-in for a jaw-dropping experience (page 108).

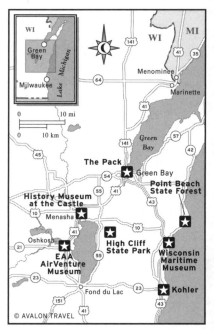

**T**hese waters truly made the state of Wisconsin, serving as the site of the first permanent nonnative settlements and the state's timber-and-water commercial nucleus. Today, you'll find picturesque lakeside resorts, quaint towns with

excellent museums, and a rich blend of European heritage. And of course, the heart and soul of the region is the football mecca of Green Bay, home to the Packers.

When the Portage Canal linking the Upper Fox and Lower Wisconsin Rivers was completed, two of the most crucial waterways in the Great Lakes system were finally joined, allowing transportation from the Atlantic Ocean all the way to the Gulf of Mexico. (The Fox River is one of the few rivers in North America to flow north.) The Fox River engineering was no mean feat for the time—it required 26 locks and dams to corral the rapids and negotiate a 200-foot drop. Within a century, though, the decrepit condition of the Fox River locks in Kaukauna earned them the distinction of being one of the 10 most endangered historic sites; Wisconsin established the Fox-Wisconsin Riverways Heritage Corridor to preserve what was left. The entire length

of the Fox River is being considered by the National Park Service for a National Heritage Corridor. In addition to the locks, some of the only extant French-style agricultural developments can still be seen—they're recognizable by their long, narrow plots perpendicular to the river, as opposed to the patchwork parallelograms of the other European immigrants.

## HISTORY

Early nomadic Paleo-Indians arrived as the glaciers retreated; this was millennia before explorer Jean Nicolet arrived in 1634. The Jesuits then attempted to found the westernmost fringe community of New France. Later, European immigrants began pouring in, harvesting timber for the rapacious needs of a burgeoning nation. For a time, with the hinterlands timber industry and the prodigious fishing harvests and shipping receipts, this was the richest part of the state.

**Previous:** a plane at EAA AirVenture Oshkosh; Kohler-Andrae State Park. **Above:** entrance to the historic Lambeau Field.

# East-Central Waters

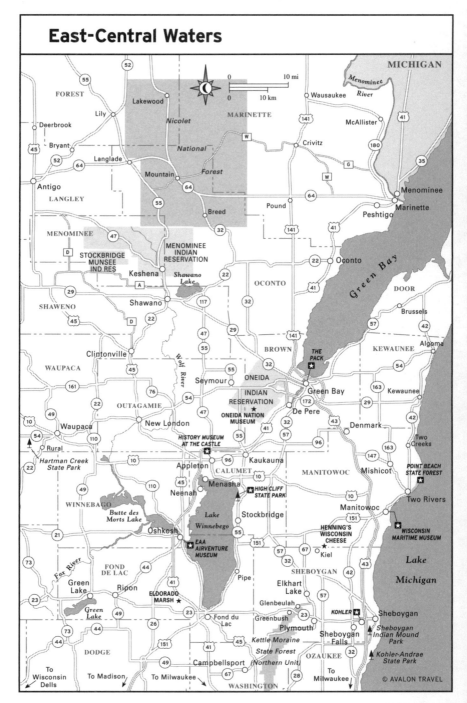

# Birth of the Republican Party

By the early 1850s, the powers within the contemporary political parties were impotent, willfully ignorant, or hamstrung on both sides regarding the issue of slavery. Antislavery activists within the Whig Party in Ripon ultimately grew tired enough to call for action. In 1852, Alvan Earle Bovay visited Horace Greeley in New York City to discuss matters. The Whigs were waning, but what was next?

Senator Stephen Douglass of Illinois provided an opportunity for a minor revolution with his Kansas-Nebraska Bill; the proposal was to extend slavery beyond the perimeters of the earlier Missouri Compromise. Bovay immediately and quietly summoned 53 other voters back to Ripon to devise a battle plan for opposing the slavery proponents. Ripon had long been a nerve center of the abolitionist movement; so strong was its opposition, in fact, that the city was the site of what's known as "Booth's War," a guerrilla skirmish between Milwaukee abolitionist Sherman Booth, who helped escaped slaves along the Underground Railroad, and the federal authorities; local citizens helped Booth and frustrated the authorities for five years.

Bovay hoped to organize the abolitionists into a cohesive force to be called Republicans—"a good name . . . with charm and prestige," he said. His oratory was effective, and the Republican Party was born on March 20, 1854, in the Little White Schoolhouse in Ripon. The official declaration of its platform came two years later in Pittsburgh; standing near the podium was Abraham Lincoln, who, four years later, would become the party's first successful presidential candidate.

The timber industry has slowed to a trickle and the shipbuilding and fishing fleets are mostly gone, but the region has some great recreation amid the faded economic glory.

## PLANNING YOUR TIME

A weekend isn't enough time for this area, unless you stay somewhere in the historic **Fox Cities** area and pick and choose by region or activity. You could also spend a night and a day in either Oshkosh or Appleton and then spend the second day at EAA AirVenture Museum in Oshkosh and the Birthplace of the Republican Party in Ripon; High Cliff State Park and Kohler-Sheboygan; or the Wisconsin Maritime Museum in Manitowoc and Point Beach State Forest in Two Rivers.

# Sheboygan

Sheboygan has come a long way in terms of visitor appeal since its days as a gritty industrial town. Over the last two decades, Herculean efforts and millions of dollars have made possible the renovation of marinas, promenades, lighted walkways, bike trails, building facades, and harbor breakwaters. *Reader's Digest* even named Sheboygan the number-one family-friendly city in the United States.

Sheboygan has never lacked fame as the self-proclaimed Bratwurst Capital of the World, and nothing comes close to Sheboygan brats. Innumerable neighborhood butchers still turn out family-secret-recipe bratwurst, and locals are devoted to their butchers. **Brat Days** (www.brat-days. com) in early August is one of Wisconsin's largest food festivals.

## History

Nearby cascades inspired the Ojibwa people to name the area Shaw-bwah-way-gun, "the sound like the wind of the rushing waters."

# Sheboygan

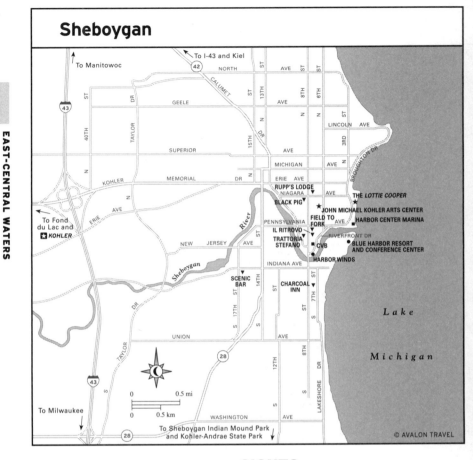

To I-43 and Kiel

To Manitowoc

To Fond du Lac and KOHLER

To Milwaukee

To Sheboygan Indian Mound Park and Kohler-Andrae State Park

© AVALON TRAVEL

Lake Michigan

0    0.5 mi
0    0.5 km

Due to its fortuitous location, equidistant from Milwaukee and Manitowoc, the village erected one of the first large piers along Lake Michigan, allowing lake schooners and ferries to bring tens of thousands of German, Dutch, and English immigrants, many of them dairy farmers, to town.

During the final wave of German immigration, between 1880 and 1890, some areas became and remain 95 percent German. Many of the immigrants were woodworkers, so several furniture and wood-product factories opened. Thus Sheboygan became known as the city of cheese and chairs.

# SIGHTS

## John Michael Kohler Arts Center

The superlative **John Michael Kohler Arts Center** (608 New York Ave., 920/458-6144, www.jmkac.org, 10am-5pm Mon.-Fri., 10am-8pm Tues. and Thurs., 10am-4pm Sat.-Sun., free) is one of Sheboygan's cultural landmarks. The wondrously progressive, eclectic grouping of galleries is devoted to contemporary art in all media, including galleries devoted to self-taught artists. The center has been nationally recognized for its unusually broad scope and its efforts to incorporate the whole community in its undertakings. This explains why industry groups consistently rate it as one of the top 10 arts centers nationwide.

## The Boardwalk

The city center's gem is this winding walkway along the Sheboygan River and Riverfront Drive, a zone of gentrification. The old fishing shanties have been transformed into antiques shops, art galleries, restaurants, and other retail outlets. A few old weather-beaten shacks remain.

## The *Lottie Cooper*

One of 62 shipwrecks near Sheboygan, the *Lottie Cooper,* a three-masted lumber schooner, went down in a gale off Sheboygan on April 9, 1894, killing one. Including one of the longest salvaged keels of a Great Lakes wreck, the vessel now rests in Deland Park, near the North Pier. It's along a lovely lakefront promenade.

## RECREATION
### Charter Fishing

Sheboygan's 300-slip **Harbor Centre Marina** (821 Broughton Dr., 920/458-6665) offers great fishing, with about three dozen licensed skippers. Prices vary but it generally costs $325-500, not including a tip or a Wisconsin fishing license, for 1-4 people for a half-day charter; some outfits offer shorter charters.

## Old Plank Road Trail

In 1843, the territorial legislature, hoping to effect permanent settlement in today's Sheboygan County region, began building the first plank road to reach all the way to Fond du Lac. It was completed in 1852. Today, the Old Plank Road Trail is a paved 17-mile multipurpose recreation trail running from western Sheboygan to Greenbush and the Kettle Moraine State Forest's northern unit (and thus the Ice Age Trail), via Kohler and Plymouth, a lovely bicycle ride in spots.

## FOOD
### American

At the casual yet upscale **Black Pig** (821 N. 8th St., 920/457-6565, www.eatblackpig.com, lunch and dinner Tues.-Sat., brunch Sun., $8-24) it's no surprise that the entire pig (organic and locally sourced) is used in almost every dish. (Worry not—several non-porcine dishes are available.)

Enjoy rib-sticking American food at **Rupp's Lodge** (925 N. 8th St., 920/459-8155, 11am-2pm and 5pm-9pm Mon.-Fri.,

the *Lottie Cooper* shipwreck

# Bratwurst: The Wisconsin Dish

Bratwurst, a Germanic legacy in Wisconsin, is the unofficial state dish. The brat (rhymes with "spot" not "spat") is pervasive: Supermarkets devote entire lengths of freezers to accommodate sausages. Many towns still have old butcher shops that string up homemade varieties.

## THE IMMIGRANT EPICURE

Strictly speaking, the bratwurst is but one of hundreds of varieties of sausage, according to the official draconian German food laws. But sausage-making was done here before the Europeans arrived by the Native Americans, who had long stuffed deer intestines and hides with wild rice, grains, meats, offal, and herbs to produce pemmican, which is, technically, a sausage.

From the earliest settlement of the region, immigrants made their own sausage. Wisconsin's bratwurst, unlike some varieties, is almost always made from pork. The internal mixture was meat, fat, and seasonings, along with occasional starches such as rice and bread. Concoctions were, and remain, highly secret.

## INFINITE VARIETIES

The Czech method includes a rice sausage and head cheese; the Norwegians make *sylte*, which is spiced and salted in brine. The main categories of Wisconsin sausage:

- **German:** The many German varieties are most often seasoned with marjoram, pepper, salt, caraway, and nutmeg.

- **Italian:** Sweeter and hotter; fennel gives it its trademark flavor.

- **Polish:** A garlic-heavy ring of two-inch-thick dark-pink bologna-esque sausage is traditionally steam-fried for dinner and then cut into sandwiches for leftovers and lunchboxes; Polish recipes often call for red cabbage and mustard sauces.

---

4pm-9pm Sat.-Sun., $5-25), which has been around for six decades. Aged hand-cut steaks are the specialty, along with standard supper club fare. Through a glass partition, you get to watch the food being prepared in the kitchen. On Friday and Saturday nights, patrons join in sing-alongs at a piano.

## Bratwurst

To sample the "best of the wurst," there are many options, including the **Charcoal Inn** (1313 S. 8th St., 920/458-6988, 6am-9pm Tues.-Fri., 6am-7pm Sat.; 1637 Greele Ave., 920/458-1147, 5am-7pm Tues.-Sat., $4-8), where they still fire up a fryer every morning to supplement the unpretentious Midwestern fare. With no choice but to give in to modern tastes, they've added turkey brats, considered sacrilege by some.

## Fish Fries

The **Scenic Bar** (1635 Indiana Ave., 920/452-2881, 4pm-9pm Tues.-Thurs. and Sat., 11am-2pm and 3:30pm-10pm Fri., 4pm-8pm Sun., $5) has standard "supper club in a tavern" fare, with a fish fry of pike, bluegill, and perch in addition to the standard cod Friday at noon and night. Most locals point this place out as the place for unpretentious fare.

## Italian

Dishing up the best Italian is the ever-friendly ★ **Trattoria Stefano** (522 S. 8th St., 920/452-8455, 5pm-9pm Mon.-Thurs., 5pm-10pm Fri.-Sat., $12-28), a casually upscale place with a bright pastel and handmade-brick setting. For years this has been a foodie must-stop. For a more subdued Italian experience, across the street is another of the owner's ventures: Il

## PREPARATION

Microwave a brat and you'll incur the wrath of any Wisconsinite. Frying one is OK, but traditionally, a brat must be grilled. Brats work best if you parboil them in beer and onions for 10-15 minutes before putting them on the grill. Sheboyganites absolutely cringe at parboiling, however. Another no-no is roughage crammed in the bun—lettuce, tomatoes, and so on; even sauerkraut, loved by Milwaukeeans, is barely tolerated by Sheboyganites.

Another option is to parboil the brats briefly, sear them in butter in a frying pan, and set them aside. Pour two cups of dark beer into a frying pan and scrape out the residue. Combine a finely chopped onion, some beef stock, the juice of one lemon, and maybe a chopped green pepper. Put the brats back in and boil for 12 to 15 minutes. Remove the brats and place them on a hot grill. The sauce can be thickened with flour or cornstarch and poured over the top. A Cheesehead will stick the sauce in a bun along with the brat and mustard.

### BRATS IN SHEBOYGAN

The place to go is **Miesfeld's Triangle Market** (4811 Venture Dr., 2 blocks north of the intersection of I-43 and Hwy. 42, 414/565-6328), where Chuck and the gang have been putting out national award-winning sausages—15 varieties have won 68 national awards—for as long as anyone can remember. The town has a celebratory fit of indulgent mayhem in August with Bratwurst Days. Some brat-related Sheboygan-specific tips:

- "double": You simply cannot eat just one brat.

- "fryer": Whatever thing you cook the brat on; Cheeseheads otherwise say "grill."

- "fry out": Used as both a noun and a verb.

- "hard roll": It looks like a hamburger bun but it's bigger and harder; sometimes called "sennel roll."

**Ritrovo** (515 S. 8th St., 920/803-7516, lunch and dinner Mon.-Sat., $9-17), dinner with excellent pizza. If that weren't enough, Stefano has also opened **Field to Fork** (511 S. 8th St., 920/694-0322, 7am-3pm Mon.-Sat., $5-14) next door to the pizzeria—think locavore deli and light lunch place; try the Coney dog.

## ACCOMMODATIONS

Nothing is cheap in Sheboygan, if you can even find a room; for some reason the town lacks motel variety and adequate nearby camping. The best bets for cheaper lodging are on I-43 at nearly every exit.

The **Harbor Winds** (905 S. 8th St., 920/452-9000, www.harbor-winds-hotel-sheboygan.magnusonhotels.com, $109) is the only place on the water in Sheboygan.

An observation deck affords a great view, the staff is friendly, and guests get a free breakfast. Service has been hit or miss, but the location cannot be beat.

The **Blue Harbor Resort and Conference Center** (725 Blue Harbor Dr., 920/452-2900, www.blueharborresort.com, $229-689) is a four-level Victorian replica with an indoor water park. The self-enclosed place boasts spas, fitness centers, two enormous restaurants, arcades, and more.

## INFORMATION

The **Sheboygan County Convention and Visitors Bureau** (CVB, 712 Riverfront Dr., Suite 101, 920/457-9497 or 800/457-9497, www.visitsheboygan.com) is along the Boardwalk.

# Vicinity of Sheboygan

## SHEBOYGAN INDIAN MOUND PARK

An archaic relic, **Sheboygan Indian Mound Park** (5000 S. 9th St., 920/459-3444, free), along the Black River region in south Sheboygan, is eerily impressive. The 18 Native American effigy mounds, in myriad geometric and animal shapes, date from AD 500. A beautiful nature trail runs along a creek.

## KOHLER-ANDRAE STATE PARK

Perhaps the best stretch of beach along Wisconsin's Lake Michigan shoreline, **Kohler-Andrae State Park** (1020 Beach Park Lane, 920/451-4080) includes two miles of windswept beach and a plank trail that meanders through the fragile Kohler Dunes Natural Area, one of the state's rarest habitats, an interdunal wetland. White-tailed deer are frequently seen among the dunes. The chilly waters off the park are home to about 50 shipwrecks, a diver's paradise; many of the recovered wrecks are on display at the **Sanderling Center** (12:30pm-4:30pm daily May-Oct.,

free) in the park. Camping is superb here, but it's almost always full on weekends. Reservations (888/947-2757, http://wisconsinstateparks.reserveamerica.com, sites for nonresidents from $25, reservation fee $10) are a good idea.

## ★ KOHLER

A planned community for workers surrounding the operations of the Kohler Company, Kohler is trim and attractive—thoroughly inspiring for a sense of community. Kohler also houses the state's most incredible resort and restaurant and puts on unforgettable factory tours.

### Sights and Recreation

The **Kohler Factory** and, to a lesser extent, **Kohler Design Center** (101 Upper Rd., 920/457-3699, www.kohler.com, 8am-5pm Mon.-Fri., 10am-4pm Sat.-Sun. and holidays, free) are must-sees. On its 2.5-hour tour, the international manufacturer of bathroom fixtures showcases the company's early factory and factory-town history, along with its wares

Kohler-Andrae State Park

in an incredible "Great Wall of China." Also featured are a theater, a ceramic art gallery, and more. Tours of the factory itself are at 8:30am Monday-Friday and require advance registration.

**Waelderhaus** ("House in the Woods," 1100 W. Riverside Dr., 920/452-4079, tours at 2pm, 3pm, and 4pm daily except holidays, free), a dwelling based on homes from the mountainous Austrian Bregenz Forest region commissioned by a daughter of the Kohler founder, contains antique furnishings and highlights such as candle-reflected water-globe lighting.

Hands down the best golf in Wisconsin—and some say in the Midwest—is found in Kohler at the **American Club Resort** (Highland Dr., 920/457-8000, www.destinationkohler.com, $185-360 for 18 holes). **Blackwolf Run** (1111 W. Riverside Dr., 855/444-2838, from $195) offers two PGA championship courses—one of them was the highest-rated gold medal course in the United States, according to *Golf* magazine. Newer are the preternaturally lovely courses of **Whistling Straits** (N8501 Lakeshore Rd., 855/444-2838, from $195), designed to emulate the old seaside links courses of Britain; it's even got sheep wandering around. The Straits Course and a challenging Dunes Course are both PGA championship courses. The Irish Course, a companion course to the first Straits course, features some of the tallest sand dunes in the United States. It's all good enough for the PGA Championship to have been played here three times. Greens fees are high and it's not easy to get a tee time.

## Food and Accommodations

Easily Wisconsin's most breathtaking resort, ★ **The American Club** (Highland Dr., 920/457-8000, www.destinationkohler.com, $350-1,300) is the Midwest's only AAA five-diamond resort. The 1918 redbrick facade of an former workers hostel and dormitory has been retained, along with the original carriage house, though both have been plushly

retrofitted. A full slate of recreation is offered, including two championship Pete Dye golf courses, one of them considered among the world's best shot-master's courses. There's also a private 500-acre wildlife preserve to explore. If that's not enough, the seven dining rooms and restaurants include the state's best—the Immigrant Room, winner of the prestigious DiRoNa Award. Here, various rooms offer the cuisine and heritage of France, Holland, Germany, Scandinavia, and England. The food is created with regional Wisconsin ingredients. Jackets are required for male diners.

If ever you splurge in Wisconsin, this is one of the places to do it; if not, consider taking the tour (2pm Mon.-Sat.).

## SHEBOYGAN FALLS

Sheboygan actually got its start near these thundering falls on the Sheboygan River. The town has a great river walk with views of the falls and two historic districts. Among the grandest bed-and-breakfasts in the area is ★ **The Rochester Inn** (504 Water St., 920/467-3123 or 800/421-4667, $129), a massive 1848 general store. The guest rooms all have parlors with wing chairs, and there are four split-level luxury suites and a grand internal spiral staircase.

## PLYMOUTH

Plymouth is just west of Sheboygan and would definitely be on a National Register of Quaint Places: The aesthetics of its early Yankee settlement remain intact. Initially a solitary tavern and stage stop, as all rail traffic passed through the little town, it eventually became the center of the cheese industry in eastern Wisconsin; the first Cheese Exchange was here.

## Sights

The local chamber of commerce has an impressively mapped and detailed historical and architectural walking tour highlighting about 50 buildings. The visitors center itself is an architectural highlight: the **Plymouth Arts Center** (E. Mill St., 920/892-8409, 10am-4pm

# Ice Age National Scenic Trail

Glaciation affected all of the Upper Midwest, but nowhere is it more exposed than in Wisconsin. Southwestern Wisconsin's Driftless Area is also the only purely unglaciated region on the planet surrounded by glacial till.

Wisconsin's epic Ice Age National Scenic Trail is a 1,200-mile course skirting morainic topography left behind by the state's four glacial epochs. It's also an ongoing project, started in the 1950s and still being pieced together. When county chapters have finally cobbled together enough municipal, county, and state forestland with donated private land for right-of-ways, Potawatomi State Park in Door County will be linked with Interstate State Park on the St. Croix National Scenic Riverway via one continuous footpath.

## THE ICE AGE SCIENTIFIC RESERVE

Technically, the trail is but a segment of the Ice Age National Scientific Reserve, established

---

Tues.-Fri., noon-3pm Sat.-Sun.) is a restored 1920s edifice that also houses a historical museum and art galleries.

### Food and Accommodations

Ignore the strip-mall ambience and go for the fish at the delightful and unbelievably friendly and helpful Italian restaurant **Sweet Basil** (645 Walton Dr., 920/892-7572, dinner Mon.-Sat., $8-25).

Historic bed-and-breakfasts are everywhere you turn. A structure that woodworkers will want to see is the **52 Stafford Irish Guest House** (52 Stafford St., 920/893-0552, www.52stafford.com, 5pm-9pm Mon.-Fri., 11:30am-9pm Sat., 4pm-8pm Sun., $120). The 19 guest rooms are decent, but the main attraction here is the food. The limited but ambitious menu changes a lot; the signature meal is an Irish beef brisket basted in Guinness—it'll wow you. The rich woods, ornate stained glass, and original fixtures give the place

a special atmosphere. Drop by Wednesday evening for rousing Irish music.

## ELKHART LAKE

Northwest of Sheboygan is one of the region's first resort areas, Elkhart Lake (www.elkhartlake.com). In the early 20th century, well-to-do Chicagoans sought it out as a quiet getaway, and later, so did high-profile mobsters such as John Dillinger. Another major draw is the international speedway **Road America** (7390 Hwy. 67, 800/365-7223, www.roadamerica.com), North America's longest natural road-racing course.

### Food and Accommodations

One of the most extraordinary meals of late is at the newish ★ **Paddock Club** (61 S. Lake St., 920/876-3288, 4pm-close Tues.-Sun., $18-38). You'll find indescribably good new American cuisine in another erstwhile gangster hangout.

One of the oldest and most established

by Congress in 1971 after decades of wrangling by forward-thinking ecologist Ray Zillmer of Milwaukee.

The reserve's nine units are scattered along the advance of the glacial periods and highlight their most salient residuals. Numerous other state and county parks, equally impressive geologically, fill in the gaps. Kames, eskers, drumlins, moraines, kettles, and all the glacial effects are highlighted in the units on the east side of the state. An interpretive center is planned for Cross Plains, Wisconsin, west of Madison.

## THE TRAIL

As of 2015, around 725 miles of official trails had been established either by the National Park Service, county chapters, or state parks; the rest are link-up trails, roads, or even main streets. The longest established stretches are in the Chequamegon and Nicolet National Forests, along the Sugar River Trail in southwest Wisconsin, through the Kettle Moraine State Forest, and along the Ahnapee State Trail in the Door Peninsula. Hiking the whole thing is possible, but it takes about three months and oodles of patience attempting to circumvent cityscapes where segments have not yet opened.

Camping is a problem along the route if you're outside an established park or forest. Do not trespass on private land, or landowners may become resistant to completion of the trail.

## INFORMATION

View the National Park Service's website (http://nps.gov/iatr) or contact the **Ice Age National Scorie Trail** (608/441-5610, www.iceagetrail.org) in Madison.

lodgings, family-run since 1916, is **Siebkens** (284 S. Lake St., 920/876-2600, www.siebkens.com, weekends $149-479), a turn-of-the-20th-century resort with two white-trimmed main buildings open in summer and a year-round lake cottage. A nod to modernity is also available in the plush new condos. The classic tavern and dining room serve up regional fare on an old porch.

Much plusher is the ★ **Osthoff Resort** (101 Osthoff Ave., 855/876-3399, www.osthoff.com, peak season weekends $280-700), with lavish comfort and fine lake views. Lola's dining room and the Aspira spa are superb, and there is a new cooking school, making for an overall awe-inspiring experience.

## HENNING'S WISCONSIN CHEESE

Nobody makes 'em like they do at the too-cool **Henning's Wisconsin Cheese** (20201 Point Creek Rd., Kiel, 920/894-3022, www.henningscheese.com, 7am-4pm Mon.-Fri.,

8am-noon Sat.), northeast of Sheboygan in little Kiel. The operation is enormous, complete with an outstanding museum of cheese making. Snap photos of the gigantic 12,000-pound wheels of cheddar cheese, as this is the only place in the United States that still makes them.

## KETTLE MORAINE STATE FOREST-NORTHERN UNIT

A crash course in geology helps preface a trip through the 29,000 acres of the northern unit of the **Kettle Moraine State Forest** (along Hwy. 67 west of Plymouth, 262/626-2116). The northern unit was chosen as the site of the Henry Reuss Ice Age Interpretive Center, on the Ice Age National Scenic Trail, because of its variegated topography of kettles, terminal moraines, kames, and eskers. Surrounded by suburban expansion, it comprises 12 state natural areas.

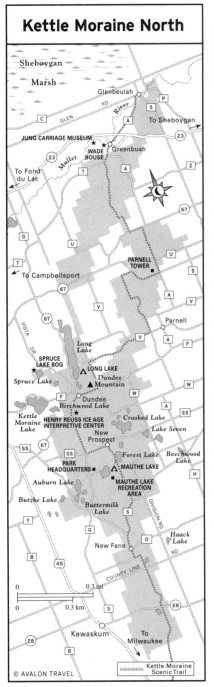

# Kettle Moraine North

Sheboygan Marsh

Glenbeulah

To Sheboygan

JUNG CARRIAGE MUSEUM

WADE HOUSE  Greenbush

To Fond du Lac

Mullet

PARNELL TOWER

To Campbellsport

Parnell

Long Lake

SPRUCE LAKE BOG

LONG LAKE

Spruce Lake

Dundee Mountain

Dundee Birchwood Lake

Kettle Moraine Lake  HENRY REUSS ICE AGE INTERPRETIVE CENTER

Crooked Lake

Lake Seven

New Prospect

Forest Lake  Beechwood Lake

PARK HEADQUARTERS

MAUTHE LAKE

Auburn Lake

MAUTHE LAKE RECREATION AREA

Butzke Lake

Buttermilk Lake

Haack Lake

New Fane

Kewaskum

To Milwaukee

0        0.3 mi

0        0.3 km

© AVALON TRAVEL

Kettle Moraine Scenic Trail

This northern swath of forest is the complement to its sibling southwest of Milwaukee. Supporters of the forest have always envisioned the two sections of forest as segments of wildlands buffering urban zones along a 120-mile eco-corridor.

## Henry Reuss Ice Age Interpretive Center

Along Highway 67 near the Highway G junction is the **Henry Reuss Ice Age Interpretive Center** (920/533-8322, 8:30am-4pm Mon.-Fri., 9:30am-5pm Sat.-Sun. Apr.-Oct., shorter hours Nov.-Mar., free). The back deck has outstanding vistas of the region's topography. The exhibits and documentary theater are well worth a stop. A self-guided 40-mile geology driving tour starts from the center. A short nature trail winds from the building outside.

## Wade House and Jung Carriage Museum

Along Highway 23 in Greenbush, the **Wade House and Jung Carriage Museum** (Hwy. T, 920/526-3271, 10am-5pm daily mid-May-mid-Oct., $11 adults) sits along the oak plank road that once stretched from Sheboygan to Fond du Lac. The state historic site is a detailed reconstruction of the original 1848 sawmill, as evidenced by the post and beam work. Environmentally friendly construction was used in the restoration.

Perhaps the Wade House's biggest draw is the impressive Wisconsin Jung Carriage Museum, with the state's largest collection of hand- and horse-drawn vehicles, many of them rideable.

## Scenic Drives

The Kettle Moraine forest offers a smashing scenic drive along ribbons of highway that include officially designated Rustic Roads. The forest has the oldest geology in Wisconsin, a 10,000-year-old outwash of the last glacial period.

To the south, the scenic drive connects with other great back roads all the way to the

Kettle Moraine Southern Unit, about 40 miles away. It's hard to get lost; just follow the acorn-shaped road signs. From Sheboygan Marsh in the north to Whitewater Lake in the Southern Unit, the drive is about 120 miles and passes through six counties.

## Recreation

More than 140 miles of trails snake through Kettle Moraine's narrow Northern Unit, including the highlight, the sublime 31-mile segment of the **Ice Age National Scenic Trail.** It runs the length of the park and connects to five other forest trails for plenty of recreational options. There are five shelters along the way; backpackers must have free permits, which are generally easy to obtain, but plan ahead for midsummer, when the permits are in demand. Permits cannot be obtained online. Call **ReserveAmerica** (888/947-2757) as far in advance as possible, and at least 48

hours prior to arrival. You can only stay in a backpack site for one night.

The best-known trail is the 11-mile **Zillmer Trail,** accessible via Highway SS; it includes a tough ridge with a great vista. Some say the best view (1,300 feet above sea level, plus 450 feet above the tower) is from **Parnell Tower,** two miles north of Highway 67 via Highway A.

**Parkview General Store** (262/626-8287), north of the Mauthe Lake Recreation Area entrance, has bicycle, paddleboat, canoe, and rowboat rentals.

## Camping

In all, 400 campsites are available, lots of them reservable. Primitive shelter camping is possible along the Glacial Trail. **Mauthe Lake** also has a tepee for rent. **Reservations** (888/947-2757, http://wisconsinstateparks.reserveamerica.com, from $23 nonresidents, plus $10 reservation fee) are a good idea. A $10 daily entrance fee is also charged.

**EAST-CENTRAL WATERS**
**MANITOWOC AND TWO RIVERS**

# Manitowoc and Two Rivers

These neighboring Lake Michigan cities were originally home to Ojibwa, Potawatomi, and Ottawa people. The tranquil harbors attracted European fur traders, and by 1795 the Northwest Fur Company had built a post here. The area prospered during the heady early decades of whitefish plunder and the still extant shipbuilding.

## Charter Fishing

Charter fishing on Lake Michigan from Manitowoc and Two Rivers is big business. Coho and king salmon, along with lake, brown, and some rainbow trout, are the most popular quarry for skippers in these waters. Average rates start at $400 for a half-day charter and up to $700 for a full-day (10-hour) charter.

## MANITOWOC

This small bight was a port of call for weary Great Lakes travelers—the earliest ones in birch-bark canoes—heading for Chicago. Drive out into the countryside and you can still see smokehouses and bake ovens on early farmsteads, log threshing barns large enough to drive machinery through, split-rail fencing, and unique cantilever house designs.

An enormous fishing industry developed and, thanks to overfishing through injudicious use of drift nets and seines, collapsed. Industry in the so-called Clipper City shifted to shipbuilding beginning in the 19th century and peaked during World War II, when Manitowoc's shipyard became one of the most important naval production facilities in the country.

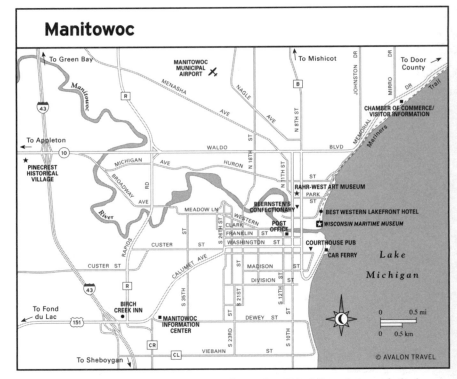

# Manitowoc

To Green Bay
MANITOWOC MUNICIPAL AIRPORT
To Mishicot
To Door County
Trail
Manitowoc
MENASHA
AVE
NAGLE
JOHNSTON DR
MIRRO DR
Mariners Trail
R
AVE
N 8TH ST
CHAMBER OF COMMERCE/ VISITOR INFORMATION
To Appleton
10
WALDO
N 8TH ST
BLVD
★ PINECREST HISTORICAL VILLAGE
MICHIGAN AVE
HURON
N 11TH ST
N 18TH ST
BROADWAY
River
RAPIDS ST
RD
AVE
MEADOW LN
WESTERN
BEERNSTEN'S CONFECTIONARY
RAHR-WEST ART MUSEUM ★ PARK ST
ST
BEST WESTERN LAKEFRONT HOTEL
POST OFFICE
S 26TH ST
CLARK ST
FRANKLIN ST
WISCONSIN MARITIME MUSEUM
CUSTER ST
WASHINGTON ST
COURTHOUSE PUB
43
CUSTER ST
CALUMET AVE
CAR FERRY
*Lake Michigan*
MADISON ST
S 35TH ST
DIVISION ST
S 21ST ST
S 12TH ST
R
To Fond du Lac
151
BIRCH CREEK INN
DEWEY ST
S 10TH ST
0    0.5 mi
0    0.5 km
CR
■ MANITOWOC INFORMATION CENTER
S 23RD ST
CL
VIEBAHN ST
© AVALON TRAVEL
To Sheboygan

## ★ Wisconsin Maritime Museum

At peak World War II production, Manitowoc eclipsed even major East Coast shipbuilding centers. Its legacy is remembered at the **Wisconsin Maritime Museum** (75 Maritime Dr., 920/684-0218, www.wisconsinmaritime.org, 9am-6pm daily Memorial Day-Labor Day, shorter hours in other seasons, $15). The museum is an amazing collection of local Great Lakes maritime history and includes the **USS *Cobia* submarine**—a National Historic Landmark and one of 28 subs built here. Pride in this industry is why Manitowoc is the only U.S. city with streets named after submarines.

## Other Sights

The **Pinecrest Historical Village** (Pine Crest Lane, 920/684-4445, 9am-4pm daily May-Oct., $10 adults) is a 60-acre collection of more than 25 buildings, dating as far back as the 1840s, that have been transported here and painstakingly restored.

The **Rahr-West Art Museum** (610 N. 8th St., at Park St., 920/686-3090, 10am-4pm Tues.-Fri., 11am-4pm Sat.-Sun., free) is an 1891 Victorian with intricate woodwork and grand beamed ceilings housing one of the finer collections of decorative art in the Midwest. A tidbit: The brass ring in the street out front is where a piece of a Sputnik crashed in 1962.

Stretch your legs on the **Mariners Trail** (www.marinerstrail.net), a 12-mile paved recreation trail between Manitowoc and Two Rivers.

## Food

Boisterous is the **Courthouse Pub** (1001 S. 8th St., 920/686-1166, 11am-9pm Mon.-Fri., 9am-9:30pm Sat., 9am-2pm Sun., $7-15), which handcrafts its own brews and has above-average pub grub, including gluten-free fare—a shocker in Wisconsin—in a painstakingly restored 1860s Greek Revival building. The proprietor is ever-friendly.

Chocolate fanatics and the dessert-minded should not miss **Beernsten's Confectionary** (108 N. 8th St., 920/684-9616, 10am-10pm daily), a renowned local chocolatier for 50 years.

## Accommodations

Most motels and hotels, including several chain operations, are clustered around the junction of I-43 and U.S. 151. The **Birch Creek Inn** (4626 Calumet Ave., 920/684-3374 or 800/424-6126, www.birchcreekinn.com, from $70) put $1 million in renovations to turn itself into a unique 1940s motor inn with a cottage complex. It's not upscale, but it's comfortable in a mom-and-pop way.

There are no luxury lodgings in town, but a solid mid-range option is the long-standing **Best Western Lakefront Hotel** (101 Maritime Dr., 920/682-7000 or 800/654-5353, $119), adjacent to the maritime museum and the only place right on the lake.

## Information

The super **Manitowoc Information Center**

(4221 Calumet Ave., 920/683-4388 or 800/627-4896, www.manitowoc.info) is prominently housed near the junction of I-43 and U.S. 151 and has a 24-hour kiosk.

## Getting There

Originally one of seven railroad and passenger ferries plying the route between Manitowoc and Ludington, Michigan, the **SS Badger** (800/841-4243, www.ssbadger.com) is a wonderful anachronism. Although it's technically a steamship—the last of its kind on Lake Michigan—you can hardly tell thanks to modern pollution controls. Crossings take four hours and depart daily mid-May-mid-October. One-way fares are $74 pp plus $74 per car. Deals are sometimes available. As a side note, for years this ferry has been embroiled in an environmental debate about whether its use and dumping of coal should preclude its further operation; so far its operators have agreed not to dump ash and can continue to sail.

# TWO RIVERS

Two Rivers is called the fishing capital of Lake Michigan, but residents are even prouder of another claim to fame: The ice cream sundae was invented here in 1881 at a 15th Street soda fountain. The mammoth historic

The USS *Cobia* stands outside of the Wisconsin Maritime Museum.

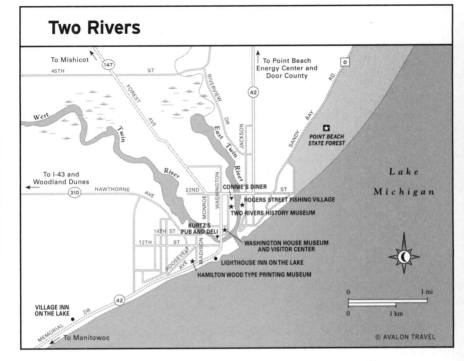

## Two Rivers

To Mishicot
45TH ST
147
FOREST AVE
West
Twin
RIVERVIEW DR
42
To Point Beach
Energy Center and
Door County
0
RD
JACKSON ST
SANDY BAY
POINT BEACH
STATE FOREST
To I-43 and
Woodland Dunes
310
HAWTHORNE
AVE
22ND
MONROE ST
WASHINGTON
River
East Twin River
CONNIE'S DINER ST
ROGERS STREET FISHING VILLAGE
TWO RIVERS HISTORY MUSEUM
KURTZ'S
PUB AND DELI
14TH ST
12TH ST
MADISON
ROOSEVELT AVE
WASHINGTON HOUSE MUSEUM
AND VISITOR CENTER
LIGHTHOUSE INN ON THE LAKE
HAMILTON WOOD TYPE PRINTING MUSEUM
VILLAGE INN
ON THE LAKE
DR
42
MEMORIAL
To Manitowoc

Lake
Michigan

0            1 mi
0        1 km

© AVALON TRAVEL

**Washington House Museum and Visitor Center** (17th St. and Jefferson St., 920/793-2490, 9am-9pm daily May-Oct., 9am-5pm daily Nov.-Apr., free), once an immigrant hotel, dance hall, and saloon, dispenses information as well as great ice cream at a mock-up of the original fountain that made the town famous.

## Sights and Recreation

Across from Washington House is the fascinating **Hamilton Wood Type and Printing Museum** (1816 10th St., 920/794-6272, http://woodtype.org, 9am-5pm Tues.-Sat., 9am-1pm Sun., $5), with vintage equipment for international wood typing. So funky are its holdings that companies like Target seek it out for lettering on clothing lines. The **Two Rivers History Museum** (1810 Jefferson St., 920/793-1103, www.2rhm.com, 11am-3pm Tues.-Sat., $2) was once a convent; it features pieces by renowned portrait artist Lester W. Bentley, born in Two Rivers in 1908.

**Rogers Street Fishing Village** (2102 Jackson St., 920/793-5905, 10am-4pm Mon.-Fri. and noon-4pm Sat.-Sun. May-Oct., $4 adults), includes artifacts from the region's U.S. Coast Guard, especially its lighthouse operations. There is a lot of shipwreck memorabilia—possibly Wisconsin's largest shipwreck exhibit—and plenty of retired vessels.

Ten miles west of Two Rivers along Highway 310 is the excellent **Woodland Dunes,** a 1300-acre nature preserve once at the edges of a glacial lake. There are nature trails and interpretive displays to explore.

## Food

Hole-in-the-wall **Connie's Diner** (1303 22nd St., 920/794-8500, 8am-8pm Mon.-Sat., from $4) was long named Phil Rohrer's, and when Phil sold it in 2011 to an assistant, many locals were worried. But the original retro has been redone in '50s style and the food hasn't declined. Try the mini burgers and raw fries.

One of the best-known restaurants in

the lighthouse at Point Beach State Forest

the region is **Kurtz's Pub and Deli** (1410 Washington St., 920/793-1222, 11am-10pm Mon.-Sat., $4-11), established in 1904 to serve the sailors hopping off Great Lakes steamers and clippers. Today, it can be called an upscale pub.

Don't forget: There's a dessert tray at the visitors center!

## Accommodations

The **Lighthouse Inn on the Lake** (1515 Memorial Dr., 920/793-4524 or 888/228-6416, www.lhinn.com, $128) is showing its age but is still comfortable. The standard guest rooms aren't large, but they have magnificent vistas of Lake Michigan—and some higher-priced rooms are quite large.

Farther south from town toward Manitowoc, the **Village Inn on the Lake** (3310 Hwy. 42, 920/794-8818 or 800/551-4795, www.villageinnwi.com, $118) is a decent family-run operation—a two-level motel with RV sites, a coffee shop, and a mini golf course on the premises.

Six miles northeast of Two Rivers, off Highway O, is gorgeous **Point Beach State Forest** (920/794-7480). You can't miss it: The majestic white lighthouse towers above the sand and pines. The wind-whipped 2,900 acres are spread along latte-colored sandy beaches, and the wicked shoals offshore have sent plenty of ships to their graves. The lighthouse is a working facility, and public access is sporadic. The preserved ridges along the shoreline, part of the reason the entire forest is a State Scientific Area, are residual effects of a glacial lake that retreated 5,500 years ago. One of Wisconsin's official Rustic Roads runs along the park—Highway O, a.k.a. Sandy Bay Road. Camping reservations (888/947-2257, www.wisconsinstateparks.reserveamerica. com, $10, sites for nonresidents from $25) are a good idea; two brilliant new sites dating to 2015 are kayak-only.

Farther north on this road is the **Point Beach Energy Center** (6600 Nuclear Rd., 920/755-6400, 11am-4pm Tues. and Sat., free). The Point Beach nuclear plant has caused some controversy in Wisconsin because of plans to store waste aboveground in concrete casks. Nonetheless, the energy center features worthwhile hands-on exhibits on energy as well as a nature trail and an observation tower.

One of nine Ice Age National Scientific Reserves in Wisconsin is the **Two Creeks State Natural Area,** a few miles north of Point Beach. Two Creeks contains the remnants of a 12,000-year-old buried glacial forest.

## DENMARK

Just off I-43 on the way to Green Bay is the Danish enclave of Denmark, previously known as Copenhagen. There's lots of old Danish architecture downtown, and more cheese shops per capita than anywhere else.

# Green Bay

## The Bay

At *la baye verte,* a haven from the volatility of Lake Michigan, the Jesuits established an official settlement of New France in 1669—the first permanent European settlement in what would become Wisconsin—at the mouth of the bay near the present-day suburb of De Pere.

The European explorers and trappers found a wealth of beavers and new networks of waterways, which meant inland access; the wilderness from here to the Fox River Valley produced more pelts than any other region in New France.

## The City

Forts erected by the French, mostly during periods of Native American unrest, gave permanence to east-central Wisconsin's most populous community, Green Bay. The fur trade was the bedrock of the city's fortunes early on, but Green Bay began growing when the Erie Canal was completed in 1825, which led to the state's first wave of European immigrants descending en masse on Wisconsin, most via Green Bay. Many put down roots immediately, working in Green Bay's burgeoning agricultural, logging, and iron smelting industries; the paper and lumber industry quickly surpassed the beaver trade.

Enormous volumes of ship and railroad cargo still travel through this firmly blue-collar town of working-class bungalows.

Most importantly, regardless of history and recent subtle gentrification, the dominant cultural ethos that underpins the city is the beloved Green Bay Packers football team. *The Sporting News,* among other national media outlets, has rated the city as having the most fans among National Football League teams. The waiting list for season tickets is about 200 years—this is a city where 60,000 people pay to watch the team *practice.*

## Orientation

Running along the bay and bisected by the Fox River, streets can sometimes be a confusing jumble. Remember which side of the river you're on, and when in doubt, head for Lake Michigan and start over.

## ★ THE PACK

One of the oldest professional football teams in the United States—and the only community-owned team in professional sports—the **Green Bay Packers** are the most important thing in this town; check out the gleeful fans from around the world in the parking lot at **Lambeau Field** (1265 Lombardi Ave., 920/569-7500 or 888/442-7225, http://packers.com). Perhaps no stadium mixes tradition with modernity more than this national treasure, where the atrium and its restaurants and shops (8am-9pm Sun.-Thurs., later on game days, 8am-midnight Fri.-Sat.) are open every day of the year; you'd be surprised how many people are wandering around at 8am. Note that all schedules change on game days, so check the website or the fan hotline (920/569-7502) for daily information.

Visitors and locals often crowd the free twice-a-day practices (usually 8:15am and 2:30pm) during the Packers' late-summer **training camp,** held at the practice facility along Oneida Street across from Lambeau Field. Sometimes practices are held indoors in the team's state-of-the-art Hutson Practice Facility, also on Oneida Street near the stadium. Practices begin in mid-July and run until preseason games begin in late August. In mid-July is the **Packer Hall of Fame Induction Ceremony,** a very big deal to fans.

A perfect Packer Country day starts by watching some of the practice sessions; people standing along the fence to watch are known as "railbirds," and it's a tradition for Packers

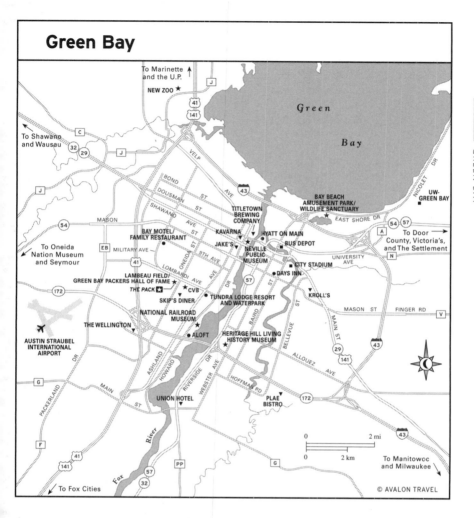

# Green Bay

players to ride local kids' bikes to and from the playing field.

On the basic hour-long **Lambeau Field Tour** (9am or 10am-4pm daily on nongame days, from $15 adults), visitors explore virtually every corner of this local landmark (except, sadly, the Packers locker room), including the press box, the visitors locker room, the skyboxes, and even the field itself.

The Lambeau Field Atrium is home to the **Green Bay Packers Hall of Fame** (9am-6pm daily, hours vary during home games, $15 adults), where fans weep at the life-size

re-creation of the 1967 Ice Bowl—the defining moment that made the team "America's team." After a multimillion-dollar facelift in 2015, it looks smashing. Kids will have to jostle with the adults in any interactive zones.

## Other Packers Sights

The most unusual sight is **Skip's Diner** (2052 Holmgren Way, 920/494-9882, 6am-2pm Mon.-Fri., 7am-noon Sat.-Sun., from $4) in Ashwaubenon. It preserves the stool sat on regularly by the ferocious Packer linebacker Ray Nitschke; the street it's on is named for a Packers coach. In 2002 a plaza was dedicated at **City Stadium** (1415 E. Walnut St., behind Green Bay East High School), where the Packers played from 1925 to 1956.

Believe it or not, in Green Bay there exists a bar dedicated to archrival football team the Chicago Bears. The **Lorelei Inn** (1412 S. Webster St., 920/432-5921, 11am-10pm Tues.-Fri., 4pm-10pm Mon. and Sat.) was originally owned by a Bears fan, as reflected in the decor. Expect good-natured rivalry. It's closed Sunday except when the Packers and Bears clash.

During training camp and on some game days, a cheery way to take in the Pack is aboard a bus on the **Packer Heritage Trail Tour** (800/895-0071, http://candmpresents. com, $25). It leaves from the **Convention and Visitors Bureau** (1901 S. Oneida St., across from Lambeau Field, 920/494-9507 or 888/867-3342, www.greenbay.com) and takes in an array of Packers sights.

## OTHER SIGHTS
### Museums

The impressive **National Railroad Museum** (2285 S. Broadway Ave., 920/437-7623, www. nationalrrmuseum.org, 9am-5pm Mon.-Sat., 11am-5pm Sun. Apr.-Dec., shorter hours

# Lombardi Time

When, not if, you visit Lambeau Field, pull out your mobile phone and check the time. Now look at the stadium clock outside. No, that isn't a mistake: The stadium's clock is intentionally set 15 minutes fast. That's because Vince Lombardi absolutely insisted that "on time" meant 15 minutes early, and hereabouts it's called "Lombardi Time."

Jan.-Mar., $10 adults) has more than 80 railroad cars and locomotives, a respected collection rivaling any in the nation. Available for close-up inspection is *Big Boy*, the world's largest steam locomotive. Train rides are available five times daily in summer. Included in the admission is a mile-long jaunt on a narrow-gauge railroad.

Perhaps the most unusual state park in Wisconsin is **Heritage Hill Living History Museum** (2640 S. Webster Ave., 920/448-5150, www.heritagehillgb.org, 10am-4:30pm Mon.-Sat., noon-4:30pm Sun. Apr.-Oct., $10 adults). More than 25 historic buildings from around Wisconsin have been reconstructed at this 50-acre site. Separated into four distinct

the entrance to Lambeau Field

thematic areas—Pioneers, Military Life, Small Towns, and Agricultural—the buildings include mock-ups of the flimsy sapling-and-bark dwellings of the early Jesuits and some of the oldest extant buildings in Wisconsin. All areas are accessible via trams.

The **Neville Public Museum** (210 Museum Place, 920/448-4460, www.nevillepublicmuseum.org, 9am-5pm Tues.-Sat., noon-5pm Sun. spring-fall, 9am-4pm Tues.-Sat., noon-4pm Sun. winter, $7 adults) contains art, history, and science exhibits. The outstanding main hall exhibit, *On the Edge of the Inland Sea*, a 7,500-square-foot diorama of a retreating glacier, is worth the admission, as is the impressive view of the city skyline. The dinosaur displays are outstanding.

## Bay Beach Amusement Park

A favorite in Green Bay is the anachronistic collection of more than a dozen rides along the bay shoreline at the **Bay Beach Amusement Park** (1313 Bay Beach Rd., 920/391-3671, 10am-9pm daily June-Aug., 10am-9pm Sat.-Sun. May and Sept.). The best part: Rides cost as little as $0.25. An exact replica of Elvis Presley's favorite ride at an amusement park in Memphis is very recent, as are more modern gravity-defying rides, and a train.

## Bay Beach Wildlife Sanctuary

Up the road from the amusement park is the excellent **Bay Beach Wildlife Sanctuary** (1660 E. Shore Dr., 920/391-3671, www.baybeachwildlife.com, 8am-7:30pm daily Apr.-Sept., shorter hours Oct.-Mar., free), a 700-acre spread with exhibits on Wisconsin fauna, including the very popular timber wolf house.

## NEW Zoo

The well-regarded **NEW Zoo** (4378 Reforestation Rd., 920/448-4466, 9am-8pm daily June-Aug., shorter hours Sept.-May, $7 adults), eight miles north of Green Bay, allows the animals greater freedom to roam. Animal compounds include Prairie Grassland, Wisconsin Native, and International—you're as likely to see a Galápagos tortoise as you are a Wisconsin red fox. The zoo has tripled in size in recent years and added many new exhibits, including a black-footed penguin zone. A children's area allows interactive experiences.

## Seymour

West of Ashwaubenon is zany Seymour, a small town that bills itself as the "Home of the Hamburger," purportedly invented here. The townsfolk fete their title with the annual **Burger Fest** (http://homeofthehamburger.org, 1st Sat. in Aug.); they try to fry a world-record three-ton burger every year. Check out the enormous burger and Hamburger Charlie on Depot Street, west of Highway 55.

# ENTERTAINMENT AND EVENTS

For local entertainment listings, check the schedules in the *Green Bay Press-Gazette* (www.greenbaypressgazette.com).

## The Arts

On the University of Wisconsin-Green Bay campus, the wonderfully modern **Weidner Center for the Performing Arts** (920/465-2217, www.weidnercenter.com) showcases national and regional musicians, plays, musicals, dance performances, and the annual midwinter Green Bay jazz fest. The city boasts its own symphony orchestra and two community theater groups.

# RECREATION

## Trails

The **Fox River Trail** is a 14-mile multipurpose trail stretching along the Fox Valley corridor to Greenleaf. The city is also the departure point for the **Mountain Bay Trail,** an eight-mile trail connecting to trails west to Wausau.

## Camping

Nearest to Green Bay, camping is north on Highway 57, toward Door County, 15 miles out of town at **Bay Shore County Park** (920/448-4466, May-Oct., $20).

# Titletown

It is always the same: Sunday morning at 11:59am, the network TV feed fades to black. Then, a still shot of the man, and slowly, with the melodrama of sports announcers, the voice-over: "The Man. Vincent T. Lombardi." Or, even more powerfully, "Titletown . . ." It incites goose bumps followed by the shaking of unwavering belief.

## THE RELIGION

If there are any awards for professional sports fandom, the Green Bay Packers football team and its beloved legions win hands down. One grizzled sportswriter wrote, "The Dallas Cowboys were only another football team; the Packers were a practicing religion."

The Packers are the only passively proselytizing franchise in all of professional sports. Hard-core travelers and football aficionados will find Packer bars and Packer fan clubs in every state in the Union and as far away as England. I've even found Packer faithful bellowing for Sunday satellite-dish equity as far away as Taiwan and Thailand.

## EARLY YEARS

The Packers were founded in 1919 as one of the handful of teams that would eventually make up the National Football League (NFL). The team was born in the back room of the *Green Bay Press-Gazette*, where the cigar-chomping sports editor, George Calhoun, and legendary ex-Notre Damer Curly Lambeau agreed to found a local team. They convinced a local industry bigwig to supply a practice field and uniforms, thus obligating the team to call itself the Indian Packing Company Footballers. This was later shortened to the Packers. Going 10-1 its first season, the dynasty had begun.

## Spectator Sports

It's impossible to arrive and get same-day tickets to regular-season Packers games; preseason games are another matter. Call 920/496-5700 for ticket information.

## FOOD

Don't forget that suburban De Pere also has some fine eateries, especially the since-1918 **Union Hotel** (200 N. Broadway, 920/336-6131, lunch Mon.-Fri., dinner daily, $15-30), the most pleasantly anachronistic environment you'll find in the state. It has outstanding service, perhaps a visit from the owner, and a comparatively extraordinary wine list.

## Brewpubs

Green Bay has a couple of lively brewpubs. Right downtown at the west end of the Fox River Bridge along Highway 29 is **Titletown Brewing Company** (200 Dousman St., 920/437-2337, 11am-10pm daily, $8-15), with

an above-average menu of quite creative fare. It's housed in a grand old depot with a soaring clock tower.

Virtually across the street, the **Hinterland** (313 Dousman St., 920/438-8050, lunch Sat., dinner Mon.-Sat., $8-18) has great beer and professionally well-made food—even caribou and wild boar.

## Fish Fry

**The Settlement** (3254 Bay Settlement Rd., 920/465-8415, 11am-close daily, from $4) bar and grill has a top-notch Friday perch fish fry. It's as much bar as grill but has good-quality food in large portions, and you'll be welcomed like a friend; it's a great local find.

## Heartland Fare

If you really want to rub elbows with the locals, check out ★ **Kroll's** (1658 Main St., 920/468-4422; 1990 S. Ridge Rd., 920/497-1111, 10:30am-11pm Sun.-Thurs.,

After literally passing the hat in the crowd for the first season, the Packers, in need of financial stability, hit on one of the most unusual money angles in sports. The community issued $5 nondividend public shares in the team; almost beyond logic, the citizens scooped up the stocks.

The only nonprofit, community-owned team in professional sports, the Packers have become a true anomaly: a small-market team with few fiscal constraints on finding and wooing talent. And they can never desert the town—if they try to move, the organization is dissolved and all money goes to a charitable foundation.

## TITLETOWN'S TITLES

After the Packers beat their opponents in the first season, they became the first NFL team to win three consecutive NFL titles, and they did it twice—1929-1931 and 1965-1967. In all, they won 11 championships through 1968 and the Lombardi years. In fact, even though the Lombardi-led teams get all the glory, the teams of the early years were even more dominant, amassing a 34-5-2 record.

Then the well went dry. Before the 1990s brought in more forceful management, the Packers suffered through their longest drought ever between NFC Central Division Championships: 24 long, unbearable, embarrassing years. Still, the fans dutifully packed the stadium every Sunday; they always believed.

But after all those doormat decades, the Packers finally won the Super Bowl again in 1997, which began an always-in-the-playoffs run culminating in yet another notch in the Titletown belt on February 6, 2011, when the Packers defeated the Super Bowl-seasoned Pittsburgh Steelers 31-25 for their record 13th NFL championship and fourth Super Bowl title. The headline in the *Milwaukee Journal-Sentinel* said it all: "Titletown Again." A more apt quote often heard after the game was, "The Lombardi trophy is coming home."

10:30am-midnight Fri.-Sat., $4-11), the best family restaurant in town, with two locations: The more convenient one is on Main Street, and the other, closer to Lambeau Field, is the older of the two and looks like a film set. They serve great walleye and perch along with legendary burgers. The Ridge Road Kroll's also features wall buzzers that diners can use to summon the waitstaff.

Kroll's competition is **Bay Family Restaurant** (Military Ave. and 9th St.; 1245 E. Mason St.; 1100 Radisson St., 920/494-3441, breakfast, lunch, and dinner daily, $6-11). The Bay uses ingredients direct from family farms and serves homemade pies and voluminous piles of hash browns.

## Italian and Pizza

Italian restaurants are the dominant international specialty in Green Bay. One of the best-known is **Victoria's** (2610 Bay Settlement Rd., 920/468-8070, lunch and dinner Mon.-Sat.,

$5-15). The portions are outrageously huge; vegetarians also have good options.

The best pizza in town is at **Jake's** (1149 Main St., 920/432-8012, 4pm-close Tues.-Sun., $4-6). It was so popular that the getting-older Jake couldn't keep up and closed; some former employees and new blood brought it back, and it's better than ever. You'll have to wait up to half an hour for a seat at times, but it's well worth it.

## Supper Clubs and Fine Dining

★ **The Wellington** (1060 Hansen Rd., 920/499-2000, lunch Mon.-Fri., dinner Mon.-Sat., $8-28) is a Green Bay institution of sorts. An exclusive spot done up as an English drawing room, it specializes in beef Wellington and excellent duck, beef tenderloin, and seafood dishes.

**Plae Bistro** (1671 Hoffman Dr., 920/632-7065, lunch Mon.-Thurs., dinner Mon.-Sat., $13-40) is a cozy little bistro serving creative

American cuisine, where you'll find fish tacos as well as tenderloin. The grilled apple-pear salad is otherworldly.

### Vegetarian

Visitors complain about the lack of vegetarian options on local menus, but **Kavarna** (143 N. Broadway, 920/430-3200, breakfast, lunch, and dinner daily, brunch Sat.-Sun., $5-10), a coffee shop with a café complex, has baked yam fries that are worth the trip.

## ACCOMMODATIONS

Don't even think of showing up in Green Bay on a weekend when the Packers are playing at home with any hope of getting lodging. Try the website of the **Visitors Bureau** (www.greenbay.com) for links and deals, or the local lodging association (www.greenbaystays.com).

### Downtown

It's possible to get a room as low as $75, though most are more, at the **Days Inn** (1125 E. Mason St., 920/430-7040, $90-189), which has a large number of amenities.

Upmarket digs are nearby at the excellent **Hyatt on Main** (333 Main St., 920/432-1234, www.greenbay.hyatt.com, from $219). It's almost a self-contained city, with everything you need, and breakfast is included.

### Southwest: Airport and Stadium

Where Lombardi Avenue swings around to meet Military Avenue is the nice **Bay Motel** (1301 S. Military Ave., 920/494-3441, $50-75), where all rooms have movies included; some have mini fridges.

A boutique hotel for chic youngsters in Packerville is **Aloft** (465 Pilgrim Way, 920/884-0800, www.aloftgreenbay.com, $115). It's Zen chic and very friendly.

The place for families is the **Tundra Lodge Resort and Waterpark** (Lombardi Ave. and Ashland Ave., 920/405-8700, www.tundralodge.com, $180-399), near Lambeau Field. Indoor-outdoor water parks let the kids

work up a sweat, then let them gorge in the buffet-style restaurant.

## INFORMATION

The **Packer Country Tourism Office** (1901 S. Oneida St., 920/494-9507 or 888/867-3342, www.greenbay.com) is across the street from Lambeau Field. It serves Green Bay east to Two Rivers, Kewaunee, and Algoma.

The **Green Bay Press-Gazette** (www.greenbaypressgazette.com) is Wisconsin's oldest newspaper, dating to 1833, and is a great source of local goings-on.

## GETTING THERE
### Air

**Austin Straubel International Airport** (GRB, Hwy. 172, Green Bay, 920/498-4800, http://flygrb.com), southwest of Green Bay off Highway 172, has flights to Chicago, Minneapolis, Detroit, and Atlanta.

### Bus

The **Bus Depot** (800 Cedar St., 920/432-4883) is served by Greyhound, with routes to most points in southern and western Wisconsin and west to Minnesota. Note that there has been talk of closing this station to consolidate with the city's bus system, so phone first.

## ONEIDA NATION

West of Green Bay are the 12 square miles of the **Oneida Indian Reservation.** Known as the "People of the Standing Stone," the Oneida were members of the League of the Iroquois and were once a protectorate of the Stockbridge-Munsee bands on the east coast. They moved westward en masse (save for a small band that still lives in New York) in the early 18th century.

One of the only repositories of the history of the Oneida people is the **Oneida Nation Museum** (W892 Hwy. EE, 920/869-2768, 9am-5pm Tues.-Fri., 10am-5pm Sat., $2 adults, $1 children). Exhibits in the main hall focus on Oneida history and culture. A longhouse and stockade are outside, as well as a nice nature trail. The Oneida powwow takes place on or near the Fourth of July.

# The Bottom of the Door

For many folks, Door County begins only when they have crossed the bridge spanning Sturgeon Bay's Lake Michigan canal. Others claim that you're not in the county until Highway 42 and Highway 57 bifurcate into bayside and lakeside routes northeast of town. Still, Door County proper includes a chunk of 15 or more miles south of the ship channel, and the peninsula also includes underappreciated Kewaunee County, east of Green Bay.

Note that Highway 57 has been undergoing dramatic changes, and this will likely continue as long as visitors flock to the Door. The road bends away from the lake and into a fast four-lane divided highway. This may creep farther up the peninsula, slowed only by the requirement not to damage archaeological sites, wetlands, and threatened species. For now, you'll find an easily overlooked little county wayside along Highway 57. At **Red Banks** wayside, a statue of explorer Jean Nicolet stands a few hundred yards from the red clay bluffs overlooking the serene bay. Historians agree that it was here that Jean Nicolet first came sloshing ashore in 1634, cracking his harquebus to impress the Winnebago people.

Highway 57 leaves much to the imagination. More adventuresome travelers might attempt to find Highway A out of Green Bay. It traverses the same route but right at the lake. Bypassing Point Sable, once a boundary between Native American nations, the road offers views of a state wildlife area across the waters. Farther north, you can see Vincent Point and, immediately after that, Red Banks. This byway continues through Benderville before connecting back to Highway 57 and crossing the Kewaunee-Door County line into Belgian territory.

## BRUSSELS AND VICINITY

Brussels and surrounding towns such as Champion, Euren, Maplewood, Rosiere, and Forestville constitute the country's largest Belgian American settlement. The architecture of the region is so well preserved that more than 100 buildings make up Wisconsin's first rural National Historical Landmark. Right along Highway 57, the homes and Roman Catholic chapels show distinctive Belgian influences, along with a lot of reddish-orange brick and split cedar fencing. On alternating weekends through the summer, the villages still celebrate kermis, the Roman Catholic mass during harvest season.

**Brussels** is the area's de facto capital; **Belgian Days** (1st week of July) has plenty of Belgian chicken, *booyah* (thick vegetable stock), *jute* (boiled cabbage), and tripe sausage. You'll find Belgian fare in a few places in Brussels, including **Marchants Food** (9674 Hwy. 57, 920/825-1244, 8am-8pm Mon.-Fri., 8am-6pm Sat., 8am-12:30pm Sun.), open daily for 50 years.

A quick side trip takes in lots of Belgian architecture. In Robinsville, 1.5 miles east of Champion along Highway K, is the **shrine grotto,** a home and school for disabled children founded by a Belgian to whom the Virgin Mary is said to have appeared in 1858.

Not Belgian per se but north of the town of Luxemburg, itself south of Brussels, near the junction of Highways A and C, is ★ **Joe Rouer's** (E1098 Hwy. A, 920/866-2585, 11am-8pm Tues.-Sun., from $5), a classic bar with legendary burgers and delicious cheese curds.

North of Brussels along Highway C, the **St. Francis Xavier Church and Grotto Cemetery** is representative of Belgian rural construction; farmers contributed aesthetically pleasing stones from their fields to raise a grotto and crypt for the local priest. The interior of the church is not available to the public.

Three miles northeast of Brussels via Highway C is the **Gardner Swamp State Wildlife Area** along Keyes Creek. The lowland forest and swamps here are a

# The Bottom of the Door

SHERWOOD POINT
LIGHTHOUSE

DOOR 44

Potawatomi
State Park

Sturgeon
Bay

Brookside

Gardner Swamp
State Wildlife Area

Green Bay

Namur

Brussels

Forestville

JOE ROUER'S

Rosiere

Dyckesville

VON STIEHL
WINERY

Champion

Algoma

Howard

THE PACK

Luxemburg

Casco

Alaska

Green
Bay

Bellevue

Kewaunee

To Two Rivers
and Manitowoc

Lake Michigan

0        5 mi
0      5 km

© AVALON TRAVEL

perfect environment for the endangered Hines Emerald dragonfly. No hiking trails exist, but it's great for bushwhacking to find wild edibles, if you have experience doing so.

## KEWAUNEE

Perched on a hillside overlooking a lovely historic harbor, Kewaunee was once bent on rivaling Chicago as the maritime center of the Great Lakes and could have given the Windy City a run for its money when an influx of immigrants descended on the town after hearing rumors of a gold strike in the area. But Chicago had the railroads, and Kewaunee, despite its harbor, was isolated, and it became a minor port and lumber town.

### Sights

Kewaunee is Wisconsin's Czech nerve center. Outlying villages have Czech-Bohemian heritage, and you'll often hear Czech spoken.

The **Kewaunee Chamber of Commerce** (308 N. Main St., 920/388-4822, www.kewaunee.org) has maps of a nifty **walking**

**tour** that takes in about three dozen historical structures. A popular photo subject is the 1909 **Kewaunee Pierhead Lighthouse** (96 Ellis St.). The structure consists of a steel frame base and a steel tower with a cast-iron octagonal lantern about 50 feet tall.

At the harbor you can take a tour ($3) aboard a retired World War II tugboat with **Tug Ludington** (920/388-4317, 10am-6pm Thurs.-Sun. summer, shorter hours in other seasons).

The central **Old Jail Museum** (Vliet St. and Dodge St., 920/388-4410, 10am-4pm Thurs.-Fri. summer, free) is near the courthouse in an old sheriff's home, part of which doubled as the jail, complete with gruesome dungeon cells. Statues of Father Marquette and solemn, pious Potawatomi are first on the tour, and you can visit the replica of the USS *Pueblo*. The ill-fated Navy ship, involved in an incident with North Korea in the 1950s, was built in Kewaunee during World War II.

Three miles west of town, the Wisconsin Department of Natural Resources operates a state-of-the-art **Anadromous Fish Facility** (N3884 Ransom Moore Lane, 920/388-1025, 10am-5pm daily, free). Detailed are the spawning practices of anadromous fish, which swim upstream to spawn, viewed through underwater panels.

Southwest of town in Montpelier Township is a **Rustic Road** scenic drive along parts of Hrabik, Cherneysville, Sleepy Hollow, and Pine Grove Roads. Nearby, south of Krok, is the only known Wisconsin rooftop windmill, a granddaddy of a historic structure. Follow the brown and yellow Rustic Road signs.

South of Kewaunee via Highway 42 and then west on Highway J is **Parallel 44 Winery** (N2185 Sleepy Hollow Rd., 920/388-4400, http://44wineries.com, 10am-5pm Mon.-Sat., noon-5pm Sun.), which produces Frozen Tundra wines.

At **Svoboda Industries,** along Highway 42 north, you'll see what is purportedly the world's largest grandfather clock, 39 feet tall.

The local **Visitors Information Center** (Hwy. 42, 920/388-4822 or 800/666-8214, www.kewaunee.org) is right on Highway 42, north of downtown, near a great marsh walk.

## Food

The local specialty is Czech and Bohemian food, including *kolace* (yeast buns with fruit filling) and *buhuite* ("BU-ta"—thin dough filled with seeds or fruit), sauerkraut rye bread, and *rohlik*. Near the bridge in town are a couple of places for great smoked fish.

## Accommodations

The **Karsten Inn** (122 Ellis St., 920/388-2228, www.karstenhotel.com, from $90), a 1912 arts and crafts structure, has grand roots and the rooms ooze history, but it always seems to be under new ownership. Check several rooms. It's reportedly haunted.

The **Coho Motel** (705 Main St., 920/388-3565, http://cohomotel.com, $77) is an amazingly clean place for the cost.

## ALGOMA

The beach-hugging drive along Highway 42 from Manitowoc to Algoma is spectacular. As you swoop into Algoma from the south, endless miles of wide empty beach begin, and neither the road nor the beach are heavily used. Today, the small town of Algoma is known mostly for sportfishing, and its marinas, holders of four state records, account for the state's most substantial sportfishing industry.

Tour Kewaunee on Tug Ludington, a retired World War II tugboat.

A passenger ferry between Algoma and Frankfort, Michigan, has been discussed for years but is still nonexistent.

## Sights

**Von Stiehl Winery** (115 Navarino St., 920/487-5208, www.vonstiehl.com, guided tours 9am-5:30pm daily July-Aug., shorter hours in other seasons, $4 adults) is the oldest licensed winery in Wisconsin, housed in what was once the Ahnapee Brewery (named after the local river), built in the 1850s, with three-foot-thick limestone walls and a ready-made underground catacomb system. The house specialty is cherry wine; many other Wisconsin fruit wines are produced, all made in a patented system that prevents premature aging and light damage. Two doors east its new **Ahnapee Brewery** (920/785-0822, hours vary) features handcrafted beers for the first time since before the Civil War.

Algoma is also the southern terminus of the **Ahnapee State Trail,** a section of the Ice Age National Scenic Trail stretching 18 miles partly along the Ahnapee River to the southern shore of Sturgeon Bay. Another trail runs from Algoma to Casco.

Algoma once had a legendary "fishing mayor" named Art Dettman. His name lives on in the restored **Art Dettman Fishing Shanty** (Church St. and Shanty Rd., 920/487-3443)—almost a museum of fishing—that's on the National Register of Historic Places. It's open by appointment only; call for information.

## Charter Fishing

Second in the state for the volume of fish taken, this is a prime place to smear on the zinc oxide and do some fishing. Early-season lake trout are generally biting in May, but June is Algoma's biggest month; rainbow trout and chinook salmon are everywhere. Steelhead and especially king salmon are added to the mix come July, and brown trout get big in August. September fishing is great. Visit the website of the **Algoma Area Chamber of Commerce** (www.algomachamber.org) for a list of all member charter operations. The lowest cost for a six-hour charter fishing tour is $350.

## Food

Several family restaurants and diners in town serve Belgian *booyah* and Belgian pie.

For espresso, coffee, tea, or light food—along with live music—in a trendy atmosphere, you can't beat the Mediterranean-influenced **Caffe Tlazo** (607 Hwy. 42, 920/487-7240, 6am-7pm Mon.-Fri., 7am-8pm Sat., 7am-3pm Sun., from $5).

Fine dining in a low-rent bar atmosphere is at **Skaliwags** (312 Clark St., 920/487-8092, www.skaligwags.com, 4:30pm-10pm daily summer, $8-25), where there is Hawaiian-inspired seafood, pasta, and great steaks. The chef also operates a food truck in town.

For a picnic basket, **Bearcat's** (Hwy. 42 and Navarino St., 920/487-2372, 9am-5pm daily year-round) has great smoked fish for cheap prices.

## Accommodations

A basic motel across the road from Lake Michigan is the **Scenic Shore Inn** (2221 Lake St., 920/487-3214, $79), with clean guest rooms and welcoming owners who have put a great deal of updating into the place.

## Information and Services

The **Visitors Information Center** (Hwy. 42, 920/487-2041 or 800/498-4888, www.algoma. org) is on the south edge of Algoma along Highway 42. It is also the departure point for historical walking tours of downtown—on your own or guided ($3).

# The Fox Cities

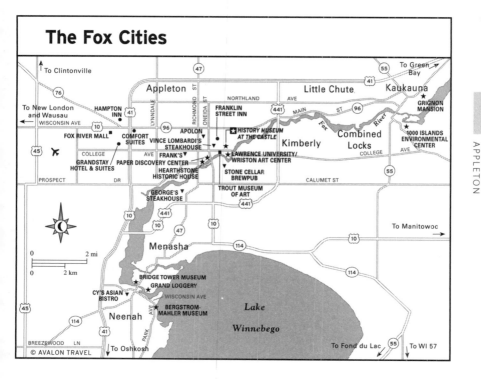

# Appleton

It has been called the Queen of the Fox Cities and the Princess of Paper Valley, although even locals might not know what you're talking about. Bisected by the Fox River, spread-out Appleton hardly seems paper-centered or industrial when you're in the gentrified downtown area.

One civic nucleus is well-respected **Lawrence University** (www.lawrence.edu), a small liberal-arts college that was the state's first coed institution of higher education and also the first to initiate a postgraduate paper-making institute.

Appleton grew up around a mill, but wheat production was far more profitable than logs. Not until after the Civil War did local industrialists turn their attention to Wisconsin's potential for paper wealth. It is still an important industry, and the region is known as Paper Valley.

## The Fox Cities and Fox Valley

Between Neenah and Kaukauna, along Lake Winnebago's northwestern cap, lie a dozen concatenate communities making up the Fox Cities region—part of but distinct from the Fox River Valley, which stretches along the Fox River-Lake Winnebago corridor and takes in all communities between Green Bay and Oshkosh. Appleton is the region's economic anchor; the smallest town is Combined Locks. All are based on the Fox River—one of the few rivers in North America that flows north. Together, the Fox Cities constitute the third-largest metropolitan area in the state (pop. 180,000), a statistic many Wisconsinites find surprising.

# SIGHTS
## ★ History Museum at the Castle

Paper may be the city's raison d'être, but folks just can't get enough of that Houdini magic. Born Ehrich Weiss in Hungary in 1874, the enigmatic Harry Houdini spent most of his life in Appleton. The **History Museum at the Castle** (330 E. College Ave., 920/735-9370 www.myhistorymuseum.org, 11am-4pm Tues.-Sun., closed holidays, adults $7.50) includes **A.K.A. Houdini,** the foremost collection of Houdini artifacts anywhere, notable for the Guiteau handcuffs, which bound President Garfield's assassin and from which the magician later escaped. The center has prepared a detailed walking tour of the city, marked with brass plaques, that takes in the sites of Houdini's childhood. Magic shows, hands-on exhibits, and more thrill kids and parents alike.

The History Museum also contains an excellent and award-winning exhibit titled *Tools of Change* about the workers and economic history of the Lower Fox region.

## Paper Discovery Center

Where else would the paper industry's hall of fame, the **Paper Discovery Center** (425 W. Water St., 920/749-3040, www.paperdiscoverycenter.org, 10am-4pm Mon.-Sat., $5), be but the Fox River Valley? In a renovated paper mill, experience every facet of paper, start to finish, with lots of activities for the kids. Seriously, it's amazing how much paper touches our lives.

## Hearthstone Historic House

**Hearthstone Historic House** (625 W. Prospect Ave., 920/730-8204, 10am-3:30pm Thurs.-Fri., 11am-3:30pm Sat., 1pm-3:30pm Sun., $8 adults) is a massive 1882 Victorian structure, the first home in the world to be lighted by a self-contained hydroelectric plant. Within Appleton's city limits, the Fox River drops almost 40 feet, much of it in angry rapids; in the late 1880s the Hearthstone, also the city's major architectural draw, pioneered the technology. The rich original appointments have been preserved, down to period electroliers and light switches designed by Thomas Edison. Hands-on displays teach visitors about electricity and allow you to operate the controls of a power plant.

## Art Galleries

Lawrence University's **Wriston Art Center** (E. College Ave., 920/832-6621, hours vary Tues.-Sat., free) features rotating and permanent exhibits of student and guest artists in traditional and mixed media. Go if just to see the building's otherworldly design.

The **Trout Museum of Art** (111 W. College Ave., 920/733-4089, www.troutmuseum.org, 10am-4pm Tues.-Sat., noon-4pm Sun., $6) has three galleries, puts emphasis on regional artists, but hosts many big-time national touring exhibitions.

## Vicinity of Appleton

In nearby New London, along the Wolf River, the **Mosquito Hill Nature Center** (N3880 Rogers Rd., New London, 920/779-6433, dawn-dusk daily) offers some good hiking trails and the very intriguing **Wisconsin Butterfly House** (11am-3pm Wed. and Sat.-Sun., $1 donation), showcasing Wisconsin's native butterfly species. The American water spaniel, bred by a local resident, also originated in New London.

Among the oldest paved trails in Wisconsin is hard-to-find number 53 on Wisconsin's Rustic Road system. Beginning in 1857, work was done on what today are Garrity, McCabe, Greiner, and Bodde Roads, northwest of Appleton along U.S. 41 at Highway JJ. Keep your eyes peeled for the signs—it's somewhat confusing. Along the way, you'll pass scenic double-arch bridges, a stone silo, and a wildlife conservation area.

# ENTERTAINMENT AND EVENTS

Pick up a copy of the free monthly *Scene* (www.scenenewspaper.com), which has a good listing of entertainment and cuisine.

the History Museum at the Castle

## Cultural Events

**Lawrence University** almost always has something happening, from a remarkable speaker series to regular performing arts productions at the **Memorial Chapel and Stansbury Theatre**, in the **Music-Drama Center** (E. College Ave. and Lawe St.). For information, contact the **Office of Public Events** (920/832-6585).

## SHOPPING
### Malls

Appleton is mall country, with so much mall floor space that bus tours make regular pilgrimages. The city sported the nation's first indoor mall, which was partially demolished in 2006. The **Fox River Mall** (4301 W. Wisconsin Ave., 920/739-4100, 10am-9pm daily), the state's second-largest indoor mall, is admirable.

## SPORTS AND RECREATION
### Spectator Sports

**Goodland Field** (2400 N. Casaloma Dr., 920/733-4152) is the home of the Wisconsin Timber Rattlers, a single-A minor league baseball franchise of the Milwaukee Brewers. It's typical family-friendly fun with zany promotions and dirt-cheap ticket prices.

## FOOD

Downtown Appleton has an amazing array of eateries; stroll a few blocks and you'll find a wide variety of options.

### Asian

For an upscale Pacific Rim-Asian fusion meal, head south of downtown to Neenah to ★ **Cy's Asian Bistro** (208 W. Wisconsin Ave., 920/969-9549, lunch Mon.-Fri., dinner Mon.-Sat., $10-16), whose remarkable food has heavy overtones of Thai. Cy is one of the friendliest proprietors you'll ever chat with at your table.

Also check out http://appletondowntown.org for listings.

## Pubs and Nightlife

Closer to Lawrence University, one place to check out is **Houdini's Lounge** (117 S. Appleton St., 920/832-8498, 11am-11pm daily), a pub with Harry Houdini as the central theme and more than 60 kinds of beer available.

**Bazil's** (109 W. College Ave., 920/954-1770, 11am-2:30am) features an amazing 135 microbrews. The **Stone Cellar Brewpub** (1004 Olde Oneida St., 920/735-0507, 11am-10pm daily) is an 1858 brewery that whips out a few tasty brands—one named for Harry Houdini.

*USA Today* called **The Wooden Nickel** (217 E. College Ave., 920/735-0661, 11am-2am) the best sports bar in Wisconsin, and it's hard to argue with that. Another pick is **Olde Town Tavern** (107 W. College Ave., 920/954-0103, 4pm-2am daily), for its wonderful beers of yesteryear (Schlitz? Really? How grandfatherly).

# Joseph McCarthy, Native Son

I have in my hands a list of 205 names that were made known to the Secretary of State as being members of the Communist Party and who nevertheless are still working and shaping policy in the State Department.

These words, uttered by Senator Joseph McCarthy, a Fox Cities native, in Wheeling, West Virginia, in what became known as the 205 Speech, thrust him into the national political spotlight. Before his political fortunes waned, he dominated U.S. politics, electrified the nation, aided Tricky Dick Nixon, and inspired a new word, *McCarthyism*. Wisconsinites still wonder how they feel about one of their most infamous native sons. Since the passage of the post-September 11 attacks Patriot Act, his name has been invoked repeatedly.

## TAIL GUNNER JOE

After a lifelong struggle with education, McCarthy graduated from the law school at Marquette University and astonished everyone by winning an elected judgeship in 1938 through sheer grassroots flesh-pressing toil. He was not a widely respected judge, and he further infuriated opponents by stumping for higher office and exaggerating, some say, his military service in the South Pacific during World War II; Tail Gunner Joe was born.

## THE JUNIOR SENATOR

McCarthy was swept up in the GOP wave of 1946 and made it to Washington DC, beating out a

## Mediterranean

One of the best dining experiences around is at ★ **Apolon** (207 N. Appleton St., 920/939-1122, 5pm-10pm Mon.-Sat., $9-20), a Hellenic-heavy pan-Mediterranean restaurant famed for its flaming cheese.

## Pizza

**Frank's Pizza Palace** (815 W. College Ave., 920/734-9131, 4pm-3am daily, $4-9) has been making every ingredient of its pizzas from scratch for more than 40 years—including the sausage—and it's still going strong. October to May, the restaurant hosts 18-piece big brass band blowouts.

## Steaks and Supper Clubs

Open for 50 years and still going strong is **George's Steak House** (2208 S. Memorial Dr., 920/733-4939, lunch Mon.-Fri., dinner Mon.-Sat., $9-30). It's strictly steaks and sea-food, with piano music nightly.

This is Packerland, so a visit to **Vince Lombardi's Steakhouse** (333 W. College Ave., 920/380-9390, 4pm-10pm Mon.-Sat.,

4pm-9pm Sun., $15-45) in the Radisson Paper Valley Hotel is a requisite for Packers football fans; the steaks are sublime.

## ACCOMMODATIONS

The rates listed here will double during Experimental Aircraft Association (EAA) events in nearby Oshkosh. Most lodgings are west of downtown.

The Appleton **Hampton Inn** (350 Fox River Dr., 920/954-9211, $115) has been rated one of the top 10 Hampton Inns nationwide and gets rave reviews.

One of the largest recreation centers in the state is at the Appleton **Comfort Suites Comfort Dome** (3809 W. Wisconsin Ave., 920/730-3800, $120). Some guest rooms have kitchens and microwaves.

A few blocks north of the Avenue Mall is the 1897 Victorian **Franklin Street Inn** (318 E. Franklin St., 920/739-3702, www.franklinstreetinn.com, from $130). Original pocket doors, oak and maple hardwoods, and original chandeliers give one of the stateliest

member of Wisconsin's La Follette dynasty. He incessantly angered the Senate with his intractable attitude, personal attacks, and rules violations. By 1949 the congressional leadership loathed him, and most assumed he was simply a lame-duck embarrassment.

What no one counted on was his shrewd prescience about the national paranoia over communism. In part, McCarthy concocted the Red Scare. He was once again reelected. His path culminated in his antics in the House Un-American Activities Committee, and McCarthyism was born.

By 1953 he had reached the zenith of his powers, attacking his peers and fending off censure attempts from his many Senate enemies. One charge finally stuck—a kickback scheme—and on December 2, 1954, he was officially censured, diminishing the junior senator from Wisconsin.

## WISCONSIN AND MCCARTHY

Strident opposition to McCarthy was ever present throughout his time in office. The newspapers in Madison and Milwaukee lobbed many editorial shells to bring him down. "Joe Must Go" recall petitions collected almost half a million signatures statewide.

Ask Wisconsinites today about McCarthy, and they'll likely dodge the question or roll their eyes and shudder. There are still those who support him. Perhaps most tellingly, Appleton, his adopted hometown, removed his bust and all other McCarthy displays from the courthouse, while favorite resident Harry Houdini is celebrated with Houdini Plaza and a huge memorial sculpture of the man in the city center.

mansions in town a nice feel. Expect superlative service.

If you're planning to mall it at the Fox River Mall during your trip and need luxury, the **Grandstay Hotel & Suites** (300 Mall Dr., 920/993-1200, $125) is an amazing option for the money, with top-notch service and amenities for bargain prices.

Downtown, the best option for comfort is the European-style hotel **CopperLeaf Boutique Hotel** (300 W. College Ave., 877/303-0303, www.copperleafhotel.com, from $145), a great deal considering the location, the freshness of the place, and amenities; guests rave about it.

## INFORMATION AND SERVICES

The **Fox Cities Convention and Visitors Bureau** (3433 W. College Ave., 920/734-3358 or 800/236-6673, www.foxcities.org) is quite far west of downtown, but the staff is definitely helpful.

## GETTING THERE
### Bus

**Greyhound** (100 E. Washington St., 920/733-2318) has frequent daily departures to major regional cities. **Lamers** (800/261-6600) bus line also has one departure daily to Milwaukee's Amtrak train station and one to Wausau.

### Air

The **Outagamie County Airport** (ATW, W6390 Challenger Dr., 920/832-5268, www.atwairport.com) is the fourth-busiest in Wisconsin, with 60 flights daily on three airlines to Chicago, Detroit, Minneapolis, Atlanta, and Phoenix.

# Vicinity of Appleton

## NEENAH-MENASHA

The twin cities of Neenah-Menasha are casually regarded as one entity, although they are governed separately. They share Doty Island, where Little Lake Butte des Mortes on the Fox River empties into Lake Winnebago.

Two Fox River channels flowing past the island and two minor promontories provided the water power that created both villages by the 1840s. Depressed industries gave way to papermaking, and within three decades Neenah-Menasha ruled the powerful Wisconsin papermaking region.

### Bergstrom-Mahler Museum

This massive dwelling was once home to early area industrialist John Bergstrom. The highlight of the **Bergstrom-Mahler Museum** (165 N. Park Ave., 920/751-4658, 10am-4:30pm Tues.-Sat., 1pm-4:30pm Sun., free) is a world-renowned collection of paperweights, many dating from the French classic era (1845-1860). The glass menagerie, as the museum calls it, is made up of 2,100 exquisite pieces.

### Downtown and the Riverfront

The scenic landscaped Fox River north channel sports walkways with a kid-friendly fountain and summer concerts; elsewhere the twin towns feature a marina and more than 30 picturesque historic buildings, many straight-up neoclassic in design. The best view is from the still-hand-operated lock on the canal. A new museum on Tayco Street, the **Bridge Tower Museum** (Tayco St. and Main St., 920/967-5155, by appointment, free), is in an 80-year-old bridge tender's tower.

Downtown Neenah's East Wisconsin Avenue gives the best glimpse of 19th-century opulence as well as great river vistas. The mansions along this stretch were part of the setting for Wisconsin native Edna Ferber's novel *Come and Get It.*

Neenah's Doty Park contains a reconstruction of **Grand Loggery** (Clark St. and 5th St., generally noon-4pm daily June-Aug., free), the home of James Doty, the state's second territorial governor. Artifacts of the Doty family and area history are scant, however.

Menasha's **Smith Park** has a few Native American burial mounds. **Kimberly Point Park,** at the confluence of Lake Winnebago and the Fox River, has a great lighthouse and some good views of the river. The big draw is the world-class **Barlow Planetarium** (1478 Midway Rd., 920/832-2848, http://fox.uwc.edu, $8 adults for public shows), on the campus of the University of Wisconsin-Fox Valley. It has virtual reality exhibits and new public shows every week; no reservations are required.

Adjacent to the planetarium is the **Weis Earth Science Museum** (1478 Midway Rd., 920/832-2925, open daily, hours vary, $3), the official Wisconsin mineralogical museum. Learn about glaciers and the stunning sandstone formations of the state.

In Menasha, the **Club Tavern** (56 Racine St., 920/722-2452, 2pm-9pm Tues.-Thurs. and Sat.-Sun, 11am-midnight Fri.) has lots of offbeat beers on tap and friendly proprietors.

## KAUKAUNA

The word *gran ka-ka-lin* is a French-Ojibwa pidgin hybrid describing the long portage once necessary to trek around the city's 50-foot cascades, which ultimately required five locks to tame. A bit more amusing: In 1793, the area's land was purchased—the first recognized deed in the state—for the princely sum of two barrels of rum.

### Sights

Not far from the pesky rapids stands **Grignon Mansion** (1313 Augustine St., 920/766-6106, www.grignonmansion.org, noon-4pm Sat.-Sun. summer, $6). Built in 1838 by Augustin

Grignon to replace the log shack lived in by rum-dealing city founder Dominique Ducharme, the house became known as "the mansion in the woods," although from the outside it doesn't look that grand. It has been thoroughly renovated, down to the hand-carved newel posts and imposing brick fire-places, and the apple orchard still stands. Several of Kaukauna's legendary locks can be visited via the grounds. Call ahead to tour the mansion; walk-in visits are not possible.

Across the river at a bight is the aptly named **1000 Islands Environmental Center** (700 Dodge St., 920/766-4733, 8am-4pm Mon.-Fri., 10am-3:30pm Sat.-Sun., free), a vital stop on the Mississippi Flyway for waterfowl and predatory birds. A huge number of mounted animals are displayed, and live versions include plenty of native Wisconsin fauna, such as great blue herons, coots, and bitterns. The acreage also supports a stand of chinquapin oak, rare in the state. Great trails run along the Fox River here.

## ★ HIGH CLIFF STATE PARK

The vista from the sheer escarpment of **High Cliff State Park** (N7630 State Park Rd., off Hwy. 55, Sherwood, 920/989-1106,

6am-11pm daily year-round), northeast of Lake Winnebago, is truly sublime. The cliff is actually the western edge of the Niagara Escarpment, a jutting, bluff-like dolomite rise stretching almost 1,000 miles to the east, through Door County and beyond to Niagara Falls. From the top, almost 250 feet above the water, you can see all of the Fox River Valley—Appleton, Oshkosh, Neenah, Menasha, and Kaukauna. Perhaps we should do as Chief Redbird of the Ojibwa did; he loved to sit on the cliff and "listen" to the lake—his statue still does today.

High Cliff was founded on an old lime-stone quarrying and kiln operation. Junked equipment and structures still stand. Effigy mounds, 28 to 285 feet long, can be found along trails; they were built by unknown pre-historic Native Americans.

## Recreation

Approximately 12 miles southeast of Appleton, High Cliff State Park maintains both a swimming beach and an 85-slip marina. Hikers have seven miles of somewhat steep trails to choose from, and cross-country skiers have access to four of those come winter. The **Lime-Kiln Trail** is just over two miles and runs from the lime kiln ruins to the lake

Grignon Mansion

and then up the east side of the escarpment. The longest trail is the mostly gentle **Red Bird Trail,** passing by the family campground.

## Camping

The park's 1,200 acres have 112 fairly isolated **campsites** (920/989-1106), most occupied early in the summer high season. **Reservations** (888/947-2757, http://wisconsinstateparks.reserveamerica.com, nonresidents from $23, plus $10 reservation fee) are advised. Nonresidents also pay a $10 daily admission fee.

# Oshkosh

Former President Jimmy Carter once said in a speech at the University of Wisconsin-Oshkosh campus, "I have never seen a more beautiful, clean, and attractive place." He was referring to this Fox River Valley city of 55,000—the one with the odd name. Situated on the western bight of Lake Winnebago and bisected by the Fox River, Oshkosh is often associated by Wisconsinites and others with two disparate images—bib overalls and bizarre airplanes. Since 1895, Oshkosh B'Gosh has turned out functional, fashionable bib overalls and children's clothing and put the city's tongue-twisting name on the international map. And yes, locals have indeed heard visitors ask "Is this Oshkosh, b'gosh?" As for the bizarre airplanes, the annual Experimental Aircraft Association's Fly-In is the largest of its kind, a not-to-be-missed midsummer highlight of itinerant edgy aviation.

## History

Strategically located, water-wise, Oshkosh was a traditional gathering spot for Native Americans. The famous Jesuit missionary Claude-Jean Allouez even came here in 1670 to preach to the Fox and Menominee people.

### SAWDUST CITY

Until the mid-19th century, the north woods of Wisconsin extended much farther south than they do today. In 1848 the first large-scale sawmills appeared. By the end of the Civil War, about 35 mills were working, with a resulting constant light shower of wood dust, at times an inch thick on the city streets, that earned Oshkosh the moniker "Sawdust City." Excavations along Oshkosh riverbanks still reveal marbled layers of compacted sawdust.

This sawdust condemned the city to a painful series of conflagrations; an 1875 fire was so bad that the city—built of the cheap local timber—was finally rebuilt with stone. Ironically, some of this stone came from Chicago, which had been devastated by fire in 1871 and had been rebuilt mostly with wood from Oshkosh sawmills.

## ★ EAA AIRVENTURE MUSEUM

The state has officially decreed the **EAA AirVenture Museum** (3000 Poberezny Rd., 920/426-4818, www.airventuremuseum.org, 10am-5pm daily, $12.50 adults) a state treasure, a consequence no doubt of the 800,000 or so visitors who converge on Oshkosh for the annual fly-in sponsored by the Experimental Aircraft Association (EAA). More than 250 airplanes of every possible type are displayed in the museum—aerobatic planes, home-built, racers, and more. Five theaters, numerous display galleries, and tons of multimedia exhibits make this well worth the admission. Kids of all ages adore the many hands-on exhibits in the Kidventure Gallery, including a g-force machine. Be there when flights are offered in old-timey planes, complete with the leather hat, goggles, and wind-blown hair. The museum is located off U.S. 41 at the Highway 44 exit, next to Wittman Regional Airport. Overall, this is perhaps the best money spent for family recreation in the region.

# Oshkosh

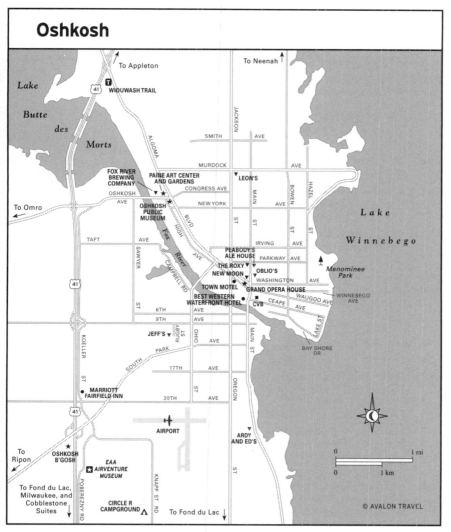

## EAA AirVenture Oshkosh

Oshkosh aviation pioneer Steve Wittman designed and built racing planes, one of which is on display at the Smithsonian. They were so impressive that he drew the attention of Orville Wright and other airplane aficionados. Soon after the EAA moved to Oshkosh, a tradition began: The gathering known as the **EAA AirVenture Oshkosh** (www.airventure.org), often referred to as the Oshkosh Fly-In or Airshow, is now a legendary jaw-dropping display of airplanes that draws hundreds of thousands of people from around the world.

It's a spectacle. The skies are filled with planes and pilots with an appetite for aviation the way it used to be done—strictly by the seat of the pants. Handmade and antique aircraft are the highlights, but lots of contemporary military aircraft are also on show. Thrilling air shows go on nonstop. In all, almost 12,000 aircraft and more than 750,000 people are on hand. Wear good walking shoes, a hat, and sunscreen, and carry water.

The Fly-In is held the last week of July and the first week of August; it runs 8am-8pm daily. The air shows start at 3pm daily. For nonmembers, admission is $45 adults per day.

## OTHER SIGHTS
### Paine Art Center and Gardens

A lumber baron's Tudor revival house, the **Paine Art Center and Gardens** (1410 Algoma Blvd., 920/235-6903, 11am-4pm Tues.-Sun Mar.-Nov., $9 adults) displays meticulously appointed rooms showcasing period furnishings and antiques, along with 19th-century French Barbizon and U.S. art. Outside are acres and acres of gardens; one, modeled after the Dutch Pond Garden at Hampton Court in England, features more than 100 varieties of roses. Legend has it the place is haunted, but the caretakers disavow any knowledge.

### Oshkosh Public Museum

In a grand 1907 English-style home, the **Oshkosh Public Museum** (1331 Algoma Blvd., 920/236-5799, 10am-4:30pm Tues.-Sat., 1pm-4:30pm Sun., $7) is one of the best public museums you'll see in a town of this size. Permanent holdings range in subject from local and natural history, china, and pressed glass to Native American ethnology and archaeology. One highlight is an eight-foot-tall Apostles Clock designed and built in the late 1800s by a German immigrant; it's considered one of Wisconsin's most treasured pieces of folk art.

### Grand Opera House

The 1883 **Grand Opera House** (100 High Ave., 920/424-2355), an architectural gem designed after the majestic halls of Italy, is worth a visit. No organized tours are offered. If someone is around, which is generally when the box office (11:30am-5pm Mon.-Fri., 11:30am-2pm Sat.) is open, you may be allowed to take a peek at the interiors.

# The Republic of Winneconne

In 1967 the state of Wisconsin issued its annual highway map. Puzzled tavern-goers in Winneconne—west of Oshkosh—tried to find their village. It was gone, absent, forgotten, ignored.

With tongues in cheek, the village board voted to secede from the state; then it declared war. The new Republic of Winneconne's banner boasted: "We like it—where?" To which the governor, in Madison, said in jest, "By the way, where *is* Winneconne?" The brouhaha continued as the little village that wouldn't be ignored went through the machinations of recreating itself as a sovereign nation. They've never been overlooked since.

### Oshkosh B'Gosh

This clothier, established in 1895, put Oshkosh on the map. Tours of the factory, where the dandy pin-striped bib overalls come together, are sadly no longer offered because of insurance liability issues. Instead, head for the **Oshkosh B'Gosh Factory Store** (Prime Outlets, 3001 S. Washburn St., 920/426-5817, 10am-9pm daily), which features outlet prices.

## ENTERTAINMENT AND EVENTS

The free monthly *The Scene* (http://scene-newspaper.com) lists happenings for Oshkosh as well as Appleton and Green Bay.

### Bars and Music

**Peabody's Ale House** (544 N. Main St., 920/230-1110, 3pm-2am daily) has live music, including blues, rock, and jazz. For a basic watering hole without the cacophony of college students downing shots, try **Oblio's** (434 N. Main St., 920/426-1063, 3pm-2am daily). It has a pressed-tin ceiling, an antique wooden bar, and photos of old Oshkosh.

## Cultural Events

Stage and theater shows can be found on the campus of the University of Wisconsin-Oshkosh at the **Frederic March Theatre** (926 Woodland Ave., 920/424-4417).

# RECREATION
## Fishing

Winnebago-region specialties are the white bass run (generally mid-late May) and sheepshead. For a one-of-a-kind, only-in-Wisconsin experience, visit in February for the sturgeon-spearing season.

## Parks and Beaches

**Asylum Point Park** (Sherman Rd.), a wildlife restoration area, has trails running from marshland to prairie to lakefront. For swimming, jump in Lake Winnebago at **Menominee Park** (Hazel St. and Merritt St.), along Millers Bay. The park also has the great **Menominee Park Zoo** (520 Pratt Tr., 920/236-5082, 9am-7:30pm daily May-Sept., free) and "Little Oshkosh," one of the country's largest playgrounds and kiddie amusement parks.

## Trail Systems

Of the 75 miles of multipurpose trails in the area, the main route is the **Wiouwash State Trail,** a crushed limestone surface meandering through woods, marshes, farm fields, and tallgrass prairie from Oshkosh to the Winnebago County line. The Oshkosh access point is along Westwind Road, just west of the Highway 41 and Highway 45 intersection northwest of downtown.

# FOOD
## Brewpub

Fratello's Cafe is part of the complex of the **Fox River Brewing Company** (1501 Arboretum Dr., 920/232-2337, 11am-10pm Mon.-Fri., 11am-11pm Sat., 11am-9pm Sun., $5). The attractive café interiors overlook the river; you can even boat up to the outdoor deck. Service can be iffy. Brewery tours are available Saturday.

## Drive-Ins

Oshkosh has two classic drive-ins. **Leon's** (121 W. Murdock Ave., 920/231-7755, 11am-11pm Sun.-Thurs., 11am-midnight Fri.-Sat. summer, from $3) is a classic neon kind of place with delectable custards (and turtle sundaes!) and a mouthwatering homemade sloppy joe-style concoction. **Ardy & Ed's** (2413 S. Main St., 920/231-5455, 10:30am-10pm daily, $3-10) has been around since 1948 and does not appear much changed. It still plays 1950s tunes, and the waitstaff still gets around aboard roller skates.

## Fish Fries

Hands down, locals pick **Jeff's** (1005 Rugby St., 920/231-7450, breakfast Sun., lunch Fri. and Sun., dinner until 10pm Mon.-Sat., $4-20) as the place to go for great seafood that's both down-home and cutting edge. The traditional perch at the Friday fish fry heads the list of seafood and steaks.

## Light Meals and Coffee

Spacious but cozy, the **New Moon** (N. Main St. and Algoma Blvd., 920/232-0976, 7am-late daily, $3-6), in a renovated 1875 beauty, is the place for coffee or a light meal. Atypical sandwiches and creative soups emphasize local and state ingredients and products. It also offers live music and poetry readings.

## Supper Clubs

**The Roxy** (571 N. Main St., 920/231-1980, 11am-10pm Mon.-Sat., 8am-10pm Sun., $7-19) is an archetypal old-style Wisconsin supper club. Casual or formal, it's steaks and fresh fish; you can also get German specials on Tuesday.

# ACCOMMODATIONS

All of the rates listed double during EAA events.

## Downtown

The least expensive option in downtown Oshkosh is the **Town Motel** (215 Division St., 920/233-0610, $50). Fresh coffee is the only extra.

# Stinking Water

Lake Winnebago dominates east-central Wisconsin. At 10 miles across and 30 miles north to south, this shallow lake—once a glacial marsh—is among the largest freshwater lakes fully within one state. It has 88 miles of shoreline and a surface area of 138,000 acres, formed more than 25,000 years ago by a lobe of the Wisconsin glacier.

The lake was always crucial to Native Americans as a part of the water transportation system along the Fox and Wolf Rivers. The name purportedly comes from a linguistic mix-up—or deliberate pejorative snub—by the French, who dubbed the Native American people they discovered here the "stinkers" (an updated translation); "Stinking Water" was a natural follow-up.

Lake Winnebago today is heavily populated with fishers and pleasure-crafters. In winter, up to 10,000 cars park on the frozen lake at any one time. If you're around in February, don't miss the annual throwback to Pleistocene days—the sturgeon-spearing season.

Drive east from Fond du Lac on U.S. 151 to skirt the eastern shoreline along what locals call "the Ledge," the high breathtaking rise above Deadwood Point. Along this route, the small town of Pipe is home to an awesome 80-foot tower. Farther north is Calumet County Park, with six rare panther effigy mounds. At the entrance to the park, stop at the Fish Tale Inn to see the largest male sturgeon ever caught on the lake. An even better place to experience the lake is High Cliff State Park, along the northeastern edge.

Another large centrally located hotel complex is the brand-new **Best Western Waterfront Hotel** (1 N. Main St., 920/230-1900, from $129), which gets high marks; it also has the largest number of amenities in town.

## West

Most Oshkosh accommodations are spread along the highway interchanges of U.S. 41 west of town. The cheapest is the new in 2013 **Cobblestone Suites** (1515 Planeview Dr., 920/385-5636, $85), southwest of town, which gets rave reviews. The economical **Marriott Fairfield Inn** (1800 S. Koeller Rd., 920/233-8504 or 800/228-2800, $129) is off the 9th Street exit and offers a pool, a whirlpool tub, and a game room.

# INFORMATION

The **Oshkosh Convention and Visitors Bureau** (100 N. Main St., 920/303-9200 or 877/303-9200, www.visitoshkosh.com) is downtown.

# GETTING THERE

The local **Greyhound** stop is at **Wittman Regional Airport** (525 W. 20th Ave., 920/231-6490); not many buses serve Oshkosh. Also stopping at the airport, **Lamers** (800/261-6600) bus line runs between Milwaukee and Wausau, with stops in Stevens Point, New London, Appleton, Oshkosh, and Fond du Lac; another Lamers bus stops here on a run between Green Bay and Madison.

# Fond du Lac

Fond du Lac often refers to itself as "First on the Lake"—a loose take on the French, which translates as "bottom (far end) of the lake."

## History

Three separate Winnebago villages predated European permanent settlement, which began in 1785. Despite its strategic location—at the base of a big lake and equidistant to the Fox and Wisconsin Rivers—the town grew painfully slowly. Well-known town father and later Wisconsin's first territorial governor, James Doty, had the town platted in 1835.

Boomtown status effectively eluded Fond du Lac—timber was too far north and receding fast. The local constabulary, the story goes, couldn't even afford a pair of handcuffs. However, a plank road, laboriously laid down from Sheboygan, became a vital transportation route from the Lake Michigan coast.

## SIGHTS

### Galloway House and Village

The stately mid-Victorian Italianate villa **Galloway House and Village** (336 Old Pioneer Rd., 920/922-6390, 10am-4pm daily Memorial Day-Labor Day, 10am-4pm Sat.-Sun. Sept., $9 adults), originally finished in 1847, features 30 rooms, four fireplaces, and much Victorian opulence. Behind it is a turn-of-the-20th-century village containing 23 restored regional dwellings and structures, including the Blakely Museum, an assortment of pioneer and early-20th-century Fond du Lac stuff, including an extensive local private Native American collection—even a mounted passenger pigeon.

### St. Paul's Cathedral

The Episcopalian English Gothic **St. Paul's Cathedral** (51 W. Division St., 920/921-3363, www.stpaulsepiscopalcathedral.org, $2) houses the Oberammergau unified collection, a priceless assemblage of wood carvings. Tours are by appointment.

### Lakeside Park

One of the better municipal parks anywhere is the 400-acre **Lakeside Park** (between Main St. and N. Park Ave. at the lakefront). The eastern part's eye-frying-white sentinel lighthouse is probably Fond du Lac's most recognizable symbol. Nearby are landscaped islands, a deer park, a mini train, a harbor, and a marina. A carousel dating from the 1920s is one of the few wooden merry-go-rounds left in the state; it still runs on a simple two-gear clutch. All the horses are pegged—constructed wholly without nails.

### Eldorado Marsh

Just a few miles west of Fond du Lac along Highway 23 and Highway C is an little-visited canoeists' paradise, the 6,000-acre **Eldorado Marsh,** which subsumes the 1,500-acre shallow flowage marsh. Locals refer to it as the "Everglades of the North." Whether that's hyperbole or not, this is a tranquil, solitary spot.

## EVENTS

Although people in Port Washington, to the southeast, might disagree, Fond du Lac claims to hold the world's largest fish fry in June—more than 5,000 fish dinners and sandwiches are generally consumed in the gluttonous three-day **Walleye Weekend** (www.fdlfest.com).

## RECREATION

### Biking

The city has a balanced system of rural trails, including the great 45-mile **Ledge Lookout Ride,** on the eastern shore of Lake Winnebago along the Niagara Escarpment. Better yet is the **Wild Goose State Trail,** of which Fond du Lac is the northern terminus. The screened limestone trail stretches 34 miles south to the

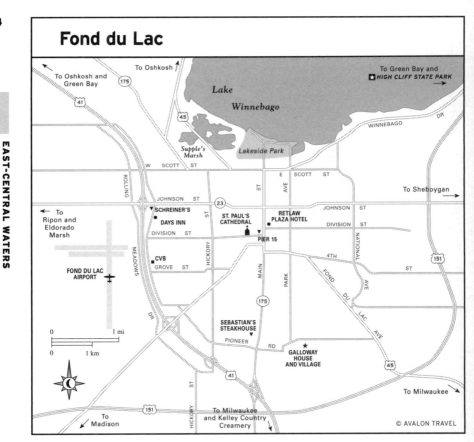

# Fond du Lac

To Oshkosh and Green Bay

To Oshkosh

175

41

45

Lake Winnebago

To Green Bay and
HIGH CLIFF STATE PARK

WINNEBAGO DR

Supple's Marsh

Lakeside Park

W SCOTT ST

E SCOTT ST

ROLLING

JOHNSON ST

To Ripon and Eldorado Marsh

23

SCHREINER'S

DAYS INN

DIVISION ST

ST. PAUL'S CATHEDRAL

RETLAW PLAZA HOTEL

PIER 15

JOHNSON ST

DIVISION ST

To Sheboygan

E ST

AVE

NATIONAL

151

MEADOWS

CVB

GROVE ST

HICKORY

4TH

ST

FOND DU LAC AIRPORT

MAIN

PARK

FOND DU LAC AVE

0     1 mi
0     1 km

DR

175

SEBASTIAN'S STEAKHOUSE

PIONEER RD

GALLOWAY HOUSE AND VILLAGE

41

45

ST

To Milwaukee

HICKORY ST

To Madison

151

To Milwaukee and Kelley Country Creamery

© AVALON TRAVEL

Horicon National Marsh, the city of Horicon, and beyond. A trail pass, which can be acquired at bike shops and some trailheads, is necessary. The trails' access points are west of downtown. Drive west on Scott Street, then north on Rolling Meadows Drive to the trailhead.

## Fishing

Fond du Lac is the southernmost access point for fishing on Lake Winnebago, the most popular fishing lake in the state. It's worth a visit during sturgeon season, when hundreds of ice fishing shanties pop up and fishing jigs give way to tridents used to spear the 10-foot-long dinosaur-looking Pleistocene-era fish.

# FOOD
## Family Dining

Arguably *the* Lake Winnebago culinary institution is ★ **Schreiner's** (168 N. Pioneer Rd., 920/922-0590, www.fdlchowder.com, 6:30am-8:30pm daily, 6:30am-2pm Mon., $3-9), a hearty American-style family restaurant serving meals since 1938. The menu is broad, the servings copious, and the specials Midwestern. But the real highlight is the bread, made fresh on-site in the bakery. The New England clam chowder is also superb.

## Ice Cream

Since the Civil War, the family of **Kelley Country Creamery** (W5215 Hwy. B,

920/923-1715, 11am-9pm daily high season, from $4) has been a dairy mainstay in these parts. You'll love their ice cream, especially sitting on a porch looking at the cows the milk came from. Head south on U.S. 41, then east on Highway B.

## Supper Clubs and Fish Fries

If it's steak you want, head for **Sebastian's Steakhouse** (770 S. Main St., 920/922-3333, dinner daily, $4-14), which is certainly good for the number of choices it gives you and for the excellent value.

**Jim and Linda's Lakeview** (W3496 Hwy. W, Pipe, 920/795-4116, www.jimandlindas. net, dinner Tues.-Sun., $12-45) serves famous fish fries and rib-sticking supper-club fare. If nothing else, come for the view of the lake—the place is 30 feet from the eastern shoreline. It's in little Pipe; take U.S. 151 east to Highway W and turn west.

## ACCOMMODATIONS

During Oshkosh's EAA fly-in, in late July-early August, you'll pay at least double these rates.

Cheapest on the west side is the **Days Inn** (107 N. Pioneer Rd., 920/923-6790, from $60), featuring a heated pool and a refreshing sense of on-the-ballness.

There's only one option near the central area, the full-service **Retlaw Plaza Hotel** (1 N. Main St., 920/923-3000 or 800/274-1712, $129). A 1930s complex, it's a bit dated, but fine at this price; during the EAA convention is another matter. It has an indoor pool, a whirlpool tub, a lounge, a restaurant, a health club, covered parking, and some suites. According to a few visitors, there is some possibly paranormal activity.

## INFORMATION

The **Fond du Lac Area Convention and Visitors Bureau** (171 S. Pioneer Rd., 920/923-3010 or 800/937-9123, www.fdl.com) is well stocked to help.

## GETTING THERE

The local **Greyhound** (920/921-4215) stop is at the **Mobil gas station** (976 S. Main St.). **Lamers** (800/261-6600) buses also stop here on their runs between Wausau and Milwaukee.

EAST-CENTRAL WATERS FOND DU LAC

# Wisconsin Gateways

**G**ive this region a miss and you'll regret it. Yes, the trees have long since been felled, replaced by agricultural tracts on the fertile glacial till, and its population centers have always battled—unfairly—the Rust Belt label. Yet within

a short bike trip one can find a bustling city life, colorful neighborhoods, gorgeous vistas from an enormous expanse of coastline, and, yes, classic pastoral dairy land.

Today a gateway to the state, this region wasn't the first entry point for Paleolithic hunters or European explorers. Lake Michigan steamships laden with European immigrants landed at Milwaukee and the southern ports, where about 90 percent of Wisconsinites live today. Major manufacturing industries,

reliant on cheap labor and water transportation, also established themselves here, giving the state its only real industrial presence.

## PLANNING YOUR TIME

Southeastern Wisconsin could easily be explored in a weekend. The easiest way is to base yourself in **Milwaukee** and explore the region on the way in. Coming from the south, **Racine** and **Kenosha** are on the way to Milwaukee.

---

**Previous:** downtown Milwaukee; Miller Park. **Above:** a sign for Cedar Creek Settlement in Cedarburg.

Look for ★ to find recommended sights, activities, dining, and lodging.

# Highlights

**★ Historic Third Ward and Riverwalk:** Milwaukee's most historic commercial district has shops, a farmers market, cafés, museums, and a cool Riverwalk (page 126).

**★ Milwaukee Art Museum:** This museum's stunning sail-like addition by Santiago Calatrava has been trumpeted in international media, but don't forget the fantastic collections inside the building (page 127).

**★ Discovery World at Pier Wisconsin:** This lakefront science and technology museum is an architectural and educational jewel in Milwaukee's downtown (page 128).

**★ Milwaukee Public Museum:** This phenomenal museum pioneered the concept of walkthrough exhibits; its massive scale may require a full day (page 129).

**★ Miller Brewing:** Miller soldiers on in the grand tradition of Milwaukee brewing. This megacomplex is a definite point of pride for Milwaukeeans (page 132).

**★ Harley-Davidson Museum:** Beer may have made Milwaukee famous, but its denizens are likely prouder of this motorcycle heritage (page 133).

**★ Cedarburg:** To Milwaukee's north is a gem of an anachronism, a preserved village with charm and lots of shops (page 147).

**★ HarborPark:** Visit fascinating museums on the beautiful lakefront of Kenosha (page 149).

**★ Racine Art Museum:** The retro-chic RAM holds the United States' most superlative collections of folk arts (page 153).

**★ Golden Rondelle Theater:** Racine's most distinctive architectural landmark is a Frank Lloyd Wright gem (page 153).

# Wisconsin Gateways

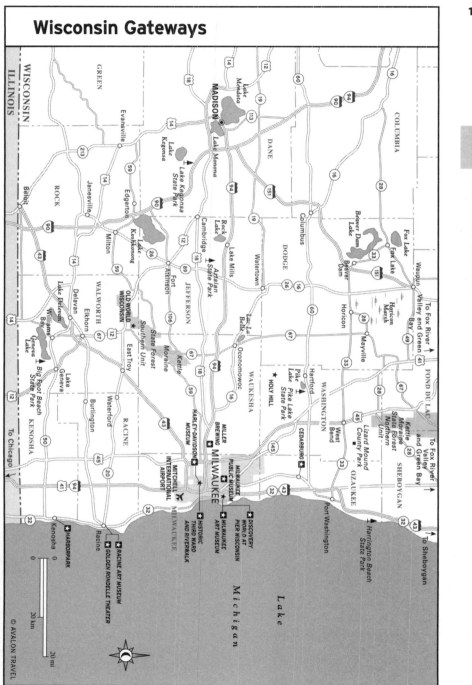

# Milwaukee

For decades, the mass media (most recently Buzzfeed) have hailed Milwaukee, a funky and utterly unpretentious amalgamation of hard-working blue and white collar people, as "underrated." The readers of *Utne Reader* once chose it as "America's Top Underrated City."

Like Cleveland and most other Great Lakes metropolises, Milwaukee doesn't get much respect. Even other Badger Staters, down the road in Madison, have an ingrained image of Milwaukee as belching smokestacks and tannery effluvia, and Milwaukeeans as beer-and-bowling knuckleheads.

Milwaukee is decidedly more lunchbox than bento box, but that's only one aspect of this wonderful mosaic of 500,000 people. It has a low-key, rootsy feel, and it rates in the top 5 percent in the nation in access to arts, attractions, and recreation. The lingua franca in the city's older neighborhoods is often a European mother tongue peppered with accented English. In fact, you'll often hear people speak of *gemütlichkeit* (warmth or hospitality in German) in Milwaukee, and it's by no means an exaggeration; stay long enough and you'll experience it.

In every weather report you'll hear the tagline "cooler near the lake." The Great Lakes establish their own microclimates and influence inland areas for miles. Temperatures along lakeside stretches endure much less extreme fluctuations than in inland communities. A popular local forecasting method is to look at the tear-shaped light atop the Wisconsin Gas Company building downtown: Gold means cold, red means warm, blue means no change, and any color flashing means precipitation is predicted.

## PLANNING YOUR TIME

Milwaukee is great for a day, a weekend, or even a few days. Most folks find lovely—and not too pricey—accommodations downtown in historic, retro, or fashionably fun hotels, and from there much of everything is walkable; you can use the skywalks downtown in winter. Even better, rush-hour traffic, excluding the interstate highways, is rarely bad, and you've almost always got a nice lake view.

If you're passing through, make an effort at least to drop in and ogle the amazing Milwaukee Art Museum and check out the Harley-Davidson Museum. If possible, plan a visit around the huge **Summerfest** music festival in late June and early July; it's a great time (but book accommodations in advance).

## NEIGHBORHOODS AND HISTORIC DISTRICTS

"Indeed, it is not easy to recall any busy city which combines more comfort, evidences of wealth and taste and refinement, and a certain domestic character, than this town on the bluffs," an impressed Easterner observed more than a century ago. The unusually high concentration of magnesium and calcium in Milwaukee clay created the yellowish tint that gives much of the city's original architecture a distinctive flair. Factories produced top-quality bricks of such eye-catching light hues that the city became known as Cream City.

**Visit Milwaukee** (414/908-6205, www.visitmilwaukee.org) offers detailed brochures covering all Milwaukee neighborhoods; it also has lists of tour companies, including **Historic Milwaukee** (828 N. Broadway, 414/277-7795, www.historicmilwaukee.org), which offers an astonishing number of expertly guided walking tours ($10).

### Yankee Hill

Yankee Hill makes other grand Milwaukee neighborhoods appear raffish. This grande dame enclave arose north of East Mason Street to East Ogden Avenue and west off the lakefront to North Jackson Street. Originally owned by Milwaukee's first resident, Solomon Juneau, this became the city's center of government, finance, and business. You'll find examples of Victorian Gothic, Italianate, and other 19th-century architectural styles.

## Juneautown

Juneautown developed into the heart of the city. Today, both Water Street and Wisconsin Avenue claim the title of most-happening area in the city. Original architectural gems such as the Milwaukee City Hall, Pabst Theater, and Iron Block remain. **St. Mary's Church** (836 N. Broadway, at E. Kilbourn Ave., Juneautown) is the same age as Milwaukee. Made of Cream City brick in 1846, it is the oldest Roman Catholic church in the city. The Annunciation painting above the altar was a gift from King Ludwig I of Bavaria.

## Kilbourntown

Speculator Byron Kilbourn refused to align his bridges with Juneautown's, and the consequences are still apparent today. The land was unimportant except as a transit point to Madison. Other than North Old World 3rd Street, much of the architecture was razed for megaprojects. The **Germania Building** (135 W. Wells St.) was once the site of a German-language publishing empire and is notable for its carved lions and copper-clad domes, endearingly dubbed "Kaiser's Helmets." Other architectural highlights in Kilbourntown include the oddly shaped **Milwaukee County Historical Center** (910 N. Old World 3rd St.); the legendary **Turner Hall** (1034 N. 4th St.); the **Milwaukee Public Museum** (800 W. Wells St.); and **Milwaukee Public Library** (814 W. Wisconsin Ave.).

## Brady Street

The most recently gentrified neighborhood, Brady Street is the area surrounding the eponymous street that spans a land bridge connecting the Milwaukee River and Lake Michigan and was originally Milwaukee's version of Little Italy. There's an appreciable quotient of hipsters and misunderstood geniuses lining the coffeehouse windows. The refurbishing has nice touches, such as the etching of Brady Street history into the sidewalk concrete.

## Bronzeville

The predominantly African American cultural and entertainment center of Bronzeville has begun making a resurgence; the district runs from North 4th Street to North 7th Street.

the Iron Block in Juneautown

# Milwaukee

© AVALON TRAVEL

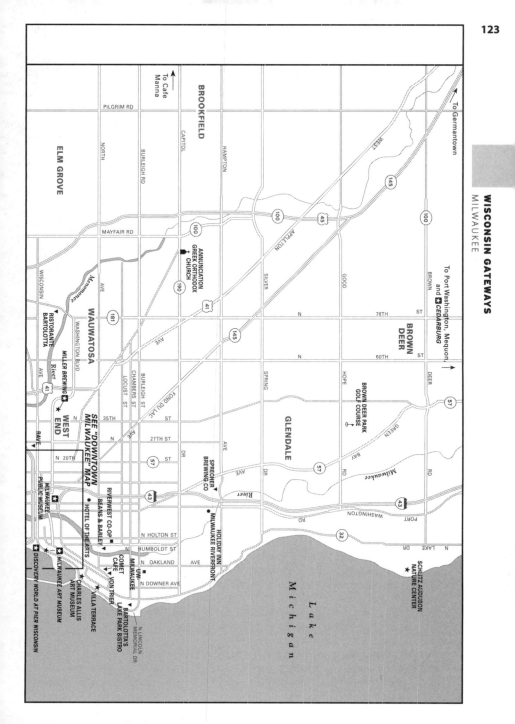

## Walker's Point

Immediately north of the Allen-Bradley clock, between 1st and 2nd Streets on West National Avenue, is a stretch of Milwaukee that smacks of a Depression-era photo essay during the day, but by night becomes one of the city's most underappreciated neighborhoods. The shot-and-a-beer crowd will find some serious restaurant action. There is major LGBT influence and even trendy nightclubs. Walker's Point is also one of the most ethnically mixed neighborhoods in Milwaukee; German, Scandinavian, British, Welsh, Irish, Serb, Croatian, and Polish immigrants once settled here, and more recently, Southeast Asian and Hispanic immigrants have arrived.

Activated in 1962, the **Allen-Bradley Clock Tower** (1201 S. 2nd St.), nicknamed "the Polish Moon," is the second-largest four-faced clock in the world, according to *Guinness World Records*. It was first until 2010, when an enormous clock in Mecca, Saudi Arabia, dethroned it. It has octagonal clock faces twice the size of the clocks of Big Ben in London. The hour hands are 15 feet 9 inches long and weigh 490 pounds; the minute hands are 20 feet long and weigh 530 pounds. It's still a crucial lake navigation marker. Stop by **Tivoli Palm Garden** (613 S. 2nd St.), originally an alfresco produce market renovated into a beer garden by Schlitz Brewing Company.

## North Point District

Virtually all of the North Point District, on the city's coastal bight, is on the National Register of Historic Places. This longtime exclusive community lies west of North Lincoln Memorial Drive and south of East Park Place to East Woodstock Place.

East of here along the lakefront is **Lake Park,** designed by Frederick Law Olmsted, planner of New York City's Central Park and San Francisco's Golden Gate Park. Prehistoric Native American burial mounds are here. At the top of North Avenue is the 1870s Victorian Gothic **North Point Lighthouse,** one of

Tripoli Shrine Temple

the few remaining water towers like it in the United States.

## West End

The West End rivals Yankee Hill's opulence. It became the city's first residential suburb, bounded by North 27th Street, North 35th Street, West Wisconsin Avenue, and West Vliet Street. Yankee bluebloods and prominent German American families competed in building the most opulent mansions. Highland Boulevard was at one time referred to as "Sauerkraut Boulevard." Architectural highlights of the area include the **Tripoli Shrine Temple** (3000 W. Wisconsin Ave.), **Central United Methodist Church** (639 N. 25th St.), Harley-Davidson's corporate headquarters, and **Miller Brewing Company** (4251 W. State St.).

## SIGHTS

Freeway upgrading is ongoing, so patience is required. Without the work, the federal

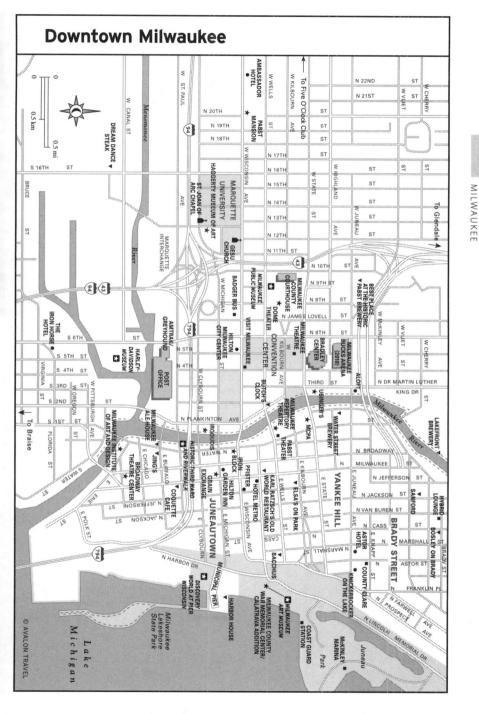

# Downtown Milwaukee

government says Milwaukee is likely to suffer Los Angeles-grade traffic by 2020.

Jaywalking is illegal, and the law is strictly enforced in Milwaukee, especially during lunchtime hours. You will be ticketed, so don't even try it. On the other hand, the police dole out equal numbers of tickets to drivers who don't yield to pedestrians.

From the west, I-94 is the primary thoroughfare; I-894 skirts the southern and western fringes north to south, and I-43 meets I-94 at the Marquette interchange downtown and then heads north.

Off the freeways, most of the sights—except the Historic Third Ward or outlying sights—are concentrated in a rough square bounded by Highway 145 to the north, I-43 to the west, I-794 to the south, and the lake to the east. The Milwaukee River splits the area down the middle and separates the city into its east and west sections. The river is also the line of demarcation for street numbering, so bear in mind where the river is to get oriented.

A comprehensive skywalk system connects the downtown convention center, the Federal Plaza, and the Shops at Grand Avenue. When it was built, one stretch, the Riverspan, was the only skywalk in the United States built over a navigable river, the Milwaukee River.

## Downtown
### ★ HISTORIC THIRD WARD AND RIVERWALK

The once bustling warehouse district suffered a catastrophic conflagration in 1892 in which more than 500 buildings burned—only one was left standing—displacing thousands of residents. Although the area was rebuilt, its earlier verve was missing until recently. The **Historic Third Ward** (http://historicthirdward.org) is now filled with antiques stores and art galleries, among dozens of cafés, upscale shops, and a few longtime holdovers. It's also the fruit and vegetable district, which is quite a sight in the morning as the trucks roll through. A quick tour on the website before you arrive is a good idea.

a view from the Riverwalk

The unofficial theater district of the city, the Third Ward has the **Broadway Theatre Center** (158 N. Broadway, 414/291-7800), which smacks of an 18th-century European opera house juxtaposed with a smaller experimental theater.

The well-regarded **Milwaukee Institute of Art and Design** (MIAD, 273 E. Erie St., 414/276-7889) is housed in an old terminal building, rebuilt in the days after the ward fire. Two galleries (generally 10am-5pm Tues.-Sat., 10am-7pm Thurs. while school is in session) display student work.

The **Riverwalk** (www.visitmilwaukee.org/riverwalk) in the Third Ward includes the **Public Market** (414/336-1111, www.milwaukeepublicmarket.org, 10am-8pm Mon.-Fri., 8am-7pm Sat., 10am-6pm Sun.), a year-round farmers market, replete with anachronistic warehouse-style buildings and early-20th-century facades.

The Riverwalk's cheekiest attraction is a statue of Arthur Fonzarelli, a.k.a. "The Fonz" from the 1970s TV show *Happy Days*, which was set in Milwaukee. When it was announced in 2007, some sniffed that it was too low-brow, and "serious" art belonged here; however, the vast majority of residents love it, and actor Henry Winkler makes regular stops to chat and take selfies with fans.

## OLD WORLD 3RD STREET AND WATER STREET

North of I-794 is another modestly gentrified zone along both sides of the Milwaukee River. To the east is Water Street, a happening mix of microbreweries, sports pubs, dance clubs, restaurants, and cultural attractions. To the west is Old World 3rd Street, with more classic Milwaukee edifices, original old hotels and factories, the Bradley Center, and more restaurants.

Also along North Old World 3rd Street is **Usinger's** (1030 N. Old World 3rd St., 414/276-9100, 9am-5pm Mon.-Sat.), known as the Tiffany of sausage makers. In a city raised on *fleisch*, Usinger's has been a carnivore's heaven since 1880, and partially explains the occasional odd smells downtown—the sweet scent of wood smoke mingling with brewer's yeast. *Food and Wine* magazine has dubbed Usinger's bratwurst the best sausage in the United States.

## LAKEFRONT

Milwaukee sits on the deepest harbor on the western edge of Lake Michigan. For miles, the city rolls like a wave along the lake. You can drive the entire lakefront on Highway 32 or bike most of it on separate county park bike paths. You'll pass nine beaches along the way.

## ★ MILWAUKEE ART MUSEUM

Among the best in the Midwest for visual arts museums is the **Milwaukee Art Museum** (700 N. Art Museum Dr., 414/224-3200, www.mam.org, 10am-5pm Tues.-Sun., 10am-8pm Thurs., $17). The museum holds one of the United States' most important and extensive collections of German Expressionist art, and ranks third in the world for its German art. The museum now houses over 20,000 paintings, sculptures, and prints. Other noteworthy exhibits include a panorama of Haitian art and the repository of Frank Lloyd Wright's documents on the Prairie School of architecture. Pieces date as far back as the 15th century, and the permanent displays are impressively diverse—old masters, Warhol, and the Ashcan School. The Bradley Wing houses a world-renowned collection of modern masters.

Milwaukee Art Museum

MAM is actually one piece of the vast **Milwaukee County War Memorial Center,** a complex comprising several parts of the immediate lakefront and assorted buildings throughout the city. The complex was originally a landmark designed by Eero Saarinen, but at MAM, the city really put itself on the map. A massive $50 million architectural enhancement to the museum by international designer Santiago Calatrava is, without exaggeration, breathtaking; don't miss it. The addition—gull-like wings that can be raised or lowered to let sunlight in, soaring above the complex—features a suspended pedestrian bridge linking it to downtown. *Time* magazine named it "building of the year." Hollywood has even used it, in 2011's *Transformers: Dark of the Moon.*

The rest of the War Memorial Center isn't in great shape, with disintegrating concrete and water leaks, to the point that in 2012 the museum announced an urgent $15 million restoration project, which was still ongoing at the time of writing.

## ★ DISCOVERY WORLD AT PIER WISCONSIN

An ultra-high-tech and fetchingly designed museum of every science, **Discovery World** (500 N. Harbor Dr., 414/765-9966, www.discoveryworld.org, 9am-4pm Tues.-Fri., 10am-5pm Sat.-Sun., $18 adults) is overwhelming in the best way. It has 120,000 square feet with 200 exhibits—including two massive aquariums, one freshwater and one saltwater—are cutting-edge. The freshwater education center is the best in the United States, and kids adore it.

Either moored outside or off on some research jaunt is the *Denis Sullivan,* a floating classroom. It's the only Great Lakes schooner re-creation and the flagship of the United Nations Environment Program. From May to September you can occasionally take a day sail ($40).

## BREWERIES PAST AND PRESENT

Milwaukee was once home to dozens of breweries churning out the secret ingredient of *gemütlichkeit.* The pungent malt scent can still pervade the city, and beer remains a cultural linchpin.

Pabst, the oldest and once the sixth-largest U.S. brewer, lives on in name (it's now popular in China), but it's no longer made in the United States. Schlitz—the "Beer That Made Milwaukee Famous"—has made a reappearance, but it's not brewed in Milwaukee. Miller is the lone megabrewer still operating here, although Milwaukeeans were upset in 2008 when, after a merger with Coors, corporate headquarters was relocated to—oh, the betrayal—Chicago.

There are microbreweries and brewpubs throughout the city. **Lakefront Brewery** (1872 N. Commerce St., 414/372-8800, www.lakefrontbrewery.com) has tours (from noon daily, more frequently Sat.-Sun., $8-10) taking in Larry, Moe, and Curly on the tanks, a cheeky start to a great tour. Lakefront brews include specialty beers such as pumpkin- and Door County cherry-flavored varieties; more impressive: It was the first brewery in the country to be certified organic, and the first to produce gluten-free beer; for this, the government had to change its definition of *beer.* It is considered the best brewery tour by local media; the brewery also has a boat dock and lies on the Riverwalk.

The brews at **Milwaukee Ale House** (233 N. Water St., 414/226-2336, 11am-10pm Mon.-Thurs., 11am-1am Fri.-Sat., 11am-9pm Sun., $6-15) are among the best—even better sipped at its great riverside location with a double-decker beer garden and great live music. This building was once a saddlery and, later, the place where the hula hoop was invented.

Farther north, find Milwaukee's original brewpub at **Water Street Brewery** (1101 N. Water St., 414/272-1195, food 11am-9pm Mon.-Sat., $5-15) with an amazing beer memorabilia collection—some 60,000 items.

Perhaps coolest of all: The former offices and interiors of the original Pabst Brewery

Pabst Mansion

space, carved panels moved from Bavarian castles, priceless ironwork by Milwaukeean Cyril Colnik, and some fine woodwork. An adjacent pavilion, now the gift shop, was designed to resemble Rome's St. Peter's Basilica.

## ★ MILWAUKEE PUBLIC MUSEUM

Among the most respected nationally and number-one nationwide in exhibits is the **Milwaukee Public Museum** (800 W. Wells St., 414/278-2702, www.mpm.edu, 9am-5pm Fri.-Wed., 9am-8pm Thurs., $17 adults). It initiated the concept of walk-through exhibits in 1882 and total habitat dioramas in 1890, with a muskrat mock-up. Today, its "Old Milwaukee" street life installation is quite possibly Milwaukee's most visited attraction. Locals blanched in 2015 when it was closed for a refreshing to add interactive spots and even a streetcar, but it's amazing. The museum's multilevel walk-through "Rain Forest of Costa Rica"—featuring its own 20-foot cascade—wins kudos and awards on an annual basis. Among the catacombs of displays on archaeology, anthropology, geology, botany, and ethnography are its jewels of paleontology: the world's largest dinosaur skull and a 15-million-year-old shovel-tusk elephant skeleton obtained from the Beijing Natural History Museum.

The museum constantly reworks itself to allow some of the six million-plus pieces in storage see the light of day. The "Live Butterfly Garden" has become the most popular exhibit. The $17 million Dome Theater and Planetarium, Wisconsin's first IMAX theater, is a big deal, as it is the only place on earth to have such advanced computer projection systems.

Wear walking shoes, as the three floors—you'll want to see them all—will wear you down.

## MARQUETTE UNIVERSITY

Although the university's namesake, 17th-century missionary Jacques Marquette, was not particularly enamored of the Great Lakes coastline, **Marquette University** (Wisconsin Ave., 414/278-3178, www.marquette.edu) was founded in 1881 as a Jesuit

have been rejuvenated into the **Best Place at the Historic Pabst Brewery** (901 W. Juneau Ave., 414/630-1609, http://bestplacemilwaukee.com), which has tours ($8) and a cool tavern (Wed.-Mon.) with all classic Milwaukee beers on tap. Even better: In 2015, Pabst announced it will recreate its famous beer varieties using recipes in archives at the University of Wisconsin-Milwaukee.

## PABST MANSION

The first stop for any historic architecture buff is the grandest of the grand—the **Pabst Mansion** (2000 W. Wisconsin Ave., 414/931-0808, www.pabstmansion.com, 10am-4pm Mon.-Sat., noon-4pm Sun. Mar.-Jan., $12 adults). Built 1890-1893 of the legendary local cream-colored bricks, it was the decadent digs of Captain Frederick Pabst, who worked as a steamship pilot while waiting to inherit the Pabst fortune. The Flemish Renaissance mansion is staggering even by the baroque standards of the time: 37 rooms, 12 baths, 14 fireplaces, 20,000-plus square feet of floor

# The Beer City

King Gambrinus, the mythical Flemish king and purported inventor and patron of beer, would no doubt be pleased to call this city home—his statue lives in the back courtyard of the Best Place at the Historic Pabst Brewery.

## THE BEGINNING

The first brewery in Milwaukee wasn't started by a German; Welshmen founded a lakefront brewery in 1840. Germans got into the act not much later with Herman Reuthlisberger's brewery in Milwaukee, and in 1844 Jacob Best started the neighborhood Empire Brewery, which later became the first of the megabreweries, Pabst. The same year saw Milwaukee's first beer garden— that all-inclusive picnic and party zone with lovely flower gardens and promenades, so essential to German culture—two years before the city's charter was even approved. The next half decade saw the establishment of the progenitors of Milwaukee's hops heritage—in chronological order, Blatz, Schlitz, and the modern leviathan Miller.

## THE RISE

Without question, the primary reason beer took off was massive immigration. Most influential were the waves of German immigrants, who earned Milwaukee the nickname "German Athens" by the 1880s. When the government levied a whiskey tax of $1 per barrel, tavern patrons immediately began asking for beer instead.

Another factor in Milwaukee's brewery success was its location; Wisconsin was a world agricultural player in herbs, hops among them. In addition, the availability of natural ice gave it an edge over other U.S. brewers. The Great Chicago Fire of 1871 also helped by devastating almost all of the competing breweries. Milwaukee became famous for beer production and consumption, and by the time of the Civil War, there was one bar for every 90 residents—and during the war, breweries again doubled their production. At one time there were nearly 600 breweries in the state. This led temperance crusader Carrie Nation to declare in 1902, "If there is any place that is hell on earth, it is Milwaukee. You say that beer made Milwaukee famous, but I say that it made it infamous."

The brewers' vast wealth allowed them to affect every major aspect of Milwaukee society and culture; ubiquitous still are the brewing family names affixed to philanthropic organizations, cultural institutions, and many buildings. So popular was Pabst beer that it could afford to place real blue ribbons on bottles by hand; so pervasive were the beers that Admiral Robert Peary found an empty Pabst bottle as he was nearing the north pole.

## THE DECLINE

After the industry's zenith, when there were perhaps 60 breweries, the number dwindled to only a dozen or so after the enactment of Prohibition, and today there is just one, Miller. In the 1950s, Milwaukee could still claim to produce nearly 30 percent of the nation's beer; as of now, the number is less than 5 percent.

Microbreweries and brewpubs have inevitably cut into the megabrewery markets. And yet microbrews are a throwback of sorts. The first beer brewed in Milwaukee came from neighborhood brewers, most of which put out only a barrel a week, just enough for the local boys. As the major breweries gained wealth, they gobbled up large chunks of downtown land to create open-atrium beer gardens and smoky beer halls, in effect shutting out the smaller operators.

Most telling of all may be the deconstruction of yet another Wisconsin stereotype: Cheeseheads, despite being born clutching personalized steins, do not drink more beer per capita than other states—the top honor goes to Nevada. It isn't for lack of trying; *Forbes* once called Milwaukee "America's drunkest city."

Another architectural treasure at Marquette is the Brobdingnagian Gothic 1894 **Gesu Church.** The vertiginous heights of the spires are marvelous, and the gorgeous rose stained glass, divided into 14 petals, is equally memorable. The entire church underwent its first restoration in summer 2012; impressive before, it's stunning now.

A fascinating holding of the **Marquette University Memorial Library** (1415 W. Wisconsin Ave., 414/288-7555) is the world-renowned J. R. R. Tolkien collection—more than 10,000 pages for *The Lord of the Rings* alone, but also thousands of other documents. Library hours vary by semester and are reduced in summer.

## North of Downtown

### CHARLES ALLIS ART MUSEUM

Overlooking Lake Michigan, the **Charles Allis Art Museum** (1801 N. Prospect Ave., 414/278-8295, www.cavtmuseums.org, 1pm-5pm Wed.-Sun., $7 adults, $12 including Villa Terrace) is in a Tudor mansion built by the first president of the manufacturing company Allis-Chalmers, a major local employer. It has a superb collection of world art, fine furniture, and nearly 1,000 objets d'art dating back as far as 500 BC and covering the entire world. The museum's plush interiors feature Tiffany windows, silk wall coverings, and loads of marble.

### VILLA TERRACE

Within walking distance of the Charles Allis Art Museum, the lavish 1923 **Villa Terrace** (2220 N. Terrace Ave., 414/271-3656, www.cavtmuseums.org, 1pm-5pm Wed.-Sun., $7 adults, $12 including Charles Allis Art Museum), in Mediterranean Italian Renaissance style, houses an eclectic collection of decorative arts, including art and handcrafted furniture from the 16th to 20th centuries. A four-year Garden Renaissance program restored a variety of botanical collections, organically melding interiors and exteriors. It is now one of the country's only

Charles Allis Art Museum

institution. The university purportedly even has bone fragments from the black-robed priest.

The primary attraction is the **St. Joan of Arc Chapel** (generally 10am-4pm Mon.-Sat., noon-4pm Sun., closed weekends when school is out), an inspiring 500-year-old relic from the Rhone River Valley of France. Transported stone by stone along with another medieval château, it was reassembled on Long Island, New York, in 1927 by a railroad magnate; the French government put an end to relocation of culturally important buildings after that. It was lovingly redone by some of the nation's premier historic architects and renovators, and it remains the only medieval structure in the western hemisphere where mass is said regularly. Stories regarding Saint Joan and the chapel may or may not be apocryphal; she is said to have kissed one of the stones while worshiping in the chapel during the Hundred Years War between France and England, and that stone has been colder than the surrounding ones ever since.

existing examples of Italian Renaissance garden art and design.

## SCHLITZ AUDUBON NATURE CENTER

On the far north side of the city, in Bayside, **Schlitz Audubon Nature Center** (1111 E. Brown Deer Rd., 414/352-2880, www.sanc. org, 9am-5pm Mon.-Thurs., 9am-8pm Fri.-Sun., $8) abuts the edge of Lake Michigan on the grounds of an erstwhile Schlitz brewery horse pasture. A six-mile network of trails winds along the beach and through diverse prairie, woodland, and wetland. An observation tower with a parapet offers lake views. The interpretive center spent $5.5 million to achieve its many environmentally friendly features, such as recirculated rainwater, sustainable wood sourced from Aldo Leopold's homestead, solar power panels, and low-flow toilets.

## South of Downtown
### CHARLES B. WHITNALL PARK

One of the larger municipal parks in the United States, at 600-plus acres, **Charles B. Whitnall Park** (5879 W. 92nd St., Hales Corners, 414/425-7303, free) is the cornerstone of Milwaukee County's enormous park system and the cornerstone of the state's proposed Oak Leaf Birding Trail, which will eventually have 35 separate parks and forests to view crucial avian habitat. Lush landscaped gardens are found inside the park at **Boerner Botanical Gardens** (414/425-1130, gardens 8am-sunset daily mid-Apr.-Oct., garden house 8am-7pm daily summer, shorter hours in other seasons, $5.50). Forty acres of roses, perennials, and wildflowers thrive here; the 1,000-acre arboretum surrounding the gardens includes the largest flowering crab apple orchard in the United States.

Also in Whitnall Park is the **Todd Wehr Nature Center** (9701 W. College Ave., 414/425-8550, 8am-4:30pm daily, parking $3), designed as a living laboratory of eco-awareness, with nature trails and an ongoing mixed-grass prairie restoration.

## ST. JOSAPHAT'S BASILICA

Just south of downtown, the first Polish basilica in North America is **St. Josaphat's Basilica** (Lincoln Ave. at S. 6th St., 414/645-5623, tours by appointment, public welcome at mass). Parishioners built the structure out of salvaged rubble from the Chicago Federal Building. The capacious dome is modeled after St. Peter's Basilica in Rome; inside is a rather astonishing mélange of Polish iconography and hagiography, relics, stained glass, and wood carvings.

## BEER CORNER

The only-in-Milwaukee award goes to **Forest Home Cemetery** (2405 W. Forest Home Ave.) and its designated sector of eye-catching monuments to the early Milwaukee brewing giants: Blatz, Pabst, Best, and Schlitz rest in peace beneath the handcrafted stones. Kooky or spooky, heritage is heritage. You can usually enter the cemetery until around 4pm Monday-Friday and on Saturday morning.

## West of Downtown
### ★ MILLER BREWING

The king of the hill in Milwaukee now is megabrewer **Miller Brewing** (4251 W. State St., 414/931-2337, www.millercoors. com, tours generally 10:30am-3:30pm Mon.-Sat., occasionally Sun., free). This slick, modern operation is the very antithesis of a neighborhood brewer. Frederic Miller apprenticed and served as a brewmaster at Hohenzollern Castle in Sigmaringen, Germany, before striking out for the United States in 1855 at age 28 and starting a small brewery. His original Plank Road Brewery, bought from the son of the Pabst progenitor and not to be confused with Miller's shrewdly named contemporary brewing operation, put out 300 barrels per year—no mean feat, but nothing stellar. Today, Miller—now merged as MillerCoors—is the second-largest brewery in the nation, with a total production of 45 million barrels a year; the warehouse is the size of five football fields. Hour-long tours take in the ultra-high-tech packaging center, the hangar-size shipping center, and, finally, the brew house. Tours end at the **Caves Museum,** a restored part of Miller's original brewery in which kegs of beer were cooled. The ineluctable Bavarian hut dispenses free samples (to those age 21 and over, of course) and features an antique stein collection and ornate woodwork.

## ★ HARLEY-DAVIDSON MUSEUM

Tours of the Harley-Davidson plant in the western suburb of Wauwatosa ended in 2009, but to replace them, the company has created paradise for you: You can't say you've seen Milwaukee without a visit to hog heaven—the **Harley-Davidson Museum** (Canal St. and S. 6th St., 414/343-4235, www.h-dmuseum.com, 10am-6pm Fri.-Wed., 10am-8pm Thurs., $20 adults), a massive, 100,000-square-foot facility. This $30 million project, the mecca of Made in America, features an interactive museum and exhibits on the history, culture, and lifestyle engendered by the company and its slavishly devoted riders. Rooms are full of vintage vehicles; not surprisingly, Elvis's bike probably gets the most attention, although it's rivaled by a permanent exhibit of a Harley-Davidson that floated to the United States

from Japan in a shipping container after the 2011 Tohoku earthquake and tsunami. The owner asked that it be placed here untouched. The museum is open 365 days a year, in true blue-collar style.

## ANNUNCIATION GREEK ORTHODOX CHURCH

"My little jewel—a miniature Santa Sophia" is how Frank Lloyd Wright described the final major work of his life, the **Annunciation Greek Orthodox Church** (9400 W. Congress St., Wauwatosa, 414/461-9400). Its imposing rondure is a landmark of Milwaukee architecture, a dramatic inverted bowl into which Wright incorporated symbolic golds and blues and the Greek cross. The blue-tiled dome rises 45 feet above the floor and spans 104 feet. During the most recent update, the congregation was involved in a heated dispute as to whether the original murals should be changed to more religious themes. Tours are not given.

## MILWAUKEE COUNTY ZOO

Believe it or not, the innovative designs of the **Milwaukee County Zoo** (10001 W. Bluemound Rd., 414/256-5411, www.milwaukeezoo.org, 9am-5pm Mon.-Sat.,

Miller Brewing

# Hog Heaven

Beer may have made Milwaukee famous, but to some, Milwaukee-born **Harley-Davidson**—the bikes, the slavishly devoted riders, and the company—truly represents the ethos of Milwaukee: blue-collar tough, proud, and loyal.

## THE COMPANY

William S. Harley and Arthur Davidson, boyhood friends in Milwaukee, were fascinated by the bicycle and German motorcycle craze around the turn of the 20th century. In 1903 they rigged a single-cylinder engine (the carburetor was a tin can) and leather-strap drive chain onto a thin bicycle frame—with no brakes. Thus began the first puttering of the company known for roaring.

The company incorporated in 1907 and within a decade became the largest motorcycle maker in the world. The Harleys' reputation for sound engineering and thus endurance—the first motorcycle lasted 100,000 miles—made them popular with the U.S. Postal Service and especially police departments. In the first Federation of American Motorcyclists endurance test, a hog scored above a perfect 1,000 points, leading to Harley dominance in motorcycle racing for decades. Constant innovations, such as the first clutch, also fueled success.

During World War I, Harley gained the U.S. government's devotion, and Harleys with sidecars equipped with machine guns pursued Pancho Villa into Mexico in 1917. Europeans also found a great enthusiasm for the machines after World War I; within five years, 20 percent of the company's production was exported.

Further, no motorcycle maker could claim the innovation or the zeal with which Harley-Davidson catered to its riders. Original dealers were instructed to employ the consumers in as much of the process as possible. Harley-Davidson open houses were legendary. *The Enthusiast*, the company's newsletter, is the longest-running continuously published motorcycle publication anywhere.

## THE BIKES

The company hit eternal fame with the goofy-looking, radically designed Knucklehead in 1936, when the public, initially dismayed by the bulging overhead valves (hence the name), soon realized its synthesis of art and engineering. It has been called the most perfect motorcycle ever made. The Sportster, introduced in 1957, also gets the nod from aficionados—it's called the Superbike. In the 1970s, the Super Glide—the *Easy Rider* low-rider's progenitor—singlehand-

9am-6pm Sun. and holidays May-Sept., 9am-4:30pm daily Oct.-Apr., $14.25 adults May-Sept., less Oct.-Apr., parking $12) have been mimicked nationally and internationally for the past five decades. It set the standard for what many today take for granted in zoological park settings. The animals' five global environments, grouped in specific continental areas with a system of moats, create juxtaposition of predator and prey. Almost 5,000 specimens live here, many of them also on the endangered species list. Perennially popular are the polar bears and aquatic animals viewable through subsurface windows. In a century-old barn is a dairy complex—an educational look at milk production. Zoomobiles ($3) roll about the expansive grounds, and mini trains ($2.50) also chug around.

The rides and animal shows have varied schedules. All rides and activities inside cost extra.

## THE DOMES

Although it's officially the **Mitchell Park Horticultural Conservatory** (524 S. Layton Blvd., 414/649-9800, www.countyparks.com, hours vary seasonally, generally 9am-5pm daily, $7 adults), everyone calls this complex "the Domes" for the conical

edly rescued the company. The modern Softail and Tour Glides are considered by Harley-Davidson to be the best ever engineered.

## GOOD TIMES, BAD TIMES

By the 1940s, two-thirds of all U.S. bikes were Harley-Davidsons. By the 1950s, swelled by demand, Harley managed to push out its main competitor, Indian Motorcycle. But somewhere along the line, something happened. Harleys had been derisively dubbed "Hardly Ablesons" because of their tendency to break down—or so said owners of archrival Indian Motorcycles.

When American Machine and Foundry (AMF) took control of the company in 1969, sales were plummeting, morale of the company's workforce hit an all-time low, and things got so bad that manufacturing was sent to separate factories around the country.

In 1981 a group of about 30 Harley employees bought the company back and virtually reinvented it. With top-of-the-line products, brilliant marketing, and a furious effort at regaining the trust of the consumer, Harley-Davidson moved steadily back into the market. By the late 1980s, the company was again profitable compared to Japanese bikes. The effects are clear: There's a veritable renaissance of the Harley craze, an extensive waiting list for bikes (all 75,000 produced in a year are spoken for up to a year in advance), and Harley groups exist in places as far away as Hong Kong. More than half of Harley owners are senior citizens, married, college educated, and have high incomes.

The contemporary Harley-Davidson headquarters is very near the site of that shed-workshop where the first bike was cobbled together. The company remains firmly committed to its downtown Milwaukee location. It has programs encouraging employees to live in the neighborhood, and it is one of the most in-touch corporations in town. Its 2008 grand opening of a new Harley-Davidson museum forever cements it as a Milwaukee brand.

seven-story, 148-foot-tall glass-encased buildings. The capacious interiors, totaling about 15,000 square feet, are split into arid desert, traditional floral, and tropical rainforest biospheres. One is relandscaped up to half a dozen times annually. Outside, the conservatory, ringed with sunken gardens, is the only structure of its type in the world.

Now the bad news: A recent study found that the structure was desperately in need of extensive repairs, so check to make sure the conservatory is open before visiting.

# ENTERTAINMENT AND EVENTS
## Nightlife

Milwaukee is no Austin, but there's a lot more music and nightlife than people realize. Then again, it's also the city where sheepshead (a local card game) tournaments might get equal billing with live music in the same bar. Milwaukee has more than 5,000 bars, which is per capita among the top 10 cities nationwide, so there's something out there for everyone. *Forbes* called it "America's drunkest city." Milwaukee is also a city of festivals. Throw a dart at a calendar, and you'll hit an enormous festival of some sort.

Only in Milwaukee: The folks at **Kochanski's Concertina Beer Hall** (1920 S. 37th St., 414/837-6552, http://beer-hall.com, 6am-2pm Wed.-Sat., 1pm-7pm Sun.) have big shoes to fill, as this was the home of legendary Milwaukee polka meister Art Altenberg, who ran his club for decades to preserve live polka music. Many nights this tradition of live music still lives on, although it might be roots rock or alt country; every Wednesday night has traditional polka music. It's authentic, and it's a hoot.

For nightlife districts, aptly named **Water Street,** stretching along the Milwaukee River, draws Marquette University students and lots of downtown business types; the rowdy nightlife ranges from a brewpub to sports bars and dance clubs. More shops, boutiques, and restaurants are rapidly moving into the formerly dive-bar **Walker's Point** neighborhood. **North Jefferson Street** and environs have the feel of a subdued scene, with more upscale bars and restaurants such as **Elsa's on Park** (833 N. Jefferson St., 414/765-0615, 11am-1am Mon.-Fri., 5pm-1am Sat. and Sun.) and **Louise's** (801 N. Jefferson St., 414/273-4224, 11am-11pm Mon.-Thurs., 11am-midnight Fri. and Sat.) to complement the upscale boutiques and galleries; it's the yin to Water Street's noisy yang.

Besides these areas, Milwaukee is one big nightspot. Along hopping North Farwell Avenue, **Von Trier** (2235 N. Farwell Ave., 414/272-1775, 4pm-2am daily) could pass for a German beer hall with its heavy wooden bench seating and a summertime beer garden. In true Bavarian and Wisconsin style, there's a buck's head affixed to the wall. Even after a couple of "refreshings," including now offering German food, Von Trier has lost none of its essence.

If you're looking for a more upscale place, try the **Hi-Hat Lounge** (E. Brady St. and Arlington St., 414/220-8090, 4pm-2am Mon.-Fri., 10am-2am Sat. and Sun.). With cool jazz wafting in the background, it's got a classy but not showy feel and an older sophisticated crowd.

Too many neighborhood taverns to count exist in Milwaukee, and everybody's got a different recommendation. The since-1908 **Wolski's** (1836 N. Pulaski St., Walker's Point, 414/276-8130, 2pm-2am Mon.-Fri., noon-2am Sat. and Sun.) is a corner tavern that defines a Milwaukee tippler's joint. You're an unofficial Beer City denizen if you drive home with an "I closed Wolski's" bumper sticker on your car.

The longtime standard for the LGBT community is **La Cage** (801 S. 2nd St., Walker's Point, 414/672-7988, 6pm-2am daily).

## The Arts

In Rand McNally's *Places Rated,* Milwaukee rates in the top 5 percent of big cities for cultural attractions and the arts. Since the 1990s, more than $100 million has been poured into downtown arts districts. Per capita, Milwaukeeans donate more to the arts than any U.S. city except Los Angeles.

### CULTURAL CENTERS

The **Pabst Theater** (144 E. Wells St., 414/286-3663, www.pabsttheater.org), an 1895 Victorian piece of opulence that still seems as ornate as ever, is a majestic draw in its own right, but it also continues to attract national acts of all kinds. Free tours (noon on Sat.) are given if show schedules don't conflict.

The **Marcus Center for Performing Arts** (MCPA, 929 N. Water St., 414/273-7121, www.marcuscenter.org) has a regular season of theater, symphony, ballet, opera, children's theater, and touring specials. It is the home of the Milwaukee Symphony Orchestra, the Milwaukee Ballet Company, the Florentine Opera Company, and others.

A detailed, painstaking postmillennial restoration of the **Milwaukee Theatre** (500 W. Kilbourn Ave., 414/908-6000, www.milwaukeetheatre.com), a historic 1909 gem, has created a state-of-the-art facility for concerts and theatrical productions.

### MUSIC

The **Milwaukee Symphony Orchestra** (700 N. Water St., 414/291-6010, www.mso.

org) is one of the nation's top orchestras. The *New Yorker* magazine, with the typical coastal undercurrent of surprise, described it as "virtuoso."

## Events

Another term of endearment for Milwaukee is "City of Festivals." Almost every week of the year brings another celebratory blowout feting some cultural, ethnic, or seasonal aspect of the city—and some are for no reason at all.

The largest party of the year is early August's **Wisconsin State Fair** (414/266-7000, www.wistatefair.com), at the fairgrounds (640 S. 84th St.) west along I-94. This fair of all fairs features carnivals, 500 exhibits, livestock shows, entertainment on 20 stages, and the world's greatest cream puffs.

### SUMMERFEST

**Summerfest** (www.summerfest.com) is the granddaddy of all Midwestern festivals and the largest music festival in the world, according to *Guinness World Records*. For 11 days in late June, top national musical acts as well as unknown college-radio mainstays perform on innumerable stages along the lakefront, drawing millions of music lovers and partiers. Agoraphobics need not consider

it. Shop around for discount coupons at grocery stores and assorted businesses, or consider a multiday pass, available at businesses all around town.

## SHOPPING

There's more to shopping in Milwaukee than the requisite cheddar cheese-wedge foam hat and cheese-and-bratwurst gift packs (although these should, of course, be on your list).

### Downtown

Downtown at its heart doesn't offer all that much in the way of shopping, other than the **Public Market** (414/336-1111, www.milwaukeepublicmarket.org, 10am-8pm Mon.-Fri., 8am-7pm Sat., 10am-6pm Sun.) on the Riverwalk in the Third Ward.

To the immediate north, North Old World 3rd Street has many good restaurants but a few long-standing shops, the highlight of which is **Usinger's** (1030 N. Old World 3rd St., 414/276-9100, 8:30am-5pm Mon.-Sat.). Sausage as a souvenir—the quintessential Milwaukee gift. Other highlights include the **Wisconsin Cheese Mart** (215 W. Highland Ave., 414/272-3544, 9am-6pm Mon.-Thurs., 9am-8pm Fri.-Sat., 11am-6pm Sun.). Farther

Pabst Theater

north, Milwaukee's Brady Street bills itself as Milwaukee's Greenwich Village and has chic boutiques.

## SPORTS AND RECREATION

Milwaukee has been rated in the top 10 percent of similar-size U.S. cities for recreational opportunities in and around the city. Don't forget that the Beer City is in the big leagues: It supports three major-league teams and a minor-league hockey team.

### Parks

Looking for something more aerobic? Consider the more than 150 parks and parkways and 15,000 acres of green spaces. Milwaukee has more park area per person than any metropolitan city in the United States and won the Gold Medal for Excellence from the National Recreation and Park Association. The place to get started is the **Milwaukee County Parks System** (414/257-6100, www.countyparks.com).

### Hiking and Biking

These are just a few of the options that the county has to offer.

A beautiful highlight is the **Oak Leaf Trail,** comprising 100 miles of multiple loops wending through the parkways and major parks of the county. The main section, around the lakefront, is an easy loop for most people. The trail begins along Lincoln Memorial Drive between Ogden Avenue and Locust Street. Signs from here point the way, but note that not all of the myriad loops are well marked or even marked. As the Oak Leaf trailhead is along the lakefront, a good option is to explore the lakeshore scenery after a day's exercise. In this area is the city's most popular beach, **Bradford Beach** (2400 N. Lincoln Memorial Dr.).

Bike and in-line skate rentals, personal watercraft, and kayaks are usually available along the lakefront at **Milwaukee Bike and Skate Rental** (1750 N. Lincoln Memorial Dr., 414/273-1343, www. milwbikeskaterental.com) in Veterans Park. Just north of McKinley Marina, **Welker Water Sport Rentals** (414/630-5387) rents personal watercraft and kayaks.

### Charter Fishing

Milwaukee leads the state in charter operations and salmonoids taken. On sunny summer days the marina and harbor areas of Milwaukee appear to be discharging a whitewashed flotilla. The **Milwaukee Convention and Visitors Bureau** (414/273-7222, www.visitmilwaukee.org) can provide more detailed information on specific charter operations.

### Bowling

An apt local joke: Wisconsin is the only state where you can factor your bowling average into your SAT score. A couple of neighborhood joints have old-style duckpin bowling. The **Holler House** (2042 W. Lincoln Ave., 414/647-9284) has the two oldest sanctioned bowling lanes (lanes 1 and 2) in the United States. A tradition of sorts here is to "donate" your bra to the rafters on your first visit! In 2012 a local ordinance was passed outlawing it since it was a fire hazard; the resulting "Are you kidding me?" brouhaha from locals quickly saw that law overturned. A true Milwaukee treasure is long-standing **Koz's Mini Bowl** (2078 S. 7th St., 414/383-0560), with four 16-foot lanes and orange-size balls; the pin setters still make $0.50 per game plus tips. An aside: Koz's was actually a World War II-era house of ill repute; the lanes were simply a cover to keep locals from asking questions.

### Golf

Milwaukee has nearly 20 golf courses within a short drive. The most prominent in the near vicinity is **Brown Deer Park** (7835 N. Green Bay Rd., 414/352-8080), an amazing public course. **Whitnall Park** (6751 S. 92nd St., 414/425-7931) and **Oakwood Park** (3600 W. Oakwood Rd., 414/281-6700) also have excellent courses.

# The Brew Crew

Not a baseball fan, or even a sports fan? It matters not; a Milwaukee Brewers game is a cultural requirement. Consider the following:

## TAILGATING

Nobody parties before a ball game like Wisconsinites. Milwaukeeans and Green Bay Packers fans have perfected the pregame tailgate party. The requisite pregame attraction is the meal of beer, grilled brats, and potato salad, eaten while playing catch in the parking lot. *Guinness World Records* recognized the Brewers' former home, Milwaukee County Stadium, as the site of the world's largest tailgate party, and the new Miller Park has nearly double the party area. The food inside the stadium is also superb: NBC Sports commentator emeritus Bob Costas has deemed the stadium's bratwurst tops in the major leagues.

## BRATWURST

But this is not the best reason to go to a game. The Brewers have the coolest stunt in pro sports: the **Sausage Race.** Grounds-crew members stick themselves into big clunky sausage outfits—a hot dog, a Polish sausage, an Italian sausage, a bratwurst, and a Mexican *chorizo*—and lumber around the field to a thrilling finish at home plate. It's so popular that players on opposing teams clamor for the opportunity to be a Milwaukee sausage for the day.

## Camping

The best public camping is 30 minutes west of Milwaukee via I-94 and south on Highway 67 in **Kettle Moraine State Forest** (262/646-3025, http://wisconsinstateparks. reserveamerica.com, year-round, from $23); it's very popular and is often fully booked May-October, so reserve early.

The nearest private campground is southwest of Milwaukee along I-43 in Mukwonago at **Country View Campground** (S110 W26400 Craig Ave., 414/662-3654, mid-Apr.-mid-Oct., $25). Country View offers a pool, a playground, hot showers, and supplies. RVs can camp at the **Wisconsin State Fairgrounds** (414/266-7035, wistatefair.com, $35), west along I-94 in West Allis, but it's crowded and noisy with freeway traffic.

## Spectator Sports

Most markets of comparable size support just one major-league franchise; Milwaukee has three. Miller Park, home of Major League Baseball's **Milwaukee Brewers** (tickets www.brewers.com) is absolutely magnificent, a synthesis of retro and techno, and worth a visit.

Except for an occasional woeful hiccup season, the **Milwaukee Bucks** (tickets 414/276-4545, www.bucks.com) are generally a competitive team in the National Basketball Association. They are slated to move into a gorgeous new arena in 2018, part of a massive downtown entertainment district.

## FOOD

You may be surprised to find that Milwaukee is a pan-ethnic food heaven spanning the gamut from fish fries in cozy 120-year-old neighborhood taprooms to four-star prix-fixe repasts in state-of-the-art gourmet restaurants.

## Downtown
### ASIAN

First off, yes, we get it, we all know Chinese food is better on the coasts. But after two decades of living in and traveling around China, I was impressed by the cuisine at **Jing's** (207 E. Buffalo St., 414/271-7788, 11:30am-9:30pm Tues.-Sat., 4:30pm-9pm Sun., $8-14), a pan-Cathay place specializing in the eastern and southeastern provinces—think sweeter rather than hotter.

The upscale Asian fusion with a heady concentration of Japanese eclectic at ★ **Umami Moto** (www.umamimoto.com) is worth the trip; it's extraordinary. At the time of writing, the restaurant had temporarily closed in order to relocate. Check the website for more information.

## COFFEE AND TEA SHOPS

Those with a java fixation should head immediately for the **Brady Street area** (http://bradystreet.org), where you'll find an inordinate number of coffee shops of every possible variety.

## FINE DINING

Nouvelle cuisine is done magnificently at ★ **Sanford** (1547 N. Jackson St., 414/276-9608, 5:30pm-9pm Mon.-Thurs., 5pm-10pm Fri.-Sat., $30-70), one of the state's most original and respected innovators of cuisine and definitely a place to cook up an excuse for a splurge. It's feted by national foodie media outlets and has garnered a wall full of awards—*Gourmet* magazine has more than once named it one of the country's top 50 restaurants. Sanford himself left the famed eatery in 2012, but fear not, it's still in good hands with longtime employees—in fact, in 2014 its chef was named the James Beard Best Chef of the Midwest.

Don't miss ★ **Bacchus** (925 E. Wells St., 414/765-1166, 5:30pm-9pm Mon.-Thurs., 5:30pm-10pm Fri., 5pm-10pm Sat., $11-22), which rivals Sanford in quality but is the antithesis of stuffy. Small-plate menus in the bar are as memorable as the lovely dining room.

Something you might never expect is to find a remarkable meal in a Milwaukee casino. The elegant and creative fare at Potawatomi Bingo Casino's ★ **Dream Dance Steak** (1721 W. Canal St., 414/847-7883, 5pm-9pm Tues.-Thurs., 5pm-10pm Fri.-Sat., $26-39) is worth the trip even for nongamblers. They switched to a more carnivore-centric menu

in 2009, but it's still one of the best in town. The casino has two other restaurants that make foodies woozy: **RuYi** (414/847-7335, 11am-midnight Sun.-Thurs., 11am-2am Fri.-Sat., $11-18) has pan-Asian cuisine, and **Wild Earth** (414/847-7626, 4pm-10pm Tues.-Thurs., 4pm-10:30pm Fri.-Sat., $13-25) has outstanding food based on Italian but taken in new directions.

## FISH FRIES

In Milwaukee you'll find a fish fry everywhere—even at the fast-food chain drive-through and at Miller Park during Friday-night Brewers games. Dozens of neighborhood taverns and bars still line their plank seating and picnic tables with plastic coverings on Friday night. The tables are arrayed with tartar sauce and sometimes pickles; hopefully you like coleslaw, as that's what you get as a side dish. A good option is at the Lakefront Brewery, where its restaurant, **Beer Hall** (1872 N. Commerce St., 414/273-8300, www.lakefrontbrewery.com, $11-14), has a wonderful Friday fish fry. Expect loads of variety, including smelt, walleye, and perch, all with rollicking polka bands.

## FRENCH

The more casual but still creative **Coquette Cafe** (316 N. Milwaukee St., 414/291-2655, 11am-10pm Mon.-Thurs., 11am-11pm Fri., 5pm-10pm Sat., $7-22), modeled after a French or Belgian brasserie, could best be called global French; the cuisine is hearty yet chic—a wonderful combination.

## GERMAN

★ **Karl Ratzsch's Old World Restaurant** (320 E. Mason St., 414/276-2720, lunch 11:30am-2pm Mon.-Fri., dinner 5pm-10pm Mon.-Sat., $8-36) has long been a Wisconsin favorite for German food. Some were worried when its longtime owner sold the restaurant to staff in 2015, but they needn't have worried. The interiors were refreshed but are still traditional—no lie, they discovered some museum-quality pieces to be displayed—and

# Fish Fries

The most important culinary experience in Wisconsin is a Friday-night fish fry. Its exact origins are unknown, but it's certainly no coincidence that in a state bordering two Great Lakes, home to 15,000 smaller lakes, and having undergone waves of Roman Catholic immigration—Catholics don't eat meat on Fridays during Lent—people would specialize in a Friday-night fish meal.

Fish fries are so popular that even local fast-food restaurants have them; the American Serbian Hall in Milwaukee serves 2,500 people at a drive-through every Friday; Chinese, Mexican, and other ethnic restaurants get in on the act; and even Miller Park has fish fries at Friday Brewers games.

Everybody has an opinion on who has the best fish fry, but realistically, how many ways can you deep-fry a perch, haddock, walleye pike, or cod? (You can sometimes find broiled options.) I've always preferred those done in church basements.

Generally set up as smorgasbords, sometimes including platefuls of chicken too, the gluttonous feasts are served with homemade tartar sauce and a relish tray or salad bar. The truly classic fish-fry joints are packed to the rafters by 5:30pm, and some even have century-old planks and hall-style seating.

The experience of a smelt fry is a special treat; the longtime tavern tradition of milk-dipped, battered, and even pickled smelt has pretty much disappeared.

it has lost none of its appeal. Try the goose or locally made sausages in addition to the spaetzle, strudel, or even some vegetarian offerings.

## ITALIAN
**Mimma's Cafe** (1307 E. Brady St., 414/271-7337, lunch 11:30am-3pm Tues.-Sat., dinner 5pm-11pm Fri.-Sat., 5pm-10pm Sun.-Thurs., $11-19) constantly gets national write-ups for its cuisine—more than 50 varieties of pasta and weekly regional Italian specialties.

## SEAFOOD
**Harbor House** (550 N. Harbor Dr., 414/395-4900, http://harborhousemke.com, lunch and dinner daily, $17-50), just north of Discovery World, is arguably the best. The fare changes with the seasons, but whether it's dreamy lobster potpie or pan-seared Great Lakes walleye, it's outstanding, as are the sublime water and city views.

## STEAK HOUSES
In the Hilton Milwaukee City Center, **Milwaukee Chop House** (633 N. 5th St., 414/226-2467, 5pm-10pm Mon.-Sat., $18-68) has, in addition to luscious steaks, a bone-in rib eye that is likely the best in town.

## VEGETARIAN AND HEALTH FOOD
For take-out health food, there are a number of co-ops and natural-foods stores in the downtown area. A favorite is the vegan-friendly **Riverwest Co-op** (733 E. Clarke St., 414/264-7933, 7am-9pm Mon.-Fri., 8am-9pm Sat.-Sun., $4-8).

**Comet Café** (1947 N. Farwell Ave., 414/273-7677, 10:30am-10pm Mon.-Fri., 9am-10pm Sat.-Sun., $6-12) means your carnivore friend can have the traditional Milwaukee mom's meatloaf with beer gravy while your vegan friend can have the vegan Salisbury steak.

## North of Downtown
### COFFEE SHOPS
The **Fuel Café** (818 E. Center St., 414/374-3835, www.fuelcafe.com) is exceedingly young, hip, and alternative; you'll find cribbage players and riot grrls. The decor is mismatched rummage-sale furniture with an arty flair, and the service bills itself as lousy.

### CUSTARD
Frozen custard is an absolute must for a Milwaukee cultural experience. The dozens of Milwaukee family custard stands were

the inspiration for Big Al's Drive-In on the 1970s TV show *Happy Days*. You really can't go wrong at any of the stands, but most often mentioned is **Kopp's** (5373 N. Port Washington Rd., 414/961-2006), which takes custard so seriously that it has a flavor-of-the-day hotline.

### FINE DINING

Opened by a prominent local restaurateur and housed in an exquisitely restored century-old park pavilion, ★ **Bartolotta's Lake Park Bistro** (3133 E. Newberry Blvd., 414/962-6300, 11am-9pm Mon.-Fri., 5pm-10pm Sat., 10am-2pm and 5pm-9pm Sun., $7-15) has somehow managed to remain rock-solid over the years as a dining highlight. Its French cuisine is superb, and if nothing else, the view from the drive along the lake is worth the time.

### VEGETARIAN AND HEALTH FOOD

A longtime standby for a low-key and decidedly body-friendly meal is **Beans and Barley** (1901 E. North Ave., 414/278-7878, 8am-9pm Mon.-Sat., 8am-8pm Sun., from $4). Very much a hip (though low-priced) eatery, it's in what looks like an old grocery store warehouse encased in glass walls, with an attached grocery and a small bar.

## South of Downtown

### CUSTARD

The south side has perhaps the most legendary custard in the city. An institution since the early 1940s is **Leon's** (3131 S. 27th St., 414/383-1784); it has the best neon. The **Nite Owl Drive In** (830 E. Layton Ave., 414/483-2524, 11am-6pm Tues.-Sat.) has been dishing up ice cream and doling out burgers by the same family for half a century; even Elvis loved to eat here.

### LOCAVORE

A fantastic element of the south's dining scene is ★ **Braise** (1101 S. 2nd St., 414/212-8843,

dinner Tues.-Sat., $17-29), a New American eatery that lives the "eat local" mantra. Small plates and butcher board items are all locally sourced and beg to be shared. It's absolutely top-notch.

### FISH FRIES

For the most unique fry anywhere, head for ★ **American Serbian Hall** (53rd St. and Oklahoma Ave., 414/545-6030, dinner Fri., $10), recognized as the largest in the nation. On Friday night this hall serves more than a ton of Icelandic-style or Serbian baked fish to more than 2,500 people (make that two tons on Good Friday). The operation got so big that a drive-through has been added, which serves an additional 1,200 patrons.

### MEXICAN

You'll find the most substantial Mexican menu, not to mention a most unpretentious atmosphere, at **Tres Hermanos** (1332 W. Lincoln Ave., 414/384-9050, 11am-10pm Sun.-Thurs., 11am-midnight Fri.-Sat., $9-20), specializing in seafood in virtually every form—particularly a soup that'll knock your socks off. There's rootsy, live Tex-Mex and *norteño* music on weekends.

Milwaukee's southeast side is a haven for unpretentious authentic Mexican eateries; some Mexican grocers have lunch counters in the back or sell delectable tamales ready for takeout. **Conejito's** (4th St. and Virginia St., 11am-midnight daily, from $4) is a neighborhood bar-restaurant with authentic atmosphere and real-deal Mexican food.

### POLISH

**Polonez** (4016 S. Packard Ave., St. Francis, 414/482-0080, 11am-3pm and 5pm-9pm Tues.-Sat., 11am-8pm Sun., $5-17) is a longtime Milwaukee favorite. It's a white-tablecloth fine-dining experience but feels casual. The pierogi and cutlets are phenomenal, as is the very good *czarnina* (a raisin soup with duck stock, duck blood, and fruit), one of seven daily soups. The Sunday brunch is unrivaled.

## SERBIAN

Enjoy top-notch Serbian food in a delightful Old World atmosphere at ★ **Three Brothers** (2414 S. St. Clair St., Bay View, 414/481-7530, dinner Tues.-Sun., from $11). The 1897 turreted brick corner house, originally a Schlitz Brewery beer parlor, was turned into a restaurant by the current owner's father, a Serbian wine merchant. Not much has changed—the high paneled ceilings, original wood, dusty bottles on the bar, mirrors, and mismatched tables and chairs remain. All of it is charming. The food is heavy on pork and chicken, with lots of *paprikash* and stuffed cabbage. The signature entrée is *burek,* a filled phyllo-dough concoction the size of a radial tire; you'll wait half an hour for this one. The restaurateurs' daughter recently added vegetarian options. The restaurant is difficult to find—this neighborhood is the real Milwaukee—and you'll likely wind up asking for directions from a horseshoe club outside a local tavern.

## West of Downtown
### ITALIAN

The name Bartolotta seems to be omnipresent in Wauwatosa. ★ **Ristorante Bartolotta** (7616 W. State St., Wauwatosa, 414/771-9710, 5:30pm-9:30pm Mon.-Thurs., 5pm-10pm Fri.-Sat., 5pm-8:30pm Sun., $16-28) is a warm and friendly eatery run by a legendary Milwaukee restaurateur and definitely worth the trip.

### STEAK HOUSES

★ **Five O'Clock Steakhouse** (2416 W. State St., 414/342-3553, 5:30pm-9:30pm Tues.-Sat., $19-32) has been around forever and is so popular for steaks that you'll need a reservation. It has the largest portions in town, all simmered in the eatery's legendary meat juice, along with old-fashioned touches such as relish trays.

## VEGETARIAN

Loads of restaurants in Milwaukee can accommodate vegetarians, but we all know that generally means a couple of pasta entrées or something with the meat left out. A favorite vegetarian restaurant that's also vegan-friendly is far west of downtown in Brookfield, but worth the drive: **Café Manna** (3815 North Brookfield Rd., Brookfield, 11am-9pm Mon.-Sat., $6-15).

# ACCOMMODATIONS

Most travelers will find lodging in downtown Milwaukee much better than they may have expected given the age of many buildings. A good trick is to check the website of the **Milwaukee Convention and Visitors Bureau** (www.visitmilwaukee.org) for frequent package deals at local hotels, even in peak seasons.

Note that the rates provided here are the lowest average rate; weekends in summer can be much more expensive at some hotels, so check around.

## Downtown

Given the severity of Wisconsin's winter, you may want to note whether your accommodations are linked via the downtown **skywalk system.**

### UNDER $50

You won't be able to stay downtown in this price range, but there's a hostel in **Kettle Moraine State Forest** (262/495-8794, $25) not too far away in Eagle, but it's open weekends only.

### $100-150

There are few options in this price range, but check the 1920 art deco **Astor Hotel** (924 E. Juneau St., 414/271-4220 or 800/558-0200, www.theastorhotel.com, from $112), which has character through and through, down to its original fixtures. Travelers report mixed experiences; some insist that it's ancient with a bucket of paint slopped on. This is one of those places where you should look at a number of the guest rooms.

No, the name is not a contradiction at **Hotel of the Arts Downtown—Days Inn** (1840 N. 6th St., 414/265-5629, www. hotelofthearts.com, $119-179); the "arts" are rotating art exhibits and special package rates for many arts group performances in town. The ceilings are high and there are glass walls; parking is included, unlike at many other hotels in town.

**Aloft** (1230 N. Old World 3rd St., 414/226-0122, www.aloftmilwaukeedowntown.com, $129-299) is possibly the trendiest place in town—think minimalist boutique, with high ceilings and windows. It has wonderful design, but keep in mind that it caters to a very young—meaning boisterous—crowd. Many mention the friendly staff.

## OVER $150

The historic apartment-condo building housing ★ **Knickerbocker on the Lake** (1028 E. Juneau Ave., 414/276-8500, www. knickerbockeronthelake.com, $150) overlooks Lake Michigan on a bluff just northeast of the funky Brady Street area—a great location. The lobby sports original marble floors and vaulted ceilings. Individually designed guest rooms are detailed with antiques but also have modern amenities such as air-conditioning and Internet access; some guest rooms have nice deck views, fireplaces, or other extras. There are well-regarded restaurants on-site. Guests have complained that the decor is outdated or are miffed that half the building is owner-occupied, but that's part of the charm.

The **Hilton Garden Inn** (611 N. Broadway, 414/271-6611, http://hiltongardeninnmilwaukeedowntown.com, $219) is in a gorgeous 1886 block that once housed an insurance company. It feels eminently refreshed but still holds its history well.

Deservedly generating lots of buzz is ★ **Hotel Metro** (411 E. Mason St., 414/272-1937, www.hotelmetro.com, $219), a plush but cute boutique hotel in an erstwhile art deco office building. Glass sinks from Wisconsin's Kohler Company are among the noticeable design highlights in the 65 oversize suites, replete with steeping tubs or whirlpool baths; downstairs is a chic sceney bar. The art deco styling includes environmentally friendly practices such as bamboo-wood flooring and wood from sustainable forests. It also has one of the best cafés in Milwaukee. Among the service highlights are bicycles for guest use, but parking is $25 per night.

The ★ **Hilton Milwaukee City Center** (509 W. Wisconsin Ave., 414/271-7250 or 800/445-8667, www.hiltonmilwaukee.com, from $229) is perhaps the best example of restored charm downtown, refurbished endlessly but carefully. This incarnation features limestone ashlar, pink granite, and buff terra-cotta; it's Milwaukee's sole Roaring '20s art deco hotel, right down to the geometric marble motifs in the lobby.

The granddaddy of Milwaukee hotels, once called the "Grand Hotel," in fact, is the ★ **Pfister** (424 E. Wisconsin Ave., 414/273-8222 or 800/558-8222, www.thepfisterhotel.com, $244 s, $264 d), built in 1893. This plush city-state-size behemoth oozes Victorian grandeur. The somewhat overwhelming lobby is done with such ornate intricacy that the hotel organizes regular tours of its displays of 19th-century art. Its state-of-the-art recreation facility outshines most health clubs. The list of attractive features and services could fill a book. Then again, many (including some professional sports figures) believe that the Pfister is haunted.

## North of Downtown

Most lodging choices in this area are found off I-43 along Port Washington Road. The best guest rooms and location are at the **Holiday Inn Milwaukee Riverfront** (4700 N. Port Washington Rd., 414/962-6040 or 844/331-7203, www.hilton.com, $111), with well-appointed one-bedroom guest rooms and a gorgeous, quiet river location. The excellent restaurant has an even better river view.

## South of Downtown

If you've got an early-morning flight or are just looking for something cheap close to downtown, head south. At least two dozen lodgings are scattered around, most along South Howell Avenue, West Layton Avenue, and South 13th Street, and all but one are neon-sign chain options. The best options for morning airport access are the **Hilton Garden Inn** (5890 S. Howell Ave., 414/481-8280, $310) or, much cheaper, a well-run **Hampton Inn** (1200 W. College Ave., 414/762-4240, $109).

Any hotel that aims to mingle business suits with biker leathers is going to raise a few eyebrows, but **The Iron Horse Hotel** (500 W. Florida St., 414/373-4766 or 888/543-4766, www.theironhorsehotel.com, from $300) actually pulls it off. It's a biker boutique hotel, appropriately a stone's throw from the new Harley-Davidson Museum. Its loft-style guest rooms are loaded with chic-but-tough design for guests with biker boots or a business laptop (or both).

## West of Downtown

You can follow the interstate highways in any direction for most chain lodgings. A nonchain option within the western suburbs is the **Ambassador Hotel** (2308 W. Wisconsin Ave., 414/342-8400, www.ambassadormilwaukee.com, $129), a remodeled 1927 art deco structure just outside downtown. It was resurrected with $12 million in upgrades, right down to the terra-cotta exterior, and it's helping the neighborhood rebound. Inside, it's historic meets state-of-the-art; sip a martini in the Envoy Lounge. The only drawback is the somewhat remote location.

## INFORMATION AND SERVICES

**Visit Milwaukee** (400 W. Wisconsin Ave., 414/908-6205 or 800/554-1448, www.visitmilwaukee.org, 8am-5pm Mon.-Fri., 9am-2pm Sat. summer, 8am-5pm Mon.-Fri. fall-spring) is in the Delta Convention Center. Additional offices are at Mitchell International Airport (414/747-4808) and by Discovery World at Pier Wisconsin (414/273-3950).

The **Milwaukee LGBT Center** (315 W. Court St., 414/271-2656, www.mkelgbt.org) is a local organization for lesbian, gay, bi, and transgendered folks.

The local sales tax totals 5.6 percent. You'll pay a 9 percent tax on hotel rooms in addition to the sales tax, 3 percent on car rentals, and an additional 0.5 percent tax on food and beverage purchases.

## Media

The *Milwaukee Journal-Sentinel* (www.jsonline.com) is a morning daily. The Friday paper has a complete listing of weekend cultural events, music, clubs, and movies. Fans of alternative views pick up weekly copies of the free *Shepherd Express* (http://expressmilwaukee.com), which is also a good source of local arts and nightlife info. The local monthly repository of everything Milwaukee is *Milwaukee Magazine* (www.milwaukeemagazine.com). Online, check OnMilwaukee.com (www.onmilwaukee.com), generally the best of the half dozen or so Web guides.

Listen to the eclectic student-run **WMSE** at 91.7 FM—it might surprise you. A local standby has always been **WTMJ** (620 AM) for news and talk.

## Bookstores

In the Milwaukee airport, I kid you not, **Renaissance Book Shop** is great for used-book lovers—and how many airports can claim a used book shop?

## GETTING THERE

### Air

**General Mitchell International Airport** (MKE, 5300 S. Howell Ave., 414/747-5300, www.mitchellairport.com) is southeast of downtown near Cudahy. It's best reached by traveling I-94 south and following the signs. From downtown, head south on North

6th Street; it should get you to Highway 38 (Howell Ave.). Nearly 50 cities are directly connected to Milwaukee on more than 220 daily flights.

Milwaukee County Transit System **buses** run to the airport; almost any bus can start you on your way if you ask the driver for transfer help. A taxi from downtown costs $15-20 and takes 20 minutes. Airport limousines cost $8-10.

## Bus

**Greyhound** (414/272-9949) is based at the Amtrak station (433 W. St. Paul Ave.). Buses leave up to a dozen times daily for Chicago; buses also go to Minneapolis, Madison, and certain points in central Wisconsin, but not to Door County.

Up the street from the Greyhound station is the **Badger Bus** (635 N. James Lovell St., 414/276-7490). Buses depart this location for Madison nine times daily. Badger Bus also serves Mitchell International Airport and Minneapolis and St. Paul when universities are in session.

The discount bus service **MegaBus** (http://us.megabus.com) runs from 4th Street just north of St. Paul Avenue, which is near the bus center in Milwaukee, to Chicago as well as to Minneapolis. Fares are around $18 to Chicago, but there are no ticket offices, terminals, or sometimes even service; it is imperative to check the website for pickup information.

## Train

**Amtrak** (800/872-7245, www.amtrak.com) offers service between Milwaukee and Chicago. At least half a dozen trains operate daily, with fares of $24 one-way off-peak Monday-Friday, $32 Saturday-Sunday. Service to Minneapolis is one train daily. The **Amtrak Station** (433 W. St. Paul Ave., 414/271-9037) also houses Greyhound.

## Boat

High-speed ferry service from Milwaukee to Muskegon, Michigan, saves you a boatload of hassle with **Lake Express** (terminal at 2330 S. Lincoln Memorial Dr., 866/914-1010, www.lake-express.com). Three round-trips make the fast 2.5-hour run across the lake, leaving Milwaukee at 6am, 12:30pm, and 7pm daily. Round-trip rates ($143 adults, $45 under age 17, $173 cars) are not cheap, but the service is outstanding.

# GETTING AROUND

## Taxi

Taxis are all metered and cost around $3 for the first mile and about $1.50 for each additional mile. **American United Taxicab** (414/220-5010) is the state's largest operation.

## Bus

**Milwaukee County Transit System** (414/344-6711, www.ridemcts.com) operates loads of buses; save 25 percent by buying a 10-pack of bus tickets. The system also has free trolley loops around downtown in summer.

## Rental Car

The major national rental-car agencies are represented at **Mitchell International Airport,** and many have half a dozen or more representatives around the city. There is a 3 percent tax on car rentals.

## Organized Tours

Increasingly popular are cabin cruiser tours on the Milwaukee River and occasionally on the Lake Michigan harbor; some providers offer dining cruises.

The venerable *Iroquois* boat tours by Milwaukee Boat Lines (414/294-9450, www.mkeboat.com, 1pm and 3pm Sat.-Sun., 1pm Mon.-Fri. June-Aug., $18 adults) departs from the Clybourn Street Bridge on the west bank of the Milwaukee River and offers scenic narrated tours. Sporadic evening tours are also offered June to September.

**Riverwalk Boat Tours and Rental** (Pere Marquette Park, E. State St. and N. Old World 3rd St., 414/283-9999, www.riverwalkboats.com) offers a number of tours, most of them themed for imbibing. You can also rent your own pontoon boat ($55 per hour).

# North of Milwaukee

## ★ CEDARBURG

What candy-facade original-colony spots such as Williamsburg are to the East Coast, Cedarburg is to Wisconsin. It has been timelessly preserved thanks to local residents who successfully fought off wholesale architectural devastation by an invasion of Milwaukeeans looking for an easy commute. Cedarburg, about 30 minutes north of downtown Milwaukee, was originally populated by German and a few British immigrants who hacked a community out of a forest and built numerous mills along Cedar Creek, which bisects the tiny community, including the only worsted wool mill and factory in what was then considered the West. Those mills, and more than 100 other original Cream City-brick buildings, have been painstakingly restored in the state's most concentrated stretch of antiques dealers, shops, galleries, bed-and-breakfasts, and proper little restaurants. Stop at the visitors center downtown for an excellent booklet on historic-structure walking tours.

The heart and soul of the town is **Cedar Creek Settlement,** an antebellum foundation mill once the village's center of activity but now a blocks-long hodgepodge of shops, restaurants, and galleries. The **Cedar Creek Winery** (262/377-8020, 10am-5pm Mon.-Thurs., 10am-8pm Sat., 10am-6pm Sun.) is also on the premises; tours include the aging cellars. West of the main drag (Washington Rd.), Portland Road features one of the original structures in Cedarburg, the enormous five-story **Cedarburg Mill,** now home to yet another antiques shop. Along Riveredge Drive is the **Brewery Works** (262/377-8230, 1pm-4pm Wed.-Sun.), a restored 1840s brewery housing the Ozaukee County Art Center.

Three miles north of town is the last remaining **covered bridge** in the state, dating from 1876. To get here, head to the junction of Highways 143 and 60 on Washington Avenue. This makes an excellent bike tour. Southeast of Cedarburg via Hamilton Road is the original settlement of **Hamilton,** with another picturesque creek-side mill.

The local **visitors center** (W61 N480 Washington Ave., 262/377-9620 or

Cedarburg's covered bridge

800/237-2874, www.cedarburg.org) has very friendly and knowledgeable staffers who will point you in the right direction.

Gorgeous lodging options exist in Cedarburg; nobody comes here to stay in a motel. **Washington House** (W62 N573 Washington Ave., 800/554-4717, http://washingtonhouseinn.com, from $200) may even be among the finest in the state. It does an amazing job of mixing classic and cutting-edge with outstanding service.

**Galioto's Twelve21** (1221 Wauwatosa Rd., 262/377-8085, lunch 11am-2pm Mon.-Fri., dinner 5pm-9pm Mon.-Thurs., 5pm-10pm Fri.-Sat., 4pm-8pm Sun., $7-26) is a smashing eatery housed in an erstwhile classic Wisconsin country tavern. The superb renovation features original beams and flickering flames in an original fireplace. The well-done dishes focus on creative comfort food; the pork chops are legendary.

## PORT WASHINGTON

Forty minutes north of Milwaukee is Port Washington, a Lake Michigan shore community with links to east-central Wisconsin. Port Washington got into the history books with its quixotic anti-Civil War draft riots, when mobs took over the courthouse and trained a cannon on the lakefront until the Army showed up and quelled the disturbance. Part Great Lakes fishing town and part preserved antebellum anachronism, Port Washington is known for its enormous downtown **marina** and fishing charters.

You can stroll along the breakers and snap shots of the art deco **lighthouse,** now a historical museum. Another renovated lighthouse is home to the **Port Washington Historical Society Museum** (311 Johnson St., 262/284-7240, 1pm-4pm daily summer). The **Eghart House** (1pm-4pm in the summer) on Grand Avenue at the library is done up in turn-of-the-20th-century style. Also along Grand Avenue, what's known as the **Pebble House,** site of a visitors center, was painstakingly built of stones scavenged from the beaches along the lake. Franklin Street, dominated by the thrusting spire of St. Mary's Church and various castellated building tops, is typical of classic Lake Michigan small towns. Upper City Park, on a bluff overlooking the water, affords lovely views of the lake and the horizon.

Port Washington claims to hold the **world's largest fish fry** annually on the third Saturday of July, although other towns in the state make the same claim.

Pebble House

The city has lots of B&Bs, including the huge shingle Victorian **Port Washington Inn** (308 W. Washington St., 877/794-1903, http://port-washington-inn.com, from $159), a gorgeous structure that gets kudos for its environmentally sound practices.

You can't beat **Twisted Willow** (308 N. Franklin St., 262/268-7600, lunch Fri., dinner Tues.-Sat., $11-25), which pulls from its own farm for its luscious American creative-comfort cuisine; try the pork loin.

Farther north on the lakeshore is **Harrington Beach State Park** (262/285-3015), mostly unknown outside the Milwaukee area. It has great lake and limestone-bluff views, an abandoned limestone quarry and a quarry lake, and hiking trails, some of which are a bit treacherous. A new **campground** (reservations at www.reserveamerica.com, from $23) relieves the serious need for public camping along Lake Michigan's southern shoreline.

# Kenosha

Though its history is one of smokestacks and work whistles and its primary employer for decades was an automobile plant, Kenosha definitely belies any blue-collar stereotype. In fact, *Reader's Digest* once declared it the second-most family-friendly city in the United States (Sheboygan, Wisconsin, was first). The city owns 8 out of 10 lakefront plots, meaning there is a lot of lakefront parkland, and you'll find an appealing array of early-20th-century buildings anchored by a downtown revitalized by green space, a promenade, a farmers market, and electric streetcar lines.

## SIGHTS

Streets run east-west and avenues north-south in a grid. The major arteries into town are Highway 50 (75th St.), Highway 158 (52nd St.), and Highway 142S.

## ★ HarborPark

At the turn of the millennium, Kenosha beaverishly set out to redo its downtown lakefront, and it is spectacular—truly one of the freshest-looking Lake Michigan cities. The cornerstone of the redevelopment is the **Kenosha Public Museum** (56th St. at 1st Ave., 414/262-4140, www.kenoshapublicmuseum.org, 10am-5pm Mon.-Sat., noon-5pm Sun. spring-summer, 10am-5pm Tues.-Sat., noon-5pm Sun. fall-winter, free). Its most exciting exhibit is on the Schaeffer mammoth,

the oldest butchered mammoth found in the western hemisphere; the bones date to 12,000 years ago, and it helped prove that humans lived here during that era—not a small detail. More recent archaeological digs in the county, along with sites in Virginia and Pennsylvania, have caused scientists to rethink the traditional Siberian land-bridge theory of how the Paleo-Indians got to North America. It's worth a visit.

Near the Public Museum is the **Civil War Museum** (5400 1st Ave., 262/653-4140, 10am-5pm Mon.-Sat., noon-5pm Sun. spring-summer, 10am-5pm Tues.-Sat., noon-5pm Sun. fall-winter, $9), focusing on the role of Wisconsin and neighboring states during the war. A recent reconstruction was well done.

Across the channel next to gorgeous Southport Lighthouse is the **Kenosha History Center** (220 51st Place, 262/654-5770, www.kenoshahistorycenter.org, 10am-4:30pm Tues.-Fri., 10am-4pm Sat., noon-4pm Sun., free). The main museum focuses on the crucial role that transportation, specifically auto manufacturing, played in the history of the city. Opened in 2010 after years of restoration work, a renovated lighthouse keeper's residence nearby presents the rich maritime history of the city, the southernmost Lake Michigan port in the state. Lighthouse tours (Sat.-Sun. mid-May-Oct., $10) are available.

# Kenosha

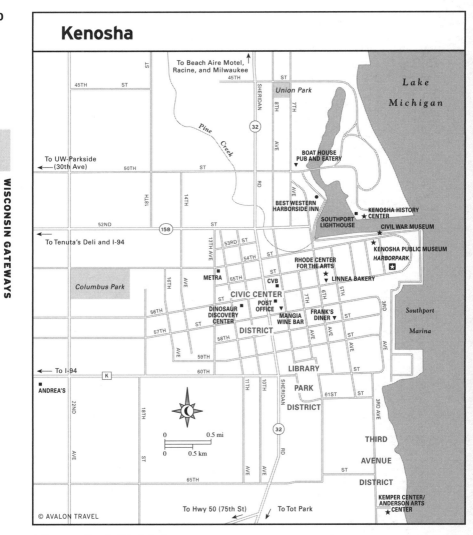

To Beach Aire Motel, Racine, and Milwaukee

45TH ST

45TH ST

SHERIDAN

8TH

7TH

*Lake Michigan*

Union Park

Pine Creek

32

AVE

To UW-Parkside (30th Ave)

50TH ST

RD

BOAT HOUSE PUB AND EATERY

18TH

14TH

AVE

BEST WESTERN HARBORSIDE INN

SOUTHPORT LIGHTHOUSE

★ KENOSHA HISTORY CENTER

52ND ST

158

13TH AVE

53RD ST

54TH ST

CIVIL WAR MUSEUM

KENOSHA PUBLIC MUSEUM

To Tenuta's Deli and I-94

RHODE CENTER FOR THE ARTS

HARBORPARK

Columbus Park

16TH AVE

METRA

55TH ST

CVB

7TH

6TH

5TH

LINNEA BAKERY

CIVIC CENTER

56TH

DINOSAUR DISCOVERY CENTER

POST OFFICE

MANGIA WINE BAR

FRANK'S DINER

3RD

*Southport Marina*

57TH ST

DISTRICT

58TH ST

AVE

AVE

AVE

59TH ST

LIBRARY

To I-94

60TH

K

11TH

10TH

SHERIDAN

PARK

ANDREA'S

22ND

18TH ST

DISTRICT

61ST ST

3RD AVE

0          0.5 mi

0      0.5 km

32

RD

THIRD

AVE

AVENUE

65TH

ST

DISTRICT

KEMPER CENTER/ ANDERSON ARTS ★ CENTER

© AVALON TRAVEL

To Hwy 50 (75th St)

To Tot Park

## Library Park District

The **Library Park District** (bounded by 59th St., 62nd St., 6th Ave., and Sheridan Rd.) was once the site of homes on the Underground Railroad, now marked by a plaque. Visitors can view the birthplace of Orson Welles (6116 7th Ave.).

## 3rd Avenue District

East of the Library Park District and fronting the lake, the **3rd Avenue District** (between

61st St. and 66th St.) is the most popular stroll for historic structures, featuring most of the ornate mansions of the wealthy early-20th-century residents.

**Kemper Center** (6501 3rd Ave., 262/657-6005, Sat.-Sun., free) is a complex of historical structures within one of seven gorgeous county parks. This park, at 18 acres the largest, is the only park in the nation listed in its entirety on the National Register of Historic Places. The antebellum Gothic Revival and

Italianate hall was originally a school for girls. Its grounds include an arboretum with more than 100 species of plants, including more than 100 types of roses and a flower and herb garden designed for those without sight. One mansion is open to the public 1pm-4pm Saturday-Sunday March-October. Also in the park is the impressive French Tudor **Anderson Arts Center** (121 66th St., 1pm-4pm Tues.-Sun. during exhibits, free).

## Civic Center District

Northwest of the Library Park District, the **Civic Center District** (roughly bounded by 55th St., 58th St., 8th Ave., and 11th Ave.) was the first district to undergo massive experimental civic rejuvenation, during the late 19th century. As part of a "City Beautiful" campaign, this district has been credited with effecting political reform. Even the post office is a neoclassical revival gem.

Possibly the most popular museum in town is the kid-friendly **Dinosaur Discovery Center** (5608 10th Ave., 262/653-4460, www.dinosaurdiscoverymuseum.org, noon-5pm Tues.-Sun., free). The usual hands-on stuff makes it fun, and there is an on-site working paleontology lab.

## ENTERTAINMENT AND EVENTS

Lots of arts performances take place at the grand **Rhode Center for the Arts** (514 56th St., 262/657-7529, www.rhodecenter.org), in a restored opera house. It's also home to the Pollard Gallery, dedicated to two artists, Nan and George Pollard. George was a portraitist who painted numerous figures in world history in the late 20th century.

## SHOPPING

Shopping in Kenosha is a sight in itself because of **Prime Outlets** (11211 120th Ave., 262/857-2101, 10am-9pm Mon.-Sat., 10am-7pm Sun.) near the junction of I-94 and Highway 165. Closer to downtown, **Andrea's** (2401 60th

St., 262/657-7732, 9am-6pm Mon.-Fri., 9am-5pm Sat., 11am-3pm Sun.) is a fourth-generation (since 1911) shop selling all sorts of home items, cards, books, and even tobacco, along with an old-timey soda fountain.

## RECREATION
### Sportfishing

In most years, Kenosha sportfishing rates number one in the state in terms of fish caught per hour, especially trout and salmon. You'll find the best opportunities to catch coho salmon, rainbow trout, king salmon, brown trout, and lake trout. Contact the **Kenosha Charter Boat Association** (800/522-6699, www.kenoshacharterboat.com) for details.

### Trails

The **Pike Trail** runs 14 miles south along Lake Michigan to the Illinois border and through **Chiwaukee Prairie** (near Carol Beach), the only unbroken stretch of mixed-grass prairie in Wisconsin. The prairie is home to more than 400 native plant species, including the endangered pink milkwort. The area is now protected as both a National Natural Landmark and a State Natural Area. The trail also goes north to Racine. Eventually cyclists will be able to ride from the Illinois border north through Milwaukee to Cedarburg, Grafton, and points north.

### Camping

The closest decent public campground is at the 4,500-acre **Richard Bong State Recreation Area** (262/878-5600, from $23), along Highway 142, one mile west of Highway 75 in Brighton and about 25 minutes northwest of Kenosha. You'll see hang gliders, parasailing, and remote-controlled planes buzzing around, which is fitting as it's named for a World War II flying ace.

## FOOD

**Mangia Wine Bar** (5517 Sheridan Rd., 262/652-4285, lunch 11:30am-2pm Tues.-Fri., dinner 5pm-9pm Tues.-Sat., 5pm-9pm Sun., $9-30) fits Italian-heavy Kenosha to a T. This basic trattoria puts out lovely wood-fired pizzas and exquisitely done pastas, meat, seafood, and roasted entrées. President Obama has been quoted calling the owner his favorite chef.

The most nostalgic Kenosha Italian experience is longtime fave ★ **Tenuta's Deli** (3203 52nd St., 262/657-9001, 9am-8pm Mon.-Sat., 9am-5pm Sun., $4-9), a good place to stop if you're in a hurry. It's got a smattering of pastas, salads, and ready-made entrées. It's also an outstanding Italian grocery store.

For scuffed newsprint on Formica-style eating, ★ **Frank's Diner** (508 58th St., near HarborPark, 262/657-1017, 6am-1:30pm Mon.-Sat., 7am-noon Sun., $3-10) is a place where factory workers coming off shift and misunderstood-genius writers pour each other's coffee. It's housed in the oldest continually operating lunch-car diner in the United States, pulled here by six horses. Forget the railcar aspect; this is roots eating, plain and simple, in a warm and welcoming Midwestern atmosphere.

If you catch a lunker, take it to the **Boat House Pub and Eatery** (4917 7th Ave., 262/654-9922, 11am-2am daily), where the staff will grill it for you.

## ACCOMMODATIONS

A few of the 115 units at the **Best Western Executive Inn** (7220 122nd Ave., 262/857-7699, $110) are multiple-room patio suites. Expect solid amenities, and service is generally quite good. You'll get great views at the **Best Western Harborside Inn** (5125 6th Ave., 262/658-3281, from $143), right on the lake. Endless upgrades have made this a rival to the other Best Western.

## INFORMATION AND SERVICES

You'll encounter solicitous and chatty folks at the **Kenosha Area Convention and Visitors Bureau** (812 56th St., 262/654-7307

Mangia Wine Bar

or 800/654-7309, www.visitkenosha.com, 8am-4:30pm Mon.-Fri.).

## GETTING THERE

Kenosha is connected to Milwaukee via Racine by **Wisconsin Coach Lines** (877/324-7767, www.wisconsincoach.com), which runs numerous buses daily; it stops at the Metra rail station (5414 13th Ave.), among other points.

You can also hop aboard Wisconsin Coach Lines' **Airport Express** (877/324-7767, www.wisconsincoach.com), which runs north to Milwaukee via Racine and south to Chicago, but it stops far west of Kenosha at the Brat Stop on the interstate.

**Metra** (312/322-6777, www.metrarail.com) offers train service between Kenosha and Chicago's Madison Street Station. Trains depart the **Metra Commuter Rail Center** (5414 13th Ave., 262/653-0141) up to eight times daily.

## GETTING AROUND

Kenosha's utterly cool electric streetcar rumbles through the downtown area to the Metra train station and back; best of all, it runs through two of the historic districts, and costs only $0.25.

# Racine

Like Kenosha, its de facto sister city to the south, Racine suffers somewhat from its association with manufacturing. But the city lakefront, once an ugly mill town with a horizon of gas tanks and brown ponds, was mostly razed and spruced up in the early 1990s. Now it's full of landscaped parks and plenty of public boat launches, and the city has the largest marina on Lake Michigan, at more than 100 acres.

In the early 20th century the city had the nation's most appreciable Bohemian influence, but it is now known for its Danish population, the largest Danish population outside Denmark. West Racine is even referred to as "Kringleville," for the Danish pastry produced in huge numbers by local bakeries.

## History

The Root River, named by early Native Americans for its gnarled knife-resistant roots, so unimpressed French voyageurs in the 1670s that they decamped here. In 1841 the town was incorporated under the name Racine, meaning "root" in French. Like Kenosha, Racine was plagued by the maddeningly shifty river mouth and resulting sandbars, so residents had to dig out and construct the first piers in 1843-1844. Initially, lake traffic was the lifeblood of the city, but by the turn of the 20th century, Racine was a leading national center for farm-implement and wagon manufacturing.

## SIGHTS
### ★ Racine Art Museum

In the city center, the impressive **Racine Art Museum** (RAM, 441 Main St., 262/638-8300, www.ramart.org, 10am-5pm Tues.-Sat., from noon Sun., $5), in a sparklingly chic edifice that's superbly meshed with its 1860s structure, is one of the best in the Midwest. With one of the top three collections—more than 4,000 pieces—of Works Progress Administration traditional arts and crafts, it is rivaled only by the Smithsonian and the American Craft Museum in New York. As an aside, this building was once a bank that was robbed by John Dillinger in 1933.

### ★ Golden Rondelle Theater

With its 90-foot arching columns, it's hard to miss the domed **Golden Rondelle Theater** (1525 Howe St., 262/631-2154), on the city's south side. The most distinctive of Racine's architectural landmarks (the Frank Lloyd Wright building across the street may be the architectural gem, but this is the one everyone stops their cars to take pictures of), it was unveiled at the New York World's Fair in 1964-1965. Afterward, Frank Lloyd Wright's company was commissioned to bring the theater to Racine and incorporate it near the SC Johnson Wax administration building, also designed by Wright. Free tours of the SC Johnson administration building depart the theater at various times on Friday; reservations are required. The Great Workroom alone is worth the tour. Also on-site is the company's Fortaleza Hall, a gorgeous glass employees hall with a small museum of company history and works by Frank Lloyd Wright.

### Other Museums

Brother to the RAM, the **Charles Wustum Museum** (2519 Northwestern Ave., 262/636-9177, 10am-5pm Tues.-Sat., free) displays regional art in a historic 1856 Italianate farmhouse on a 13-acre spread of parkland and formal gardens.

# Racine

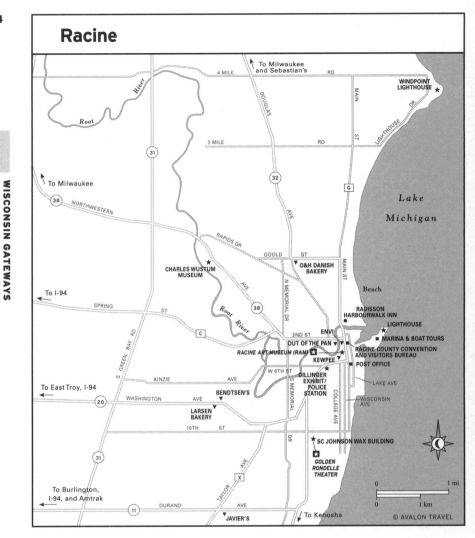

The **Dillinger Exhibit** (Racine Police Department lobby, 730 Center St., 262/635-7700, 7am-6pm Mon.-Fri., 8am-2pm Sat.-Sun., free) isn't a museum but a fun look at the bad old days of cops and robbers. On November 20, 1933, four brazen robbers held up a downtown Racine bank, stole $27,700, and relieved a security guard of his machine gun. When Dillinger was finally taken down in Arizona, the gun was recovered—complete with Dillinger's signature on the stock. The gun is part of the exhibit.

## Windpoint Lighthouse

Many visitors associate Racine with the eye-catching red beacon atop the breakwaters across from Reefpoint Marina. Racinians would rather be associated with **Windpoint Lighthouse** (north of town between Three Mile Rd. and Four Mile Rd.). Believed to be the oldest (built in 1880) and tallest (112 feet) lighthouse on the Great Lakes, it is still in use today. You can't go inside, but you can stroll the grounds at most hours of the day.

## Scenic Drives

The city of Racine boasts a historic chunk of roadway: Three Mile Road, beginning at 108th Street and running east to 80th Street, was laid out in the early part of the 19th century and has remained virtually untouched and unwidened. It still has old oaks and rail fences at its verges and makes for a beautiful drive.

State Rustic Roads are everywhere you look. One heads north of Racine along Honey Lake Road, Maple Lane, and Pleasant View Road to Highway D and Highway 83, passing along the way a woodland preserve, dairy farms, and marshes with muskrat houses. Backtrack to Highway DD and it connects to another Rustic Road adjacent to the **Honey Creek Wildlife Area.** This route also passes the **Franklyn Hazelo Home,** which is on the National Register of Historic Places. Southeast of Burlington off Highway 142 via Brever Road or Wheatland Road, a Rustic Road passes under an expanse of oak and black walnut trees. Highlights include old barns, an old farmhouse, marshes, and lots of great fishing

along the **Fox River,** accessible from Hoosier Creek Road.

Northeast of Waterford, via Highway 164 and Highway 36, is Loomis Rustic Road, originally an 1840 territorial road that's little changed. Along the way, you'll pass **Colonel Heg Memorial Park,** commemorating Wisconsin's highest-ranking Civil War officer. A park museum describes the region's settlement by Norwegians, and an 1830s cabin sits nearby.

## Burlington

Burlington, a town of 8,900 people, is about 25 miles west of Racine. For its size, it certainly has a lot of liars: As the home of the world-famous Burlington Liar's Club, it hosts an annual yarn- and fib-spinning festival; the town's chamber of commerce also distributes a brochure about the town's **Tall Tales Trail.**

Also called Chocolate Town USA, Burlington is home to a Nestlé plant, many streets named after candy bars, and the **Chocolate Experience Museum** (Chamber of Commerce Office, 113 E. Chestnut St., 262/763-6044, 9am-5pm Mon.-Fri., 10am-2pm Sat., free).

Burlington is also the hometown of Dallas Cowboys' quarterback Tony Romo; given

the Racine Art Museum

Cheesehead football fans' enmity for the Cowboys, it's galling to admit that.

The **Spinning Top Exploratory** (533 Milwaukee Ave., 262/763-3946, www. topmuseum.org, by appointment, $5) has more than 1,500 examples of yo-yos, tops, and anything else that revolves. The by-reservation-only tour features videos, demonstrations, and games as well as a look at prototype tops used in a feature film on the subject.

## ENTERTAINMENT AND EVENTS

On Memorial Day weekend in May, little Burlington whoops it up during **ChocolateFest** (www.chocolatefest.com).

Racine's **Fourth of July celebration** (www.racine.org) is the largest in the state, replete with the longest parade in Wisconsin. If you're very lucky, it'll be a year when mock 19th-century clipper ships are sailing around.

The granddaddy of all events is mid-July's **Salmon-a-Rama** (www.salmon-o-rama. com), during which more than 4,000 anglers from 25 states land about 18 tons of fish, and another 200,000 people crowd the lakefront for a huge blowout of a festival. It's the largest freshwater fishing festival in the world.

## RECREATION
### Charter Fishing
Racine has one of the most productive charter operations on Lake Michigan. It also has the largest marina on the Great Lakes at more than 100 acres. Six different species of salmon and trout cohabit near three reefs lying outside the harbor. In July 2010 a man caught a Wisconsin-record and likely a world-record 41.5-pound brown trout off Wind Point. For more information, contact **Fishing Charters of Racine** (800/475-6113).

### Biking
The county has a 117-mile on-road marked bicycle trail; some sections are on a multiuse trail. Six county scenic multiuse trails exist.

The **North Shore Trail** runs to Kenosha and links up with the **Racine-Sturtevant Trail.**

### Canoeing
The Root and Fox Rivers and Honey Creek, west of Racine, are good for canoeing. **Riverbend Nature Center** (3600 N. Green Bay Rd., 262/639-0930, 8am-4pm Mon.-Sat., 10am-4pm Sun.) rents out canoes for $15 for the first hour and $5 for every additional hour after that.

### Camping
**Sanders County Park** (4809 Woods Rd., 262/886-8400, spring-fall, $23) has 50 campsites, along with a playground and hiking trails.

## FOOD
### Bistro
★ **Sebastian's** (6025 Douglas Ave., 262/681-5465, 5pm-9pm Mon.-Sat., $6-18), just north of downtown, has long been a fine bistro. Cuisine varies by season, but expect classics like bone-in rib eye done in varied styles using produce from its adjacent garden.

An outstanding casual spot for world fusion fare is **Out of the Pan** (550 State St., 262/632-0668, 11am-3pm Mon.-Fri., 5pm-10pm Tues.-Sat., brunch Sun., $9-26). The restaurant is creative, hip, and friendly, and the Sunday brunch is simply superb.

### Burgers
Not a greasy spoon per se, ★ **Kewpee** (520 Wisconsin Ave., 262/634-9601, 7am-6pm Mon.-Fri., 7am-5pm Sat., from $1) rates a nod as the best burger joint in perhaps all of southern Wisconsin. Devotees regularly come from as far away as the Windy City. Dating to 1927, this onetime teen hangout doesn't have much in the way of ambience now. It's as fast as fast grub gets, but you can't beat the burgers or malts. It's standing-room-only at lunchtime.

### Kringle
Racine is still lovingly called Kringleville, and for good reason: Many travelers leave

town with white wax-paper bags stuffed with *kringle*, a flaky, ovoid kind of coffeecake filled with a variety of fruit and almond paste or pecans. Family bakeries vie annually for top honors of best *kringle*, and they still make it the Old World way—some taking three days to prepare the dough alone. Aficionados say that the pecan *kringles* are best, and you should always go for the thinnest slice on the plate, since it always has the most filling.

**O&H Danish Bakery** (1841 Douglas Ave., 262/637-8895, 5:30am-6pm Mon.-Fri., 5am-5pm Sat.) does the most advertising and probably ships the most *kringles;* even President Obama made a stop here in 2010. But insiders say that ★ **Larsen Bakery** (3311 Washington Ave., 262/633-4298, 6am-5pm Mon.-Fri., 6am-4pm Sat.) or ★ **Bendtsen's** (3200 Washington Ave., 262/633-0365) have the best.

Another Danish highlight is *æbleskiver,* a lovely spherical waffle.

## Mexican

**Javier's** (2815 Durand Ave., 262/598-9242, lunch and dinner Mon.-Sat., $6-18) is best described as fusion Mexican. There are wonderful Mexican standards, but you may also find baked chicken pasta or whatever else Javier thinks up. Javier's also rates a mention for being quite possibly the friendliest eatery in the region.

## Molecularly Hip

**Envi** (316 Main St., 262/770-4297, 5pm-2am Wed.-Sat., from $6) is a bar, club, lounge, and restaurant with features you might expect in Milwaukee or Chicago. They have their fingers in many hip areas, like molecular gastronomy, raw foods, and sustainable ingredients; try the local honey in a mixed drink.

# ACCOMMODATIONS

The only over-the-water hotel on southern Lake Michigan is a good one. The ★ **Radisson Harbourwalk Inn** (223 Gaslight Circle, 262/632-7777 or 800/333-3333, $139 s, $149 d) has guest rooms affording gorgeous lake views and suites with a whirlpool tub on the balcony. Boaters can dock at the slips, and the on-site restaurant is well regarded. Extras include 24-hour room service, in-room coffeemakers, airport transfers, and more.

# INFORMATION AND SERVICES

The nonprofit tourism organization **Real Racine** (14015 Washington Ave., 262/884-6400 or 800/272-2463, www.realracine.com) is just west of the interchange of Washington Avenue and I-94.

# GETTING THERE
## Train

There's no train service to downtown Racine, but trains stop eight miles west of town at the **Amtrak Station** (2904 Wisconsin St.) in Sturtevant. Racine city buses travel to Sturtevant. Kenosha's Metra trains don't yet extend north to Racine.

## Bus

**Airport Express** (877/324-7767, www.wisconsincoach.com) makes stops in Racine on its routes to and from Chicago's O'Hare Airport and Milwaukee's Mitchell International Airport. **Wisconsin Coach Lines** (877/324-7767, www.wisconsincoach.com) also stops in Racine on its run between Milwaukee and Kenosha. Buses stop at the **Racine Transit Center** (1400 State St.)

# Background

# The Landscape

Topographically, Wisconsin may lack the jaw-dropping majesty of other states' vaulting crags or shimmering desert palettes, but it possesses an equable slice of physicality, with fascinating geographical and geological highlights—many of them found nowhere outside Wisconsin. And Door County is a most precious slice of that, with a minimum of drama; the stereotype of Midwesterners as taciturn and "aw-shucks" stems from an innate sense of the land itself.

## Where in the World...?

Where is Door County? Well, start with where the state is. Sticklers might say "the eastern north-central United States," and in one guidebook an outlander classified it simply as "the north," but Wisconsinites themselves consider their state part of the Midwest, specifically the Upper Midwest. Some prefer to call it a Great Lakes State, especially as the Door Peninsula juts into Lake Michigan.

## The Basics

For Door County, extend your left hand, palm outward. It pretty much makes the shape of Wisconsin, and your thumb is Door County. Trace your hand down to your wrist to visualize a map of the scope of this book; one-third of the U.S. population lives within a day's drive of this area.

Wisconsin is by no means at high elevation, but the state's rolling topography is chock-full of hills and glacial undulation. Door County's salient feature is its high perch atop the Niagara Escarpment, but if you're coming from anywhere near the Appalachians, Rockies, or Sierra Nevada, what is called a "mountain" by a Midwesterner would hardly register as a hill elsewhere.

Even excluding all the access to the Great Lakes, approximately 4 percent of the state's surface is water—and Door County has some lovely streams and lakes of its own, not to mention Lake Michigan and Green Bay.

## GEOGRAPHY

Wisconsin was once at the earth's equator. Shifting tectonic plates created the Canadian Shield, which includes about two-thirds of eastern Canada along with Wisconsin, Minnesota, Michigan, and New York. A glacial lake flooded the Wisconsin range, the northern section of present-day Wisconsin, about 500 million years ago.

More recent glaciation during four glacial periods over two million years is responsible for Wisconsin's one-of-a-kind topography. The final ice age, occurring 70,000 to 10,000 years ago, was called the Wisconsin period, when Wisconsin had five lobes of glaciation penetrating what is now the state, reducing the landscape to knobs and slate-flat land and establishing rivers and streams. Only the southwestern lower third of the state escaped the glaciers' penetration, resulting in the world's largest area surrounded completely by glacial drift.

## Eastern Ridges and Lowlands

Wisconsin has six geographical zones, and Door County is in the Eastern Ridges and Lowlands. Bordered by Lake Michigan on the east and north, this 14,000-square-mile region was comparatively richer in glacial deposits, and the fertile soils attracted the first immigrant farmers. The impeded waterways were ideal for floating timber to mills.

The Kettle Moraine region southeast of

---

**Previous:** Cave Point County Park; a deer at Kohler-Andrae State Park.

Lake Winnebago in east-central Wisconsin provides a textbook look at glacial geology.

# CLIMATE

Contrary to what you may have heard, Wisconsin weather isn't all that bad. Temperatures can range from 105°F to -30°F, which spices things up, and come late February, most people are more than ready for the snow to go; but overall it isn't terrible.

Wisconsin is near the path of the jet stream, and it lacks any declivity large enough to impede precipitation or climatic patterns. Its northerly latitude produces seasonal shifts that result in drastic temperature fluctuations. It's not unusual for farmers near Lake Geneva in southeastern Wisconsin to be plowing while ice fishers near the Apostle Islands in the north are still drilling holes in the ice. Door County is famed for its equable climate. It is cold and hot, but Lake Michigan acts as a climate conditioner, keeping the temperatures from swinging too wildly.

Door County's northern coast

## Temperature and Precipitation

The state's mean temperature is 43°F, not a terribly useful statistic. You'll find 100°F in the shade in August, -40°F or colder in winter with the wind chill, and everything in between.

The average precipitation is 38.6 inches annually. Northern counties experience more snowfall than southern ones, and places near the Great Lakes can have precipitation when the rest of the state is dry. Snow cover ranges from 140 days per year in the north to 85 days in the south. Snowfall ranges from 30 inches in the far south to 120 inches or more near Lake Superior. Door County gets 45-50 inches of snow.

## "Cooler Near the Lake"

Wisconsin has two contiguous sea-size bodies of water that create their own lakeside microclimates. Get used to hearing "cooler near the lake" in summer and "warmer near the lake" in winter. This moderating influence is particularly helpful for the orchards and gardens of Door County on Lake Michigan and Bayfield County on Lake Superior. On the other hand, it also means more precipitation: One freaky day in 2009, Milwaukee's south side had 14.8 inches of snow, while 30 miles west it was sunny all day.

## Tornadoes

Generally, not many things in Wisconsin's natural environment can kill you; there are no hurricanes or grizzly bears. But the state does endure tornadoes, generally averaging six serious twisters and many more near-misses or unsubstantiated touchdowns each year. The good news for Door County visitors is that the Door has only had six twisters in the last 50 years, and it is in the green zone (the safest) for tornado danger, as is the Lake Michigan shoreline as far south as Chicago. East-central and southeastern Wisconsin away from Lake Michigan, however, are in the yellow zone, where you should pay attention during storms.

**Tornado season** begins in March and

# Average Temperatures

Listed in degrees Fahrenheit.

| Location | July high/low | January high/low |
|----------|---------------|------------------|
| Appleton | 81/63 | 25/10 |
| Fond du Lac | 80/61 | 25/10 |
| Green Bay | 80/58 | 23/6 |
| Kenosha | 81/60 | 29/13 |
| Manitowoc | 77/62 | 26/14 |
| Milwaukee | 81/59 | 28/12 |
| Oshkosh | 81/63 | 26/10 |
| Racine | 78/64 | 30/16 |
| Sheboygan | 82/62 | 30/14 |
| Sturgeon Bay | 76/56 | 26/11 |

peaks from late May to July, with June the riskiest month. A secondary spike occurs during September and occasionally into mid-October. Many of the midsummer tornadoes are smaller and less intense than the ones in April-June or in September.

A **tornado watch** means conditions are favorable for the development of a tornado. A **tornado warning** means one has been sighted in the vicinity. In either case, emergency sirens sound almost everywhere in Wisconsin; you might want to get an emergency weather radio and keep it with you.

Seek shelter in a basement and under a table if possible. Avoid windows. If there is no basement, find an interior room, such as a bathroom, that has no windows. Avoid rooms with outside walls on the south or west side of a building. If you are driving, position your vehicle at a right angle to the tornado's apparent path. If it overtakes you, you have a dilemma; experts disagree about whether to stay in the car with your seatbelt on or to get out and lie flat in a ditch.

## Thunderstorms and Lightning

Lightning still kills 200 to 300 people per year nationwide, more than tornadoes and hurricanes combined. Wisconsin averages two serious thunderstorms per year, with a midsummer average of two relatively modest storms each week. Don't let this lull you into complacency in fall, however; ferocious thunderstorms have struck as late as Halloween, replete with marble-size hail, flash floods, and tornadoes.

Thunderstorms are often deadlier than tornadoes, particularly when you're driving or in open areas. Lightning is serious stuff—remember, if you're close enough to hear thunder, you're close enough to get fried. The cardinal rule when lightning is present: Do the opposite of what your gut instincts tell you. Avoid anything outside—especially trees. If you cannot get indoors, squat on the balls of your feet, hugging your knees in a balled position, reducing your contact with the ground and your apparent size. If indoors, stay away from anything that has a channel to the outside: telephones, TVs, radios, even plumbing.

## Snowstorms

Technically, four inches of snow in a 24-hour period qualifies as heavy snowfall, but a Wisconsinite would laugh off such a paltry amount. Lake Michigan, that same body that moderates temperatures in Door County, can also create "lake effect snow," when the moist air near the shoreline can dump tremendous amounts of snow in a short time compared to inland areas.

Six inches of snow in 8-12 hours will cause serious transportation disruptions and definitely close airports for a while. The snow generally begins to stay in mid-late October in northern Wisconsin, and in early December in southern Wisconsin, although snow has fallen as early as September and as late as May on occasion.

If you're in Wisconsin in the winter, you'll probably be driving in the stuff. Even the hardiest winter drivers need to practice caution, and if you're a novice at winter driving, don't learn it on the road, especially on a crowded highway at dawn or dusk.

Most importantly, slow down. Be cautious on bridges, even when the rest of the pavement is OK; bridges are always slippery. In controlled skids on ice and snow, take your foot off the accelerator and steer into the direction of the skid. Follow the owner's manual advice if your car is equipped with an antilock braking system (ABS). Most cars come equipped with all-season radials, so snow tires aren't usually necessary (even though they are outstanding), and tire chains are illegal in Wisconsin.

During nighttime snowstorms, keep your lights on low beam. If you get stuck, check your owner's manual for the advisability of "rocking" the car; be sure to keep the front wheels clear and pointed straight ahead. Don't race the engine; you'll just spin your wheels into icy ruts. Winterize your vehicle, and carry an emergency kit that includes anything you may need to spend the night in a snow bank; many people have learned this the hard way while trapped in a blizzard on an interstate highway for 10 hours. And if you see someone stuck in a snow bank, do stop and help push them out.

The **Department of Transportation's** **website** (dot.state.wi.us) updates winter driving conditions four times daily November-late March. You can also call the state's toll-free roads hotline; dial 511 on your mobile phone or go to www.511wi.gov. It's a brilliant service that Iowa and Minnesota also participate in; hopefully Illinois and Michigan will join soon.

## Wind Chill and Frostbite

The most dangerous part of winter in Wisconsin is the wind-chill factor—the biting effect of the wind that makes the air colder and more lethal. For example, when the temperature is 30°F and the wind is blowing at 40 mph, the temperature with wind chill is actually -6°F; at a temperature of 0°F, a 40 mph wind makes it -54°F.

When the wind chill sends temperatures low enough, exposed skin is in immediate danger. Lots of Badgers can recount tales of serious cases of frostbite that they swear they can still feel today when the weather changes. The most serious cases of frostbite—you may have seen photos of mountain climbers with black ears and fingers—can require amputation. Worse, without proper clothing, you're at risk for hypothermia.

# ENVIRONMENTAL ISSUES

A state that produced both John Muir and Aldo Leopold must have a fairly good record of being green. If you overlook the first century of statehood, when the area, like much of the world at the time, was pillaged at full bore for its natural resources, Wisconsin has in fact been ahead of its time environmentally. The state government initiated exceptionally far-sighted environmental laws beginning in the 1950s, when tourism was seen as a burgeoning major industry. The state was the first to meet the requirements of the 1972 Clean Water Act; it had enacted similar legislation at the state level half a decade earlier. Former Wisconsin governor and U.S. senator Gaylord Nelson founded Earth Day in 1970.

## Superfund Sites and Dirty Water

Still, things could be better. Wisconsin has more than three dozen sites designated by the federal Environmental Protection Agency (EPA) as Superfund sites, areas so contaminated that large amounts of money are allotted to clean them up. The Wisconsin Department of Natural Resources (DNR) has found that about 900 miles of rivers in the state have failed environmental standards since the mid-1990s, and another 50 or so lakes were questionable or worse. Twenty-two percent of rivers and streams fail, in one way or another, to meet the state's clean-water goals. Fish-consumption advisories have been in effect since 2000 for well over 300 lakes and rivers. Although these problems involve less than 5 percent of rivers and an even smaller percentage of lakes, they are still major issues of concern.

Wisconsin has some of the country's strictest groundwater laws and is cited by the EPA as one of three exemplary states, but not enough local water sources pass muster. Land use, particularly agriculture, forestry, and construction, often creates eroded soils and runoff polluted with fertilizers and toxins. But agriculture isn't the only source of contaminants; urban runoff causes up to 50 times as much soil erosion, and whatever is dumped on the street can wind up in the groundwater.

Contaminated sedimentation from decades of abuse remains a secondary problem. Pulp and paper mills discharged almost 300 million gallons of wastewater, most of it untreated, into surface water. In east-central Wisconsin, the EPA was asked to declare 39 miles of the Fox River—the heart of the paper industry—a Superfund site because 40 tons of an original 125 tons of toxic polychlorinated biphenyls (PCBs) that were dumped remained in the river from factory waste discharge.

As a result of other pollution, the Wisconsin DNR issues almost 200 "boil water" notices annually; one county found half of its 376 wells to be seriously contaminated by pollutants such as atrazine and nitrates. More than 90 percent of the state's lakes have been affected by pollution in one way or another, including sedimentation, contamination, and, the most common and difficult to handle, eutrophication—when increased nutrients in the water lead to algal blooms and nuisance weeds, which eventually kill off other aquatic life.

With so many visitors, Door County may be loved to death, with human water use depleting the water table and its ability to recharge. Due to its bedrock and soil types, Door County is especially susceptible to drinking water contamination should something toxic find its way onto the topsoil.

## Mercury and Other Toxins

Toxic environmental pollutants are among the most pernicious silent crises in the health of forests today. Government statistics estimate that 1,200 Wisconsin children are exposed to elevated levels of mercury each year. The federal Centers for Disease Control and Prevention say 1 woman in 10 in the United States already has dangerous levels of mercury in her blood.

Mercury pollution isn't a problem in Lake Superior or Lake Michigan, but fish consumption advisories exist for the lakes because of PCBs, toxins that can cause cancer. And a recent shocking discovery is that dioxin is the likely culprit of crashing lake trout populations rather than invasive species or overfishing. Bottom feeders such as carp and catfish show PCB contamination levels of 0.11 and 0.09 ppm, respectively; predators such as bass and walleye both have much higher levels, the latter a whopping 0.52 ppm. A simple rule of thumb is that the larger a fish is, the less safe it is to eat. Check the **Department of Natural Resources' website** (http://dnr. wi.gov) for fish consumption advisories. The recommended daily intake of fish for women of childbearing years, nursing mothers, and children under age 15 is extremely low. For men and women beyond childbearing years, consumption of predator and bottom-feeder

# America's Dairyland

Dairying was not the first gear in the state's agricultural machine; wheat was. Wisconsin was a leading world wheat producer and exporter through the 1870s. The initial forays in the state into home butter and cheese production were derisively called "western grease." Wisconsin cattle were initially hybrids of hardier species, and milk production was hardly a necessity.

## THE BIRTH OF A STEREOTYPE

In the 1850s, transplanted New York farmers organized the first commercial cheese-making factory systems, and the first experiments in modern herd management and marketing were undertaken. One New Yorker, Chester Hazen, opened a cheese factory in Ladoga in 1864; in its first year, it produced 200,000 pounds of cheese. Within a few years the state had nearly 50 factories, and in some places the demand for milk outstripped the supply.

Subsequent immigrants found the topography reminiscent of Europe and the glacial till profoundly fertile. Old World pride mixed with Yankee ingenuity created an explosion in Wisconsin dairying. The first dairy organizations were founded after the Civil War, and a dairy board of trade was set up in Watertown in 1872. The state's dairies shrewdly diversified the cheese-making and took the Western markets by storm. By the 20th century, a stereotype was born: Jefferson County, Wisconsin, was home to 40,000 cows and 34,000 people.

## W. D. HOARD

A seminal figure in Wisconsin's rise to dairy prominence was the previously unknown W. D. Hoard. In 1870, Hoard began publishing *The Jefferson County Union,* which became the mouthpiece of Wisconsin farmers. The only central source for disseminating information, the paper's dairy columns became *Hoard's Dairyman.* It was the most influential publication in Wisconsin's dairy industry.

Hoard had never farmed, but he pushed tirelessly for previously unheard-of progressive farming techniques. Through his publications, farmers learned to be not so conservative, to keep records, and to compare trends. Most significantly, Hoard almost singlehandedly invented the specialized milk-only cow. He became such a legend in the industry he was elected governor in 1889.

The University of Wisconsin followed Hoard's lead and established its College of Agriculture's experimental stations in 1883. The renowned department would invent the butterfat test, dairy courses, cold-curing processes, and winter feeding.

## KEEPING THEM ON THE FARM

Dairying in Wisconsin is a $26.5 billion industry, accounting for 10 percent of the state's total economic output and half its agricultural output. It is more crucial to the state's economy than citrus is to Florida or potatoes are to Idaho.

Nearly 30 percent of all the butter and cheese consumed in the United States is produced in Wisconsin. It produces 2.3 billion pounds of milk per year on average; if it were a country, it would have the world's fourth-largest production. Wisconsin cheese makers have won 33

---

fish species is recommended at one meal per week. If you eat fish only during vacation or otherwise sporadically, you can double these amounts. To increase your chances of eating a cleaner fish, eat smaller pan fish such as sunfish and crappy rather than predators such as walleye and northern pike, and always trim off the skin and fat.

## Mall Sprawl

With 90.1 people per square mile, Wisconsin ranks in the middle among American states for population density. Two-thirds of the residents live in the 12 southeastern counties, however, creating a serious land-use and urban-sprawl issue. In southeastern Wisconsin, agricultural land is being

percent of World Cheese Championship first prizes; California, less than 5 percent. At the 2014 U.S. Cheese Championship, Wisconsin swept the awards in 10 categories, won first place in more than one-third of all categories, and saw one-quarter of its cheeses in Best of Show finals. One of these cheeses was selling for more than $200 a pound the next year. In the 2016 World Cheese Championship, it took home Best Overall for one cheese; Wisconsin is the only U.S. entrant to win in the past 30 years, and it has done so twice.

Wisconsin is the only state to require a master's license to make cheese, and 90 percent of milk produced in the state is used for cheese. Wisconsin has more than 25 percent of the U.S. cheese market today, while California has 20 percent, and while experts have long predicted California production would eclipse Wisconsin's, Wisconsin maintains its lead in specialty cheeses with 650 varietals, double the number made in California.

And yet, things have been far from easy. In 1993 California surpassed Wisconsin in whole-milk output. The number of family dairy farms has dwindled from a post-World War II figure of 150,000 to less than 14,000 in 2015; at one point the state was losing an average of 1,000 dairy farms per year.

Badger State politicians blame the dairy industry's problems on outdated federal milk-pricing guidelines, which see farmers in other states paid higher rates than Upper Midwest farmers. The farther you get from Eau Claire, Wisconsin, the higher the price paid for milk—up to $3 more per 100 pounds: A Wisconsin farmer earns $1.04 for 100 pounds of milk while a South Florida farmer earns $4.18 for producing the same thing. Wisconsin farmers even resurrected "milk strikes," dumping their milk in protest. Recent legislation has actually strengthened the system and solidified regulations favoring corporate farms.

Although it's in decline, Wisconsin is in little danger of losing its cultural underpinnings of rural Americana. Supplying so much of the cheese in the United States still means it has a huge market—and predicted rises in U.S. cheese consumption will help. Badger farmers are also finding ways to slow the rate of farm loss. One innovative program involves rural villages banding together, pooling resources, and buying family farms to keep them operational. Also, experts have rated the state first in diversity in farming practices. The results? Recently the number of cows in the state has again begun to rise, and cheese production has increased at a steady 2 percent per year.

Economists also say that California's cheese industry is dangerously linked to the stock market, since many of its consumers have disposable income that varies—every time the stock market hiccups, California's markets quake, but Wisconsin's don't. California cheese makers are mostly huge factory operations, unlike the typical small family operations in Wisconsin. Seventy-five percent of Wisconsin cheese makers grew up in an operation in which a grandparent had worked in the industry; only 20 percent of California's cheese makers can say that.

Wisconsin agriculture will never have to worry about its water, unlike California agriculture, where climate projections paint a dire picture in terms of water availability for the enormous farm operations of the Golden State. So even though it may not be able to compete in whole numbers, Wisconsin is still America's Dairyland.

converted to urban use at a rate of 10 square miles per year. All of southern Wisconsin may be in danger—Scenic America declared three sites (Vernon County's Kickapoo River Valley, Washington County around Erin, and the Mississippi River bluffs) as some of the worst examples of rural landscape degradation; then again, things are not as bad as in Colorado, where the entire state made the list. Door County also has debates on development issues; these days it's hard to tell where one village ends and the next begins.

The northern forests are being encroached on as flight from burgeoning urban areas continues. This sprawl results in diminished air quality from use of commuter automobiles, loss of farmland and wildlife habitat, more toxic runoff, and continued soil erosion.

## Give 'Em Hell

Pick an issue and Wisconsinites will passionately, but politely, be involved, for or against. The long-standing tradition of grassroots activism in the state is alive and well, especially on environmental issues. And it often isn't stereotypical granola eaters versus timber cutters; in fact, on many environmental issues, hunters, fishers, and snowmobilers work for common ground with their traditional "enemies," the tree-huggers of liberal Madison. It's no coincidence that the Progressive Party of Fightin' Bob La Follette was founded here.

## Visually Busy

Another pollution issue that merits scrutiny is that Wisconsin's lovely countryside is scarred by the visual pollution of "litter on a stick," meaning billboard advertising. States and communities across the nation have tuned in to the fact that not only is it disgustingly ugly, it can also distract drivers. The state has nearly 15,000 of these ugly popsicles; only three other states have more billboard advertising than Wisconsin.

# PLANTS AND ANIMALS
## Plants

The Eastern Transition and Great Lakes Forest Zones cover most of Wisconsin. Both are primarily mixed meadow and woodland, a far cry from the time before the Europeans arrived, when 85 percent of the state was covered by forest and the rest by tall grass. By the mid-19th century, those numbers had dipped to 63 percent forest, 28 percent savanna, and 9 percent grassland. Today, the state's forest cover is 37 percent, and precious little of that is original. Of the two million acres of prairie that once covered the state, only 2,000 scattered acres survive. In all, Wisconsin has more than 2,100 species

of plants, approximately a tenth of which are classified as rare, and some of them are threatened.

Four major vegetation types cover the state: **boreal forest,** a subarctic coniferous spread near Lake Superior; **deciduous forest,** the second-largest swath of Wisconsin woodlands; **mixed forest,** consisting of species of both, throughout the state; and **nonforest and grasslands,** found throughout the southern third of the state into west-central Wisconsin along the Mississippi River.

Before the Europeans arrived, Wisconsin had a huge expanse of wetlands, including more than 10,000 acres along Green Bay alone. Today, that amount has dwindled by more than half, a sad indicator of rapacious development and overuse, but it still constitutes the largest amount of wetlands remaining on the Great Lakes.

## Animals

Wisconsin lies within three well-defined life zones conducive to species diversity: the Canadian, the transition, and the upper austral or Carolinian. In total, Wisconsin has 73 species of mammals, 339 native bird species, and more than 200 species of amphibians, reptiles, frogs, bats, butterflies, and insects.

Of Wisconsin's two large mammals, the ubiquitous **white-tailed deer** is a traffic and garden nightmare. The other resident big mammal, the **black bear,** is still relatively common in the northern woods and has also been seen farther south, but you won't likely see a bear in Door County.

Wisconsin lies in the middle of several migratory waterfowl flyways, so birding is a big activity. **Tundra swans, sandhill cranes,** and **Canada geese** are three of the most conspicuous species. The latter are so predominant at the Horicon Marsh National Wildlife Refuge in southeastern Wisconsin that ornithologists make pilgrimages here each spring and fall.

## Threatened, Endangered, Exterminated

The last plains buffalo was shot five years before Wisconsin even became a territory. Next to become extinct here were the Richardson's caribou, the American elk, the cougar, the Carolina parakeet, the passenger pigeon (the world's last one was shot in Wisconsin), the peregrine falcon, the pine marten, the trumpeter swan, the whooping crane, the wild turkey, the moose, the fisher, and, in 1922, the common wolverine.

Jump forward to today. First, the bad news: Wisconsin has more than 200 species of flora or fauna listed by state or federal agencies as either endangered or threatened. The state ranks in the middle for species diversity and at-risk status—0 percent of mammals are at risk, but 6.2 percent of fish are at serious risk; the rest are in the middle. But all is not lost. Wisconsin instituted preservation measures long before the federal government did and is consistently recognized by environmental groups for at least trying to stem the carnage. The fisher, falcon, pine marten, trumpeter swan, and wild turkey have been reintroduced to varying degrees of success. Most amazing was the return of a nesting pair of **piping plovers** to the shores of the Apostle Islands National Lakeshore in 1999. In the entire Great Lakes, only 30 nesting pairs exist, all of them in Michigan. As a result, the U.S. Fish and Wildlife Service has proposed setting aside nearly 200 miles of Lake Superior and Lake Michigan shoreline, including 20 miles of Door County shoreline, for critical habitats, and possibly to establish a colony.

One of the most visually arresting birds—the white pelican—has also made a recent comeback. You might spot one in the Horicon Marsh National Wildlife Refuge. The most intriguing question now is whether **cougars** are hunting prey in the woods. Since 1994 more than 300 sightings have been reported, some in Door County and environs, and many have been confirmed, even though the last cougar supposedly perished in 1908; today's cats are

most likely migrants from the Black Hills of South Dakota.

If there is one endangered fish all Badgers worry about, it's the **perch,** especially the yellow perch. In a state that considers the fish fry to be almost a religious experience—and there is no better fish than perch for a fish fry—plummeting lake perch stocks, especially in Lake Michigan, freaked out the fish-loving population in the early 1990s. But since the start of the millennium, the DNR has said the numbers being seen were cause to be "cautiously optimistic." And trout lovers rejoice—blue-ribbon-status streams have increased 1,000 percent in 20 years.

Still, the picture could be much better. Even as many species are rebounding, other native species are added to the threatened and endangered lists every year. Just under 3 percent of native plants are now threatened or endangered, and 25 percent of the state's species are nonnative.

### Birder Heaven

The area's flyways have always been crucial to the survival of avian species. With the reintroduction of so many—along with wetlands restoration and protection—the state has fantastic birding opportunities. The statewide **Oak Leaf Birding Trail** (www.dnr.state.wi.us) has 35 prime birding spots; the terminus is Whitnall Park in Milwaukee. Even better is the newer **Great Wisconsin Birding and Nature Trail,** which covers the whole state; check the **Wisconsin Bird Conservation Initiative** (http://wisconsinbirds.org) for more information.

### Zebra Mussel

One culprit in the decline of Lake Michigan's yellow perch population could be this pesky little mollusk, the species that best represents what can happen when a nonnative species is introduced into an ecosystem. Most likely transplanted by a visiting freighter from the Caspian Sea in the mid-1980s, the zebra mollusk is a ferocious and tough little Eurasian mollusk that loves the warmer waters and phytoplankton of the Great Lakes. It loves to breed in warm areas, such as at the discharge pipes around power plants. They breed so rapidly that they create unbelievably dense barnacle-like crusts that do serious damage. Worse, they are being blamed for the decline and decimation of native species as they literally suck all the nutrients out of an area. Great Lakes states are frantically fighting to keep them from spreading into inland lakes and streams.

## Asian Carp

This tough-nut alien species is literally poised to invade Lake Michigan via Illinois, which is doing everything short of poisoning its rivers to keep it out. If it gets into Lake Michigan, it could mean doom for indigenous species.

# History

## EARLY ARRIVALS

The Siberia-to-Alaska Beringia theory, which posits that the progenitors of North America's first human residents arrived over a land bridge that rose and submerged in the Bering Strait beginning as long as 20,000 years ago, was seriously challenged in the late 1990s. Provocative new anthropological discoveries in North and South America have led some scientists to reconsider the theory. A Wisconsin archaeologist was one of the first to present new evidence from finds at digs in Kenosha County. The last of the glacial interludes in the Pleistocene epoch, called the Two Rivers, probably saw the first movement into the state of early Paleo-Indians about 11,500 years ago. That time frame is based on examinations of fluted points as well as a rare mastodon kill site, the Boaz Mastodon, which revealed the hunting techniques of the Paleo-Indians in Wisconsin.

Glacial retreat helps explain why the Paleo-Indian people entered the area from the south and southwest rather than from the north. Nomadic clans followed the mastodon and other large mammals northward as the glaciers receded.

### Later Inhabitants

Solid archaeological evidence establishes definite stages in Wisconsin's earliest settlement. The **Archaic** period lasted approximately 8000-750 BC. People still lived transiently, pursuing small game and fish in the newly formed lakes. Around 2000 BC, these Native Americans became the first in the New World to fashion copper.

The later **Woodland** people, with semipermanent dwellings, are generally regarded as the first Native Americans in the region to make use of ceramics, elaborate mound burials (especially in southern Wisconsin), and, to a lesser extent, domesticated plants such as squash, corn, pumpkins, beans, and tobacco. From around 750 BC until European exploration, the Woodland period was a minor golden age of dramatic change for indigenous people. Around 100 BC, the Middle Woodland people experienced cultural and technological proliferation simultaneous with the period of Ohio's and Illinois's Hopewell societies, when villages formed and expanded greatly along waterways.

The people who lived at the end of the Woodland period have been classified into two additional groups: the **Mississippian** and the **Oneota.** The former's impressive sites can be found from New Orleans all the way to Wisconsin and parts of Minnesota. Mississippian culture showed high levels of civic planning and complex social hierarchies, and it lasted at least until the Spanish arrived.

## EUROPEAN CONTACT

The Spanish, Portuguese, and English all blazed westward in an effort to circumvent the Arabs, reach the courts of the Great Khan, and establish ways to appropriate the riches of new lands. Along the way, indigenous people were to be "pacified" under papal hegemony. After England's naval power grew under the Tudor monarchs and began conflicting with the French, the New World became a battleground for the European powers.

## New France: Black Robes and the Fur Trade

Thanks to the Reformation, the French, relative latecomers to maritime and expansionist endeavors, were conveniently freed of papal dicta for divvying up the new continent and its inherent wealth. With the Spanish in the Caribbean and Gulf Coast and the up-and-coming English having a foothold in the mid-Atlantic colonies, France was effectively forced to attempt to penetrate the new land via the northern frontier.

Jacques Cartier first opened the door to the Great Lakes region with his "discovery" of the Gulf of the St. Lawrence River in 1534. The insular French monarchy left the scattered outposts to languish for another 40 years, except the fur traders, who found some success.

The French did establish sparse settlements in the early 16th century, but they were dismayed by the lack of ready riches, the roughness of the land, and the bitter weather. The original fur traders had one superlative talent: forging relationships with the Native Americans, who became enamored of French metal implements, especially firearms. Eventually, the French found their coveted mother lode in beaver pelts.

Paris hatmakers discovered that beaver pelts—especially those softened for a year worn around the waists of Native Americans—made a superior grade of felt for hats, and these soon became the rage in Paris and other parts of Europe, becoming the lifeblood of the colonies, sustaining the region through the mismanagement and vagaries of both British and French rule.

Facilitating both the fur trade and French control over the colonies were the missionaries of the Society of Jesus—the Jesuits. These "Black Robes," as the Huron and Ottawa people called them, first arrived during a time of religious fervor in France. The Franciscans had originally come to the New World as missionaries, but they found the task of conversion too daunting for their small order. The Jesuits became the foundation on which New France operated. The traders needed them to foster harmony with Native American traders, and more importantly, the often complicated French systems of operation required that all day-to-day affairs be carried out at the local level. By 1632 all missionary work in French Canada was under the auspices of the Jesuits.

The Jesuits also accompanied voyageurs (explorers) as New France attempted to widen its sphere of influence westward. Eventually, the Black Robes themselves, along with renegade fur traders, were responsible for the initial exploration and settlement of present-day Wisconsin.

## THE FRENCH IN WISCONSIN

Samuel de Champlain, who first arrived in Quebec in 1603, was the province's most famous and effective leader, despite his obsession with finding the legendary route to the Great Khan. After arriving and hearing of the "People of the Stinking Waters" (the Winnebago people), which he surmised to mean an ocean-dwelling people, he dispatched the first Europeans from Acadia to explore the wild western frontier.

Although there is speculative evidence that Étienne Brûlé, Champlain's first explorer, may have poked around Wisconsin as early as 1620—the same year many assume the pilgrims founded the new colonies—most historians credit Jean Nicolet as the first European to turn up in Green Bay, landing at Red Banks in 1634. Garbed in Chinese damask and using thunder-stick histrionics to impress the indigenous people—the Potawatomi people he met immediately dubbed him "Thunder Beaver"—Nicolet efficiently and diplomatically forged immediate ties with the locals, who guided him throughout the region to meet other communities.

As before, Nicolet couldn't rouse the wilted interest of the French royalty—all it wanted was bags of Chinese silk—and France once again neglected their part of the New World. Legitimate French fur traders were scooped by Pierre-Esprit Radisson and Médard Chouart des Groseilliers, two pesky *coureurs-de-bois* (renegade trappers) who couldn't be bothered to get licensed by the crown. They delved farther into Wisconsin than any had before but had nowhere to trade their furs after being blacklisted by the ruling powers in New France. This led them to England, which gave them a charter to establish the Hudson's Bay Company north of New France—one reason for the later conflict between France and Britain. In 1666 these two were followed by Nicholas Perrot, who extended Nicolet's explorations and consequently opened the French fur trade with Native Americans in Wisconsin.

The seasoned priest Claude Allouez simultaneously founded the first mission at La Pointe in the Apostle Islands and founded St. Francois Xavier, Wisconsin's first permanent European settlement, at De Pere, south of Green Bay.

The most famous Jesuit explorer was the priest Jacques Marquette, who, along with Louis Jolliet, was sent by La Salle in 1673 to discern whether the Mississippi River emptied into the Gulf of Mexico. The first Europeans to cross Wisconsin, they made it to the Mississippi on June 17, 1673, and went as far south as Arkansas, where they saw Indians with European goods, confirming both a route to the gulf and the presence of the Spanish. The French hesitated in buttressing their western frontier—and it wound up costing them dearly.

## Conflict with the British and British Rule

The fate of New France and thus Wisconsin was determined not in the New World but in Europe, as Louis XIV, who had reigned during the zenith of French power, frittered away French influence bit by bit in frivolous distracting battles.

The French never fully used the western edges of the Great Lakes, and James II's rise to the throne in England marked the end of France's never exactly halcyon days in the Great Lakes. James II forced Louis XIV into wild strategies to protect French interests in the New World—strategies that led to further exploration of the hinterlands but also drove France to overextend itself and, eventually, collapse in the region.

At the behest of the Jesuits, who hoped to corral some recalcitrant Native American communities, the French crown closed trade completely in the Great Lakes interiors, cutting off possible ties to the English or the Spanish. Louis XIV correctly reckoned that whoever the Native Americans sided with would end up controlling the new lands. This naturally drained royal coffers, and he decided instead to keep the Native Americans, the English, and the Spanish in check by exploring as far inland as possible and trying to establish a line of garrisons from Montreal all the way to New Orleans.

France succeeded in this second plan but in the process alienated the uneasy Native Americans that had sworn loyalty to France and, worse, aroused the ire of France's bitterest enemies—the Iroquois and the Fox people. Wars with the Fox, which raged 1701-1738, temporarily sapped the determination of the French, but they had enough pluck and military might to string forts along the Mississippi River to look for inroads into territories already held by the British in the Ohio River Valley. By 1750, British colonists in the western Great Lakes outnumbered the French 20 to 1, and many Native Americans, discovering that the British made higher-quality goods more cheaply, switched to the British side.

The French and Indian War (1755-1763) was a thorough thrashing of the French by the British and greatly determined

European spheres of influence in North America.

Under the British, little changed in daily life; the English never even had an official presence in what is now Wisconsin. One Englishman of note, however, was Jonathan Carver, a roguish explorer who roamed the state 1766-1768 and returned to England to publish fanciful, lively, and mostly untrue accounts of the new lands west of the inland seas.

The French had been content simply to trade and had never made overtures for the land itself. But the British who did come—many barely able to conceal their scorn for the indigenous people—began parceling up property and immediately incited unrest. Pontiac, an Ottawa chieftain, led a revolt against the British at Muscoda.

Additionally, the British monarchy's finances were in disarray from the lengthy conflicts with the French in North America and with other enemies in European theaters. And then the monarchy decreed that the colonies could foot their own bill for these new lands and instituted the Stamp Act.

## NATIVE AMERICAN RELATIONS

Unfortunately, none of the foreign settlers consulted the indigenous residents before carving up the land. The United States practiced a heavy-handed patriarchal policy toward the Native Americans, insisting that they be relocated west—away from white settlers on the eastern seaboard—for the betterment of both sides. Simultaneously, the new government instituted a loony system designed to reprogram Native Americans to become happy Christian farmers. Land cessions, begun around the turn of the 19th century, continued regularly until the first general concourse of most western Native Americans took place, in 1825, at Prairie du Chien, Wisconsin, at which time the first of the more draconian treaties was drawn up. The first Native Americans from New York—the Oneida, Stockbridge, Munsee,

and Brothertown people—were moved to Wisconsin beginning in 1823. The cocktail of misguided U.S. patronization and helplessly naive Native American negotiations turned lethal when many came to realize what had been done to them.

The first skirmish, the so-called Winnebago War of 1827, was nothing more than a frustrated attempt at vengeance by a Winnebago chieftain, Red Bird, who killed two settlers before being convinced to surrender to avert a war. The second was more serious—and more legendary.

## THE WISCONSIN TERRITORY

The Northwest Ordinance of 1787 established many of the borders of present-day Wisconsin; Thomas Jefferson had initially envisioned dividing the region into 10 states. Later, before the War of 1812, Wisconsin became part of first the Indiana Territory and then the Illinois Territory as the Northwest was chiseled down. In 1818 the Illinois Territory was further divided to create the Michigan Territory. Finally, in 1836, the Wisconsin Territory was established, taking in all of modern Wisconsin, the Upper Peninsula of Michigan, Iowa, Minnesota, and parts of North and South Dakota.

Well-publicized battles with Native Americans put Wisconsin on the map. This, combined with the wild mining operations in the southwestern part of the state, burgeoning lumber operations along the Great Lake coast, and discovery of fertile soils outside Milwaukee, ensured Wisconsin's status as the Next Big Thing. The new Erie Canal provided immigrants a direct route to this new land. By 1835 there were 60,000 eager settlers pushing through the Erie Canal each year, and most were aiming for what became, the following year, the Wisconsin Territory. Two years later, in 1838, when the chunk of Wisconsin Territory west of the Mississippi was lopped off, more than half of the 225,000 settlers were in Wisconsin. With the enforcement of Indian land cessions, up to three billion acres became available for government surveyors; the first land title sales started in 1834. Wisconsin had fully arrived—and it still wasn't even a state.

## STATEHOOD: GROWING PAINS

Wisconsin's entry into the Union as the flag's 30th star was a bit anticlimactic; there wasn't even a skirmish with the British over it. In fact, the populace voted on the issue of statehood in 1841, and every year for nearly the entire decade, but distinctly disinterested voters rejected the idea until 1848, when stratospheric levels of immigration impelled the legislature to more animated attempts, and the first measures passed.

Incessant immigration continued after statehood. Most newcomers arrived from New England or Europe—Ireland, England, Germany, and Scandinavia. The influx of Poles was still decades away. Milwaukee, a diminutive village of 1,500 at the time of territorial status, burgeoned into a rollicking town of 46,000 by the start of the Civil War, by which time the population of the state as a whole was up to 706,000 people.

During the period leading up to the Civil War, Wisconsin was dominated by political and some social wrangling over what, exactly, the state was to be. With the influence of Yankee immigrants and the Erie Canal access, much of Wisconsin's cultural, political, and social makeup finally resembled New England. In fact, New York legislation was the model for many early Wisconsin laws. The first university was incorporated almost immediately after statehood, and school codes for primary and secondary education soon followed—a bit ahead of the Union as a whole.

Abolition was a hot issue in Wisconsin's early years. It reached top-level status after the annexation of Texas and the Mexican-American War. As a result of this and many other contentious issues, Ripon, Wisconsin, became the founding spot of the Republican Party, which soon took hold of the legislature and held fast until the Civil War.

During the Civil War, despite being among the first states to near enlistment quotas, Wisconsin suffered some of the fiercest draft rioting in the nation. Many new immigrants had decamped from their European homelands for precisely the reasons for which the government was now pursuing them. Eventually, 96,000 Wisconsinites would serve.

### Post-Civil War: Immigrants, Dairy, and Industry

After the Civil War and through the turn of the 20th century, Wisconsin began getting its economic bearings while politicians wrestled over issues as disparate as temperance, railroads, and immigrants' rights. The latter hot potato galvanized enormous enclaves of German Americans into action; they mobilized against anti-immigration laws sweeping through the legislature. Despite the mandates, such as one banning the German language in schools, successive waves of immigrants poured into the state.

The first sawmills had gone up in Wisconsin at the start of the 19th century. Yankee and British settlers built them to use the timber they were felling in clearing farmland. One area of the Chippewa River possessed one-sixth of all the pine west of the Adirondacks—and Wisconsin pine was larger and harder than that in surrounding states. Easily floated down streams and rivers, pine became an enormous commodity on the expanding plains. In Wisconsin, even the roads were fashioned from pine and hardwood planks. By 1870, more than one billion board feet of lumber was being churned out of the state's 1,000-plus mills each year, easily making Wisconsin the country's largest timber producer, which paid one-fourth of all state wages. In time, more than 20 billion board feet were taken from the shores of Green Bay alone; one year, 425 million board feet were shipped through the port of Superior. Wisconsin wood was used in other parts of the expanding country to make homes, wagons, fences, barns, and plank roads. As a result, by the turn of the

# Mr. and Mrs. La Follette

While **Robert La Follette Sr.** dominated Wisconsin politics for most of three decades, he didn't do it alone: He and his wife, Belle, were an inseparable team, both passionate crusaders for social justice.

**Belle La Follette** (1859-1931) was behind Bob in every way, and in many cases, it could be said, *was* Bob. Her grandmother inculcated in her a fierce determination to obtain the education she herself had been denied. It was at the University of Wisconsin that this very independent woman caught the eye of her soul mate, Bob La Follette. The two flaunted many of society's constricting traditions. They were the first couple in Wisconsin to delete the word *obey* from their marriage vows. Belle later became the first woman to graduate from the University of Wisconsin law school.

Her postcollege life was supporting Bob and maintaining her own crusading career as a journalist, editor, and suffrage leader. She marched in the state's first major suffrage parade and became a leading researcher and writer on practices of segregation, welfare, and other social issues. In addition to all that, she lectured, acted as her husband's attorney, and raised the La Follette brood.

She knew Bob would need an enlightened insider, so she chose to study law. She immersed herself in the issues and became his most trusted adviser. When Bob La Follette died, she rejected public life; instead, she devoted herself to the *Progressive* magazine, which Bob had founded. Her own activism may be best remembered in her moving, eloquent 1913 speech to a transfixed the U.S. Senate Committee on Woman's Suffrage, during which she quoted Abraham Lincoln in asking, "Are women not people?"

BACKGROUND HISTORY

20th century, more than 50 million acres of Wisconsin and Minnesota forest had been ravaged—most of it unrecoverable. By 1920 most of the state was a cutover wasteland.

Land eroded, tracts of forest disappeared and weren't replaced, and riparian areas were destroyed with dams for "float flooding." Worse, the average size of pine trees was shrinking rapidly, and the lumber barons expressed little interest in preparing for the ultimate eradication of the forests. The small settlement of Peshtigo and more than 1,000 of its people perished in a furious conflagration made worse by logging cutover in 1871, and in the 1890s vast fires swept other central and northern counties.

Badgers began to diversify. A handful of years after the Civil War, the state kicked its wheat habit (by 1860, Wisconsin was producing more wheat than any other state in the United States) and began looking for economic diversity. Wheat was sapping the soil fertility in southern Wisconsin, forcing many early settlers to pick up stakes once again and shift to the enormous golden tracts of the western plains states. Later, when railroads and their seemingly arbitrary pricing systems began affecting potential income from wheat, farmers in Wisconsin began seriously reviewing their options. Farmers diversified into corn, cranberries, sorghum, and hops, among others. Sheep and some hogs constituted the spectrum of livestock, but within two decades, the milk cow would surpass everything else on four hooves.

Butter production initially led the new industry, since it was easier to keep than milk. But technology and industrialization, thanks in large part to the University of Wisconsin Scientific Agriculture Institute, propelled Wisconsin into milk, cheese, and other dairy-product prominence. The institute was responsible for extending the dairy season, introducing several highly productive new methods, and the groundbreaking 1890 Babcock butterfat test, a simple test of chemically separating and centrifuging milk samples to determine its quality, thereby ensuring farmers were paid based on the quality and not just the weight of the milk.

By 1880, despite less-fertile land and a shorter growing season than other agricultural states, Wisconsin ranked fourth in dairy production, thanks to university efficiency, progressive quality control, Herculean efforts in the fields, and the later organization of powerful trade exchanges. The southern half of the state, with its minerals in the southwest and rich loamy soils in the southeast, attracted European agrarian and dairy farming immigrants and speculators. "America's Dairyland" made it onto state license plates in the 1930s.

## THE PROGRESSIVE ERA

Wisconsinites have a fickle political history. Democrats held sway in the territorial days; then, in 1854, the newly formed Republican Party took the reins. The two monoliths—challenged only occasionally by upstarts such as the Grangers, the Socialists (Milwaukee consistently voted for Socialist representatives), Populists, and the Temperance movement—jockeyed for power until the end of the century.

The Progressive Party movement, formed of equal parts reformed Democrats and Republicans, was the original third-party ticket, molted from the frustrated moderates of the Wisconsin Republican Party keen on challenging the status quo. As progressivism gained steam, the citizenry of Wisconsin—tireless and shrewd salt-of-the-earth workers—eventually embraced the movement with open arms, even if the rest of the country didn't always. The Progressive movement was the first serious challenge in the U.S. political machine.

### Fightin' Bob: Legacy of Progressivism

One thing about the Wisconsin political mosaic that warrants kudos is its inveterate inability to follow categorization. Whether politically prescient or simply lacking

patience, the state has always ridden the cutting edge. These qualities are best represented physically by the original Progressive, Robert La Follette, a.k.a. "Menace to the Machine." One political writer in the early 20th century said of La Follette: "The story of Wisconsin is the story of Governor La Follette. He's the head of the state. Not many governors are that." The seminal force in Wisconsin, La Follette eschewed the pork-barrel status quo to form the Progressive Party. The La Follette family dominated state politics for two generations, fighting for social rights most people had never heard of.

## EARLY 20TH CENTURY

Robert La Follette's most infamous personal crusade was his strident opposition to U.S. participation in World War I, due equally to Wisconsin's heavily German population and La Follette's vehement pacifism. He suffered tremendous regional and national scorn and was booted to the lower echelons of politics. Interestingly, when the United States officially entered the war, Wisconsin was the first state to meet enlistment requirements. Eventually, La Follette enjoyed something of a vindication with a triumphant return to the Senate in 1924, followed by a final presidential run.

Also a political activist, Bob's wife, Belle La Follette, mounted a long-standing crusade for women's suffrage that helped the 19th Amendment get ratified; Wisconsin was the first state to ratify it. In other political trends starting around the turn of the 20th century, Milwaukee began electing Socialist administrations. Buoyed by nascent labor organizations in the huge factory towns along Lake Michigan, the movement was infused with an immigrant European populace not averse to social radicalism. Milwaukee was the country's most heavily unionized city, and it voted Socialist—at least in part—right through the 1960s. The Progressive banner was picked up by La Follette's sons, Phil and Robert Jr., and the Wisconsin Progressive Party was formed in 1934. Robert Jr. took over for his father in the U.S. Senate, and Phil dominated Wisconsin politics during the 1930s. Despite these efforts, the movement waned. Anemic and ineffective from internal splits and World War II, it melded with the Republican Party in 1946.

Dairying became Wisconsin's economic leader by 1920 and gained national prominence as well. The industry brought in nearly $210 million to the state, wholly eclipsing timber and lumber. This turned out to be a savior for the state's fortunes during the Depression; dairy products were less threatened by economic collapse than either forest appropriation or manufacturing, though farmers' management and methodology costs skyrocketed. Papermaking, in which Wisconsin is still a world leader, ameliorated the blow in the jobless cutover north- and east-central parts of the state. Concentrated fully in southeastern Wisconsin, heavy industry—leather, meatpacking, foundries, fabrication, and machine shops—suffered more acutely during the Depression. Sales receipts plummeted by two-thirds and the number of jobs fell by nearly half in five years. Brewing was as yet nonexistent.

## SINCE WORLD WAR II

Wisconsin's heavy-manufacturing cities drew waves of economic migrants to its factories after World War II, and agribusiness receipts grew despite a steady reduction in the number of farms. The state's economic fortunes were generally positive right through the mid-1980s, when the state endured its greatest recession since the catastrophic days of the Depression. Wisconsin companies were bought out by competitors in other states. In the early 1990s, agribusiness, still one of the top three Wisconsin industries, became vulnerable for the first time to California milk production.

The one industry that blossomed like no other after the war was tourism. Wisconsin politicians with foresight enacted the first sweeping environmental legislation, and resort owners instituted effective PR campaigns. By the late 1950s Wisconsin had become a full-fledged four-season vacation destination, and by the early 1990s tourism had become a $6 billion industry in the state; a cabinet-level Department of Tourism was established and regional travel centers were set up in other states.

# Government and Economy

## GOVERNMENT

Wisconsin entered the Union as the 30th state under President James K. Polk on May 29, 1848. Wisconsin has a bicameral legislative system, with a 99-member Assembly elected every two years and a 33-member Senate elected every four years. The governor wields veto power and also has a powerful weapon in the line-item veto. Wisconsin has always relished its penchant for progressive, and occasionally even radical, politics.

## ECONOMY

Wisconsin may be "America's Dairyland," but it isn't only that; the state's economic trifecta is agriculture, manufacturing, and tourism. Wisconsin is an international exporter, tallying $6 billion in receipts in 15 to 20 foreign markets. Leading exports include computers, industrial machinery, and transportation equipment.

Since 1990, the state had had one of the country's fastest-growing per capita income levels, topping $18,000, and had been one of the top 10 states for fastest-growing economies. However, since the 2008 recession, Wisconsin has failed to continue this trend. Any economic growth is tempered somewhat by the state's high income taxes.

The state has the highest percentage of the workforce nationwide in manufacturing (16 percent); manufacturing accounts for

# The Butter Battle

To demonstrate the importance of the dairy industry in Wisconsin, consider the Butter Battle, also called the Oleo Wars. Oleomargarine, or margarine, was developed in 1895, but it wasn't until 1967 that selling or buying it in Wisconsin was decriminalized. Dairy farmers initially feared that the buttery nondairy spread would ruin them; later they would march and protest for a ban on anything resembling butter that wasn't a dairy product. Of course, margarine smuggling started, and diet-conscious consumers would cross the state line into Illinois to the "margarine villages" that sprouted alongside border service stations. Butter's most partisan supporter was Gordon Roseleip, a Republican U.S. Senator from Darlington, whose rantings against margarine could occasionally overshadow Joseph McCarthy's anticommunist paranoia. But the good senator doomed the butter industry in 1965 when he agreed to take a blind taste test between butter and margarine—and chose the margarine. His family later admitted that he had been unknowingly consuming margarine for years; he was obese and his family had switched to margarine, hoping to reduce his weight.

$37.1 billion, up to 30 percent of Wisconsin's income. The industry produces small engines, metals, paper products, printing, processed food, mineral extraction equipment, electrical machinery, and transportation equipment. The paper product industry is particularly strong, number one in the nation since 1953, accounting for 12 percent of the national total, to the tune of $12.4 billion. One of every 11 jobs in the state is tied to paper.

The newest industry, economically speaking, is tourism, which really got started after World War II. The state now rakes in more than $12 billion annually.

Agriculture is the linchpin: 41 percent of the state economy remains devoted to agricultural products. The industry is worth more than $80 billion, with 25 percent of that from dairying. Interestingly, it's the fastest-growing state for organic farming (a 91 percent increase from 1997 to 2010); it ranks first nationwide in the total number of organic dairy farms and second in organic farms.

# People and Culture

## THE PEOPLE

Wisconsin's population is just over six million. With 90.1 people per square mile, the state ranks 24th nationally in population density. General population growth in the state is 3.9 percent annually, unusual because the upper Great Lakes area as a whole shows steadily declining numbers, though this decline is slowing. At the turn of the 20th century, it was the most ethnically diverse state in the Union, and most residents had family ties to Germany.

While still predominantly European American, the state has a fast-growing nonwhite population—12 percent and growing fast.

## Native Americans

Wisconsin has one of the most diverse Native American populations of any state, taking into account the number of cultures, settlement history, linguistic stock, and affiliations. The state is home to six sovereign Native American nations on 11 reservations, not all of which are demarcated by boundaries. In addition to the six nations, Wisconsin historically has been the home of the Illinois, Fox, Sauk, Miami, Kickapoo, Satee, Ottawa, and

Mascouten people. The total Native American population is around 40,000, or 1 percent of the population.

The largest native group is the **Ojibwa,** also rendered historically as Chippewa and now Ojibway, Ojibwe, and Ojibwa. Ethnologists, historians, linguists, and even community members themselves disagree on the spelling. *Ojib* means "to pucker up" and *ub-way* is "to roast," and the words together denote the nation's unique style of moccasin stitching. Wisconsin has five Ojibwa communities. The Ojibwa inhabited the northern woodlands of the upper Great Lakes, especially along Lakes Huron and Superior.

The Algonquian **Menominee** have been in Wisconsin longer than any other people. The Menominee once held sway south to Illinois, north into Michigan, and west to the Mississippi River, with a total of 10 million acres. Known as the "Wild Rice People"—the early French explorers called them "Lords of Trade"—the Menominee were divided into sky and earth groups and then subdivided into clans. Although the hegemony of the Menominee people lasted up to 10,000 years in Wisconsin, they were almost exterminated by eastern Canadian indigenous people fleeing Iroquois persecution and by pestilence imported by the Europeans. Today, the population has rebounded to around 3,500, and the Menominee reservation constitutes an entire Wisconsin county.

The Forest County **Potawatomi,** also Algonquians, are the legacy of the Native Americans that were most successful moving into Wisconsin, beginning in the 1640s. Originally inhabitants of the shores of Lake Huron, the Potawatomi people later moved to Michigan, Indiana, and places along the St. Joseph's River. The name means "People of the Fire," or, more accurately, "Keeper of the Fire," after their confederacy with the Ojibwa and Ottawa people. Potawatomi lands stretched from Chicago to Door County, and they were among the people who greeted explorer Jean Nicolet when he arrived in 1634. Wisconsin's band of Potawatomi was one of the few to survive forced relocation to Oklahoma in 1838.

Wisconsin's only Mohicans, the **Stockbridge-Munsee** people, live on a reservation bordering the Menominee. The Stockbridge (also called Mahican, meaning "wolf") originally occupied the Hudson River Valley and Massachusetts all the way to Lake Champlain. The Munsee are a branch of the Delaware people and lived near the headwaters of the Delaware River in New York, New Jersey, and Pennsylvania.

The **Oneida** belonged to the Iroquois Five Nations Confederacy, comprising the Mohawk, Oneida, Onondaga, Cayuga, and Seneca people. The Oneida, originally from New York, supported the colonists in the American Revolution but were forced out by the Mohawks and land-grabbing settlers along the Erie Canal after the war. Beginning in the 1820s, the Iroquois-speaking Oneida people merged with the Mahican, Mohegan, Pequot, Narragansett, Montauk, and other groups in Wisconsin. The Green Bay area is where most reside in Wisconsin today.

The Winnebago Nation has reverted to its original name, **Ho Chunk,** or, more accurately, **Ho Cak** (meaning "big voice" or "mother voice"), in an attempt to restore rightful cultural and linguistic heritage to the nation. Also known as Otchangara, the group is related to the Chiwere-Siouxan Iowa, Oto, and Missouri people, although their precise origin is unknown. After being forcibly relocated to Oklahoma, they returned to central Wisconsin and dared the federal government to remove them again; they're still here.

An excellent resource about Native Americans is the website of the **Great Lakes Intertribal Council** (www.glitc.org).

## European Americans

At statehood, only 10 nationalities were represented in Wisconsin; by 1950, more than 50 could be counted. The vast majority of these were European, and Wisconsin is still 88 percent Caucasian.

# Wisconsin Linguistic Primer

The source of the majority of Wisconsin place-names is illiterate and occasionally innumerate trappers and traders struggling to filter non-European words and speech through Romance and Germanic languages. Place-names generally fall into several categories: corrupted Native American words, whose origins are the most difficult to identify; practical monikers pertaining to local landforms or natural wonders; and memorials to European American "founding" fathers.

Even the origins of the word *Wisconsin* are difficult; a historical linguist has called Wisconsin's name the most cryptic of all 27 states with Native American names. As early as 1673, the missionary priest Jacques Marquette named the river, from which some say the state's name derived, Meskousing ("red stones"), perhaps because of a red coloration of the banks. "Ouisconsin" appeared on a Jesuit missionary map in 1688. But most widely accepted is the Ojibwa word for the state, *wees-kon-san,* meaning "gathering place of waters."

## WISCONSINISMS

Perhaps the most famous example of a Wisconsinism is "bubbler," for a drinking fountain. The *Dictionary of American Regional English* from the University of Wisconsin, Madison, says that the other truly Wisconsin word is "golden birthday," when your age matches the date of the month you were born: for example, if you were born on January 13, your 13th birthday is your golden birthday. Other words and phrases in common Midwestern or national usage that started in Wisconsin include "flowage" (water backed up behind a dam), "hot dish" (casserole), and "ishy" (icky).

Milwaukee colloquialisms—though some vociferously deny it—include "bumbershoot," for umbrella, and "ainah hey?" for "Isn't that so?" In other parts of the state the same phrase is rendered "inso?" You'll also hear "down by"—everything is "down by" something. "Grease yourself a piece of bread and I'll put you on a hamburger" is a Milwaukeeism if ever there was one. Wisconsinites also seem somewhat averse to liquid consonants, like the *l* in Milwaukee; it's "M'waukee" as often as not.

## HOWZAT AGAIN?

The phonology of Wisconsin English contains only one dramatic sound: the "ah," seriously emphasized and strongly run though the nasal cavity, as in "wis-KHAN-sin." Note that it's never, ever pronounced "WES-khan-sin." Check MissPronouncer.com (www.misspronouncer.com) to learn the pronunciation of the state's town names:

- **Fond du Lac**—FAHN-duh-lack
- **Green Bay**—green BAY, not GREEN bay
- **Kenosha**—kuh-NO-shuh
- **Manitowoc**—MAN-ih-tuh-wock or MAN-uh-tuh-wock
- **Muscoda**—MUSS-kuh-day
- **New Berlin/Berlin**—new BER-lin
- **Nicolet National Forest**—nick-oh-LAY (or nick-ul-ET)
- **Oconomowoc**—oh-KAHN-uh-muh-wock (or uh-KAHN-uh-muh-wock)
- **Oshkosh**—AHSH-kahsh
- **Racine**—ruh-SEEN
- **Ripon**—RIP-pin
- **Sheboygan**—shuh-BOY-gun

A decidedly **German** state, Wisconsin boasts more residents claiming Teutonic roots (54 percent) than anywhere else in the country. So thick is the German milieu of Milwaukee (34 percent) that German chancellors visit the city when they're in the United States for presidential summits. Wisconsin has more than 50,000 native speakers of German—quite remarkable for a century-old ethnic group. Germans came in three waves. The first arrived 1820-1835 from both Pennsylvania and southwestern Germany. The second wave, 1840-1860, came mostly from northwest Germany and included the legendary "48ers"—enlightened intellectuals fleeing political persecution. During this wave, as many as 215,000 Germans moved to Wisconsin each year; by 1855, fully one-third of Wisconsin's Germans had arrived. The third wave occurred after 1880 and drew emigrants mainly from Germany's northeastern region to southeastern Wisconsin, where they worked in the burgeoning factories.

The state's **French** roots can be traced back to the voyageurs, trappers, and Jesuit missionaries. They started the first settlements along the Fox and Wisconsin River Valleys. Although Wisconsin shows no strong French presence in anything other than place-names, the Two Rivers area still has an Acadian influence.

As the **British** and the French haggled and warred over all of the Wisconsin territory, many crown-friendly British Yankees did move here, populating virtually every community. The **Irish** began arriving in the late 19th century in numbers second only to the Germans. Irish influence is found in every community, especially Milwaukee's Bay View, Erin in Washington County, Ozaukee County, Adell and Parnell in Sheboygan County, and Manitowoc County.

Pockets of **Welsh** and **Cornish** are found throughout the state, the latter especially in the southwestern lead-mining region of the state. A distinct **Belgian** influence exists in Kewaunee County, where Walloon can still be heard in local taverns.

**Poles** represent the primary Eastern European ethnic group. The largest contingent is in Milwaukee, where kielbasa is as common a dietary mainstay as bratwurst. Most Poles arrived 1870-1910. At that time, Poland was not recognized as a country, so Ellis Island officials erroneously categorized many of the immigrants as Prussian, Austrian, or Russian. While 90 percent of Wisconsin's Polish immigrants moved into the cities, about 30 percent of those who arrived farmed, mostly in Portage and Trempealeau Counties; the latter is the oldest Polish settlement in the United States. **Czechs,** another large Eastern European group, live mostly in north and east-central Wisconsin, especially Kewaunee and Manitowoc Counties.

Many **Norwegians** also emigrated to the Upper Midwest, primarily Minnesota and Wisconsin. Most were economic emigrants trying to escape Norway's chronic overpopulation. Most Norwegians in Wisconsin wound up in Dane and Rock Counties. **Finnish** immigrants to the United States totaled 300,000 between 1864 and 1920, and many of these settled in the Upper Peninsula of Michigan and northern Wisconsin. **Swedes** were the smallest Scandinavian contingent, the original settlement comprising a dozen families near Waukesha.

By the turn of the 20th century, Wisconsin was home to almost 10 percent of all the **Danes** in the United States—the second-largest national contingent. Most originally settled in the northeast (the city of Denmark lies just southeast of Green Bay), but later immigrants wound up farther south. To this day, Racine is nicknamed "Kringleville" for its flaky Danish pastry.

The **Dutch** settled primarily in Milwaukee and Florence Counties beginning in the 1840s, when potato crops failed and protests flared over the Reformed Church. These southeastern counties today sport towns such as Oostburg, New Amsterdam, and Holland.

In 1846, a large contingent of **Swiss** from the Glarus canton sent emissaries to the New

World to search out a suitable immigration site. Eventually, the two scouts stumbled upon the gorgeous, lush valleys of southwestern Wisconsin. A great deal of Swiss heritage remains in Green County.

**Italians** began arriving in the 1830s—many Genoese migrated north from Illinois lead camps to fish and scavenge lead along the Mississippi River—but didn't arrive in substantial numbers until the early 1900s. Most settled in the southeast, specifically Milwaukee, Racine, and especially Kenosha.

Perhaps unique to Wisconsin is the large population of **Icelandic** immigrants, who settled on far-flung Washington Island, northeast of the Door Peninsula. It was the largest single Icelandic settlement in the United States when they arrived in 1870 to work as fishers.

### African Americans

Some theories hold African Americans first arrived in Wisconsin in 1835, in the entourage of Solomon Juneau, the founder of Milwaukee. But records from the early part of the 18th century detail black trappers, guides, and explorers. In 1791-1792, in fact, black fur traders established an encampment estimated to be near present-day Marinette. Although the Michigan Territory was ostensibly free, slavery was not uncommon. Henry Dodge, Wisconsin's first territorial governor, had slaves but freed them two years after leaving office. Other slave owners were transplanted Southerners living in the new lead-mining district of the southwest. Other early African Americans were French African immigrants who settled near Prairie du Chien in the early 19th century. Wisconsin's first African American settlement was Pleasant Spring, outside Lancaster in southwest Wisconsin; the State Historical Society's Old World Wisconsin in Eagle has an exhibit on it.

After the Civil War, the African American population increased, and most chose to live in rural, agricultural settings. Large-scale African American migration to Milwaukee,

Racine, and Kenosha took place after World War II, as northern factories revved up for the Korean War and, later, the Cold War. Today, the vast majority of Wisconsin's nearly 300,000 African Americans, around 6 percent of the state population, live in these urbanized southeastern counties. The African American population is one of the fastest growing, increasing by 25 percent per decade.

### Latinos

Wisconsin's Latino population has doubled in the last two censuses. **Puerto Ricans** began arriving in Milwaukee after World War II as blue-collar laborers. **Mexicans** represent one of the more recent immigration waves, many of them having arrived in the mid-1960s, though Mexican immigrants have been in the state since as far back as 1850. Mexicans today live mostly in southeastern Wisconsin—Milwaukee, Madison, and especially Racine.

### Asians

Wisconsin has upward of 77,000 residents of Asian descent, about 2 percent of the population. One of the fastest-growing elements, **Laotian Hmong,** began arriving during the Vietnam War and settled mostly in Appleton, Green Bay, the Fox River Valley, Manitowoc, Eau Claire, La Crosse, and pockets in southeastern Wisconsin. The state also has substantial **Chinese** and **Korean** populations.

## CULTURE
### Art Museums and Galleries

Everyone who comes here knows about Milwaukee's Santiago Calatrava-designed **Milwaukee Art Museum,** but don't forget about Racine's excellent **Racine Art Museum.** Further, there is a lot of art outside the two population centers. Essential art attractions include Sheboygan's **John Michael Kohler Arts Center,** respectable for its community-focused efforts. All of Door County is noteworthy as home to more galleries and art retreats than one would think possible in such a small place—it's even home to some of the country's oldest theatrical troupes.

## Food

Banish those visions of tuna casserole dancing in your head. Midwestern cuisine—real, original fare handed down through the generations—is more eclectic and more representative of American heritage than better-known, better-marketed cooking styles. And you'll find a whole mess of it within the pages of this book.

If you search out the latent Americana in Wisconsin cooking, you'll be amazed. Wisconsin's best cooking is a thoughtful mélange of ethnicities, stemming from the diverse populace and prairie-cooking fare that reflects a heritage of living off the land. Midwest regional cuisine is a blend of originally wild food such as cranberries, wild rice, pumpkins, blueberries, whitefish livers, catfish cheeks, and morel mushrooms incorporated into standard old-country recipes. Added to the mix are game animals such as deer, pheasant, and goose. Many Midwesterners simply shoot their own rather than raising them or buying them from a grocery wholesaler. It's a home-based culinary style, perfected from house to house through generations of adaptation.

### CHEESE

Wisconsin produces more than 500 varieties and more than one-third of the nation's cheese, leading in cheddar, colby, brick, muenster, limburger, and many Italian varieties. And yes, people here really do eat a great deal of it; Wisconsinites are loyal dairy eaters, and laws prohibiting the use of margarine remained on the books until 1967.

The most common cheese is the ever-versatile **cheddar.** For something different, eat it with fruit (apples are best) or melt it on hot apple pie. **Colby** cheese was invented in the northern Wisconsin town of the same name. It has a very mild, mellow flavor and a firm, open texture. It's most often eaten breaded and deep fried, but try cubing it in fruit or vegetable salads. Firmer, with a smooth body, **colby jack** cheese is marbled white and yellow—a mixture of the mellow colby cheese along with the distinctive broad taste of **monterey jack,** a semisoft, creamy white cheese.

Wisconsin effectively brought **swiss** cheese to prominence in the United States more than a century ago. Swiss cheese fans should head for the town of Monroe in southwestern Wisconsin, where you'll find the greatest swiss you've ever tasted, as well as a milder **baby swiss.** While there, slip into a tavern or sandwich shop and really experience Wisconsin culture by sampling a **limburger** sandwich—the pungent, oft-misunderstood swiss on pumpernickel with onions and radishes. Wisconsin may be the last place on earth where it's couth to munch limburger in polite company; it is definitely the last place in the world making the cheese.

Another Wisconsin original is **brick cheese,** a semisoft cheese with a waxy, open texture. Creamy white, young brick has a mild flavor; when aged, it becomes sharp. It's perfect for grilled cheese sandwiches or with mustard on pumpernickel bread.

Two transplants the state produces to near perfection are **gouda** and **edam** cheeses, imported by Western Europeans. They're semisoft to firm and creamy in texture, with small holes and mild, slightly nutty flavor.

Finally, for the most authentic cheese-eating cultural experience, go to a bar and order **cheese curds,** commonly breaded and deep fried. When bought at a dairy or a farmers market, cheese curds leave a distinctive squeaky feeling on the teeth and are a perfect snack food. Another unique cheese dish, especially in Green Bay, is beer cheese soup.

The **Wisconsin Milk Marketing Board** (www.eatwisconsincheese.com) is a wonderful place to peruse the "Joy of Cheese" and to request a copy of the fantastic *Traveler's Guide to America's Dairyland,* a scenic agricultural tour of the Dairy State, highlighting each cheese factory, dairy, or store that offers tours. The foodie sections are superb.

## SUPPER CLUBS

What, exactly, is a supper club? What the zocalo is to Latin Americans, the sidewalk café to Parisians, the beer garden to Bavarians, so is the supper club to Wisconsinites. Every Badger State community has one, and it's the social and culinary underpinning of Wisconsin. Indeed, although supper clubs exist in many Midwestern states, Wisconsin has far more.

Equal parts homey, casual meat-and-potatoes restaurant and local kaffeeklatsch, supper clubs traditionally have three obligatory specialties: prime rib, always on Saturday, although some serve it every day; home-style chicken; and most importantly, a Friday-night fish fry. No fish fry, no business. Most menus feature steaks in one column, seafood in the other. Regional variations buttress these basics with anything from Teutonic carnivore fare to Turkish food. This being Wisconsin, venison occasionally makes an appearance. One side dish will always be a choice of potato. If it's a true supper club, a relish tray comes out with the dinner rolls. On it you'll find everything from sliced vegetable sticks to pickles to coleslaw—and sometimes an indescribably weird "salad" concoction such as green Jell-O with shaved carrots inside.

No two supper clubs look alike (the only prerequisites are an attached bar and perhaps faux wood paneling somewhere), but all can be partially covered by clichés such as "rustic," "cozy," and "like someone's dining room." Nicer supper clubs will have crackling fireplaces; low-end joints feel more like run-down family restaurants in both decor and menu. The coolest ones have animal heads dangling above the diners; the tackiest ones feature overdone nautical decor. Wear a suit and you'll be conspicuous; jeans are perfectly acceptable. In many places—especially Madison—Badger red is de rigueur on football Saturday. Beware impostors: In recent years, "supper club" has been adopted by fancy restaurants on both coasts, but a co-opted supper club is not the real thing. If you ever see a dress code posted, you're not at a real supper club.

## A Drinking Life

I'm from Wisconsin, and I can testify that Badgers drink a lot. Alcohol is the social lubricant of the state, and many out-of-staters are a bit wide-eyed when they move here. We rank fourth nationally in per capita consumption, and 69 percent of the drinking-age population report participation in legal imbibing. Madison and surrounding Dane County have one of the highest percentages of binge drinkers in the United States, but Milwaukee actually took that crown in 2009. Wisconsin is also number one in driving under the influence. At last count, the state had more than 13,000 taverns, by far the most per capita in the country. One town of 69,000, for example, has more bars than all of Memphis.

### BEER

Wisconsinites do not drink more beer per capita than residents of any other state in the country; that's Nevada, and alas, the days of quaffing a brew with breakfast and finding a beer garden on every street corner are long gone.

Wisconsin beer-drinking began with the hordes of European immigrants. The earliest brewery has been traced back to an 1835 operation in Mineral Point, but there may have been one a few years before that, although what most early southwestern Wisconsin brewers were making was actually top-fermented malt liquor. Surprisingly, Germans did not initiate Milwaukee's legendary beer-making industry; it was a couple of upstarts from the British Isles. But massive German settlement did set the state's beer standard, which no other state could hope to match. By 1850, Milwaukee alone had almost 200 breweries, elevating beer-making to the city's number-one industry. Throughout the state, every town, once it had been platted and while waiting for incorporation, would build three things—a church, a town hall, and a brewery, not necessarily in that order.

The exact number of breweries in the state in the 19th century isn't known, but it is easily in the thousands; up to 50 years ago, local brew was still common. At that time, beer-making went through a decline; industry giants effectively killed off the regional breweries. But by the 1970s, a backlash against the swill that big brewers passed off as beer sent profits plummeting. In stepped microbreweries and brewpubs. The nation is going through a renaissance of beer crafting, and Wisconsin is no different; Madison and Milwaukee have numerous brewpubs and a few microbreweries. In other parts of the state, anachronistic old breweries are coming back to the fore, usually with the addition of a restaurant and lots of young professional patrons. Time will tell if this trend marks a permanent national shift toward traditional brews, made according to four-century-old purity laws, or if it's simply a fad.

Some local standards still exist. **Leinenkugel's,** or Leinie's, is the preferred choice of North Woods denizens, closely rivaled by **Point,** which is brewed in Stevens Point. In the southern part of the state, Monroe's Joseph Huber Brewing Company puts out the college-student-standard cheap but tasty **Huber**—the Bock is worth the wait. In Middleton, west of Madison, the **Capital Brewery** has been restored to its early-century standards.

## BRANDY

What traditionally has made a Badger a Badger, drink-wise? Brandy, of any kind. When the Wisconsin Badgers play a football game on the road, the 30,000-plus Cheeseheads who follow generally get newspaper articles written about their bratwurst, postgame polka dancing, and prodigious brandy drinking. In 1993, when the rowdy Badger faithful descended on the Rose Bowl in a friendly invasion, Los Angeles hotels ran out of brandy; by the time the Badgers returned in 1999 and again in 2000, local hoteliers had figured it out. The state has slipped to second place behind Washington DC, of all places, in per capita consumption, but Korbel still sells just under half its brandy here.

Wisconsinites are decidedly not connoisseurs of brandy; you'll never hear discussions of "smoky" versus "plump" varieties or vintages. Try to chat somebody up about cognac versus brandy in a bar and you'll probably be met with an empty stare. (Cognac is a spirit distilled from the white wine grapes of Cognac in France; brandy is a more general term for a spirit distilled from wine.)

Here's how to make Wisconsin's fave drink: Put ice cubes in a glass. Add two ounces of brandy (any kind you want), one lump of sugar, and one dash of cocktail bitters. Fill the rest of the glass with water or white soda. Top off with fruit or mushrooms.

# Essentials

# Transportation

## GETTING THERE
### Air
The major U.S. airlines have direct domestic flights into Wisconsin, but you often have to stop first in Chicago, Minneapolis, or another major hub. Ticket prices vary wildly depending on when you travel and, more important, when you buy the ticket.

Milwaukee's **General Mitchell Airport** (MKE, www.mitchellairport.com) is the only international airport in the state and has the most direct flights from around the country, including the most to and from Chicago. Green Bay's **Austin Straubel Airport** (GRB, http://flygrb.com) is another choice for access to Door County; it has daily flights to Atlanta, Chicago, Detroit, and Minneapolis.

### Bus
**Greyhound** (800/231-2222, www.greyhound. com) operates in major Wisconsin cities, but only along major interstate routes; this includes Green Bay, which means you have to rent a car to get to Door County.

### Car
The well-worn route from Chicago is I-94 north, then in Milwaukee I-43 north to Green Bay, then Highway 57 into the Door. The average travel time from Chicago is four hours. Of course, it's recommended that you hop off that mad dash and explore the regions leading to Door County described in this book.

### Water
The **SS** *Badger* (www.ssbadger.com), the only active passenger and car steamship left on the Great Lakes, runs daily in season between Manitowoc, Wisconsin, just south of Door County, and Ludington, Michigan.

Milwaukee has the high-speed **Lake Express** ferry (866/914-1010, www.lake-express.com) to Muskegon, Michigan, a nice way to avoid the congestion and white-knuckle driving on outer Chicago's interstate arteries.

## GETTING AROUND
### Highways
In *Midwest Living* magazine reader surveys, Wisconsin's roads have ranked the best in most categories, including best roads overall and best maintained. It would seem the state's 110,300 miles of roads are all in pretty good shape. Surprising, then, was the 2015 report by the US Department of Transportation calling the state's roads fourth worst. Huh? Here's the deal: Where you're going in this book, roads are fantastic (outside of one stretch of I-94 between Sheboygan and Door County, which is a thumper—the road is uneven). The vast majority of bad roads are middle-of-nowhere local roads where virtually no one lives. Best of all, in Wisconsin there are no toll roads. The stretch of I-94 running through Milwaukee is one of the nation's 10 most congested highways. The state Department of Transportation is now operating a 20-year plan to improve existing multilane highways and expand certain two-lane highways. These two-lane roads are crucial, as they constitute only 4 percent of the state's highways but carry 42 percent of the traffic.

County highways are designated by letters. You can determine the size and condition of the road in advance by the letters designating it. The roads are less important if they have more letters. So Highway RR will be narrower than Highway R, and possibly in worse repair. County roads are generally paved, but don't be surprised if they're not.

---

**Previous:** the *Island Clipper* on its way to Washington Island; biking the Sunset Trail in Peninsula State Park.

# Roadkill

Driving in Wisconsin, you will see a large number of deer as well as deer carcasses on the roadside that have been hit by cars. The area south of Door County is the most dangerous for collisions.

## DEER DISPLACEMENT

The fertile croplands and suburban gardens that replaced the state's original meadows and forests have also brought huge numbers of deer, to the point that some suburban areas ringed with rural lands have higher deer concentrations than public parklands. Some wildlife biologists now worry that the social capacity of the land, meaning the number of deer that humans can tolerate, has been maxed out in some areas. The primary cause is a lethal modern combination of an abundance of crops available for the deer to eat and refusal to allow hunting on private land, which results in no thinning of the herd. And it's not the same old divisions in this debate—some environmentalists are pro-deer hunting, as enormous deer populations destroy fragile and rare flora when feeding in winter.

## THE NUMBERS

Wisconsin has the seventh highest number of car-deer crashes in the United States. The Department of Natural Resources estimates the deer population statewide at 1.4 to 1.9 million. Annually, nearly 20,000 car-deer crashes are reported, causing 6 to 12 deaths and 400 to 700 injuries among humans; many more collisions go unreported. Statewide, deer account for more than 15 percent of car crashes since 1978, but the numbers have fallen since the mid-1990s, when deer populations exploded. In 1999, the worst year, half of all crashes involved deer. A conservative estimate of total damage, including cars and agricultural losses, is over $100 million per year. Thankfully, less than 2 percent of car-deer crashes result in human fatalities.

## AVOIDING COLLISIONS

Driving in Wisconsin, at some point you're going to meet a deer on a highway. October and November are statistically the worst months for collisions, along with high numbers in May and June as well. Crashes happen mostly after 8pm April to August; the rest of the year, they typically occur 5pm-7pm. Deer, like much wildlife, are most active around dawn and dusk, but they are active day and night. Most crashes occur on dry roads on clear days. And the old adage about them freezing in the headlights is absolutely true. The best thing you can do is pay close attention, don't speed, and keep an intelligent stopping distance between you and the next car. Use your peripheral vision, and if you see one deer, expect there to be more. If one appears, do not swerve or slam on the brakes, even if this means hitting the deer. Experts agree that braking or swerving only creates more danger for you and other motorists.

## REGULATIONS AND ETIQUETTE

Wisconsin permits radar detectors in cars. There is a mandatory motorcycle helmet law for people under age 18. All vehicle passengers are required by law to wear seatbelts. Car seats are mandatory for children under age four.

The speed limit on Wisconsin interstate highways is 70 mph, reduced to 55 mph in metropolitan areas. Milwaukee's fringes are well patrolled for speeding, so be forewarned.

Drivers in Wisconsin tend to be very courteous, to the point that some grumble about the "methodical" pace of Wisconsin traffic. The interstate arteries surrounding larger cities, especially Milwaukee, are the only places conducive to speed.

The largest issue you'll find in Door County is simply the amount of traffic, which can be pretty heavy in peak periods. While driving in Door County you should always assume that a car (or bike) will be coming around every bend.

The state Department of Transportation maintains a **road condition hotline** (800/762-3947, http://dot.wisconsin.gov/travel) detailing the conditions of all major roads across the state; it also lists construction delays. Dial 511 on your mobile phone to access it.

It's important to winterize your vehicle while driving in Wisconsin. Always keep your antifreeze level prepared for temperatures of -35°F (half water, half fluid usually suffices). Most important: Keep a full tank of gas—it helps prevent freeze-ups in the line and lets you run your car if you're stuck in a ditch.

# Recreation

"Work hard, play hard" is the ethic in Wisconsin. There's always a trail, a lake, or an activity within shouting distance. A state park lies within an hour's drive of every Wisconsin resident, a deliberate feature of the state park system; they've been dubbed the most diverse in the Midwest. A few of them—Door County's **Peninsula State Park,** for example—rival the best major state parks in the nation. Since 2000, Wisconsin's state park system has been a finalist in the national Gold Medal Parks award for the best in the country.

The **Ice Age National Scientific Reserve** highlights crucial zones of the state's 1,200-mile-long Ice Age National Scenic Trail. It begins in Door County.

State parks and forests require a **park sticker,** which you can buy daily ($8 residents, $11 nonresidents) or annually ($28 residents, $38 nonresidents). **Camping fees** in state parks ($16-30 residents, $21-35 nonresidents) vary by the location, with electricity and prime sites costing more; some primitive camping is free. Camping reservations in state parks are advisable, and a must for holiday weekends in summer; be prepared to reserve 11 months ahead of time for the most popular parks. The **Wisconsin Department of Natural Resources** (DNR, 608/266-2181, www.dnr.wi.gov) is an invaluable source of information on state lands and environmental issues. A separate entity, **ReserveAmerica** (888/947-2757, www.wisconsinstateparks.reserveamerica.com), handles reservations for

a $10 fee, and charges fees for cancellations or changes.

Wisconsin's massive multiuse trail system is also run by the Department of Natural Resources, and a **trail pass** ($5 daily, $25 annually) is required; note that some trails are not state trails but county trails, and you'll need a different pass. Also note that hikers do not need to buy a pass; only those using bicycles, horses, skis, or ATVs do.

## BIKING

*Bicycling* magazine rates Wisconsin one of the top three states for cyclists. A labyrinth of rural farm-to-market roads includes more than 10,000 miles of established, mapped, and recommended bike routes, and Door County has some beautiful roads, including rails-to-trails rides, multiuse recreation trails, and backcountry farm roads. Only the two main highways on the peninsula are less than ideal for cycling due to traffic congestion. Essentially, pick a road that isn't Highways 42 or 57, and you'll get lovely views!

Within Door County, car-less road highlights for bikers include the gorgeous **Sunset Trail** in Peninsula State Park, which passes gorgeous marsh, meadow, and forested lands—with a few scenic cliff views—and offers exactly what its name implies. Peninsula State Park also has off-road biking. For wilderness off-road biking, the trails at **Newport State Park** are sublime—all of them.

Outside of Door County proper, the loveliest views of Lake Michigan are found along the **Mariners Trail** between Manitowoc and Two Rivers.

Visitor information centers dispense excellent free cycling maps and booklets. Two helpful organizations are the **Bicycling Federation of Wisconsin** (www.bfw.org) and the **Wisconsin Off-Road Bicycling Association** (www.worba.org). **Trail passes** ($5 daily, $25 annually) are required for cyclists age 16 and over.

# HIKING

The **Ice Age National Scenic Trail** is an only-in-Wisconsin hiking experience that begins in Door County's Potawatomi State Park. Another wonderful segment is found in the **Kettle Moraine State Forest-Northern Unit** in East Central Wisconsin.

In **Potawatomi State Park,** the Ice Age National Scenic Trail's initial miles are linked with the Tower Trail, which takes in superb bluff views, variegated forest sections, and leisurely beach strolls. In **Whitefish Dunes State Park,** the Red Trail offers grand sand dune experiences, while the Black Trail connects to gorgeous sea caves. The myriad trails at **Peninsula State Park** include scrambling along bluffs on the Eagle Trail. You simply cannot go wrong with any trail at **Newport State Park** and its designated wilderness hiking trails, but step for step the views of the Europe Bay Trail are likely the best. Requiring two ferry rides, the isolated Thordarson Loop Trail of **Rock Island State Park** captures all the highlights and stunning views.

Not within a state park, the **Ridges Sanctuary** near Baileys Harbor is a private biotic reserve that harbors loads of unique and/or threatened species.

# FISHING

Wisconsin ranks in the top five states nationwide for the number of fishing licenses sold annually. Door County is legendary for **smallmouth bass** in addition to **Great Lakes fishing,** which has grown into an enormous industry with entire fleets devoted to working the well-stocked waters. Not all the fish in the Great Lakes are native species. Restocking began in response to early-20th-century overfishing and the decline of fish stocks due to exotic species, and now the state Department of Natural Resources stocks more than 2.1 million coho and chinook salmon, 1 million lake trout, and 2 million brook, brown, and steelhead trout. Kewaunee-Algoma and all of the Door Peninsula are popular fishing areas and include some record takes.

A time-honored tradition of Wisconsin winters is driving the truck out on a frozen lake to a village of shanties erected over holes drilled in the ice, sitting on an overturned five-gallon pail, stamping your feet quite a bit, and drinking a lot of schnapps. **Ice fishing** is serious business: Up to two million angler-days are spent on the ice each year, and ice fishing accounts for up to one-fifth of the state's annual catch.

For information on fishing licenses and regulations, contact the **Wisconsin Department of Natural Resources** (877/945-4236, http://dnr.wi.gov).

# HUNTING

Hunting, like fishing, is a well-established business in Wisconsin, but it's more a local pursuit than one visitors come for. (And not many out-of-towners, honestly, come to Door County for it.) The nine-day deer season generates $250 million for state coffers. Hunters are often conservation-oriented, and many species owe their continued existence to hunting and conservation groups.

Hunting for **deer** is a rite of passage in the state. Other popular hunts include **goose, duck, pheasant,** and **ruffed grouse.**

# SKIING

Forget downhill skiing if you've ever been to the Rockies, but cross-country ski buffs can indulge in gorgeous skiing throughout the region at virtually any county or state park. **Peninsula State Park** has the most popular ski trails (and a warming house), but **Newport State Park** has the most trails, which are all quiet and isolated.

## SNOWMOBILING

Snowmobiling is a big deal here. In some communities, snowmobiling accounts for more business than fishing. Some cities have passed ordinances giving snowmobiles rights similar to those of cars on city streets. Restaurants and nightspots often list their addresses according to the snowmobile route you'll find them on. It's less popular in Door County than in other parts of the state, but the county has 250 miles of snowmobile trails to explore. Check out http://map.co.door.wi.us for a map and links to snowmobile clubs.

## CANOEING AND KAYAKING

Kayakers enjoy the magnificence of Door County from the Green Bay side (quieter and calmer) and the Lake Michigan side (think sea, not lake). Overall, 250 miles of Great Lake coastline await. Every single town in Door County has kayaking options. The must-do for kayakers is to visit **Cave Point County Park,** most easily visited via next-door Whitefish Dunes State Park. Also worthy are **clear-bottomed kayak tours,** most commonly done in Baileys Harbor.

Never take a canoe on Lake Michigan, no matter what you see locals doing. For safe

canoeing, a good option is **Kangaroo Lake** near Baileys Harbor.

## GOLF

Among the courses most often pursued in this book are **Blackwolf Run** in Kohler and, to a lesser extent, the wonderful golf course in at **Peninsula State Park.**

## CAMPING

Some of the best and most popular camping in Wisconsin is in Door County at four of its five state parks: **Potawatomi, Peninsula, Newport,** and **Rock Island.** Whitefish Dunes State Park has no camping. Potawatomi and Peninsula attract the majority of campers; Peninsula State Park is more visited than Yellowstone National Park. Newport State Park is for solitude as it has only hike-in, bike-in, and paddle-in campsites. Rock Island is superbly isolated since it requires two ferry rides, allows no vehicles (not even bikes), and has no pesky critters to mess with your food at night.

**Reservations** (888/947-2757, http://wisconsinstateparks.reserveamerica.com, additional $10 fee) are taken at all of the above parks. You can reserve up to 11 months in advance, and it's necessary for summer

ESSENTIALS
RECREATION

kayaks at Rock Island State Park

weekends and especially holidays. No waiting lists are kept. A vehicle admission sticker ($11 daily, $38 annual for nonresidents) is necessary at Peninsula, Potawatomi, and Newport State Parks but not Rock Island State Park. Rates for nonresidents are Potwatomi, $23-33 without or with electricity; Peninsula, $25-35, depending on electricity and water view; and Newport, $25.

Should the state parks be full, a recommended private campground is the well-run **Rowleys Bay Resort** in Rowleys Bay.

# Information and Services

## VISITOR INFORMATION

The **Door County Visitors Bureau** (1015 Green Bay Rd., Sturgeon Bay, 800/527-3529, doorcounty.com) is the place to go for visitor information; http://doorcountynavigator.com is useful as well.

For information on anything and everything in the state, contact the **Wisconsin Department of Tourism** (800/432-8747, www.travelwisconsin.com), which has a good website and offers fantastic printed guides.

Few websites are overly helpful, but for culture, arts, and history try **PortalWisconsin. org** (http://portalwisconsin.org); an interesting idiosyncratic site is **Wisconsin Online** (www.wisconline.com).

### Media

The only publication that covers Wisconsin on a macro scale, with Door County as a highlight, is the online magazine **Wisconsin Trails** (www.wisconsintrails.com), with a nice balance of road warrior and nostalgia. It dispenses with the political and social and just focuses on where and when to go, providing lots of good cultural bits and stunning photography. **Midwest Living** magazine, another monthly, regularly features Door County.

### LGBT Resources

In 2012 the Door County Chamber of Commerce and its visitors bureau began a campaign to attract LGBT travelers. One very new Door County-specific resource to help is www.lgbtdoorcounty.com. Milwaukee's **LGBT Community Center** (www.mkelgbt.org) can provide visitor information for that city.

### Maps

You can get a decent Department of Transportation state road map free by calling the state **Department of Tourism hotline** (800/432-8747). The best maps for exploring Door County and the rest of the state are in the *Wisconsin Atlas and Gazetteer,* available from any outdoors store and even local supermarkets.

## MONEY

Wisconsinites are highly taxed, but in general travelers don't have to share the burden; the state doesn't even have toll roads. Prices in general are lower in Wisconsin than in the rest of the country, and gasoline is usually cheaper than anywhere else in the Midwest except Iowa. Once you get out into rural areas, prices for goods and services are absolutely cheap—except in Door County, which is pricier because of its popularity.

Wisconsin's sales tax is 5 percent. Door County tacks on an additional 0.5 percent. There are also additional hotel room taxes.

Credit cards are widely accepted, although not universally.

## COMMUNICATIONS
### Telephone

Door County and East-Central Wisconsin are in area code 920. Milwaukee is 414, and southeastern Wisconsin is 262.

### Internet Access

Public libraries generally have computers available with Internet access. Coffee shops mostly offer wireless access if you have your

# Travel Green Wisconsin

In 2007, in a U.S. first, Wisconsin launched its **Travel Green** (www. travelgreenwisconsin.com) program, designed to highlight businesses, lodgings, and attractions for their efforts to reduce the environmental impact of tourism and to highlight the fact that this can be done. Find hybrid car rentals, restaurants that follow sustainability protocols, and more.

own computer, and some accommodations also offer wireless access, but don't absolutely count on it.

# WEIGHTS AND MEASURES
## Voltage

Electrical outlets in the United States run on a 110-120 volts AC at 60 hertz. Most plugs are either two flat prongs or two flat plus one round. Transformers and adapters for 220-volt appliances are available in hardware and electronics stores.

## The Metric System

Let's just say metric doesn't come up a whole lot in Wisconsin. Overseas visitors can refer to the U.S.-Metric Conversion Table in the back of this guide for help with distances, speed limits, and temperature conversions.

## Time Zones

Wisconsin is in the central time zone, which is six hours earlier than Greenwich mean time in winter, and five hours earlier than Greenwich mean time when daylight savings time is in effect (Mar.-Oct.). if you travel into Michigan, including the Upper Peninsula, you enter the eastern time zone, which is one hour later than central time year-round.

# Resources

## Suggested Reading

Few of the pan-Wisconsin books cover much of Door County, but those listed below all have material on the regions covered by this book.

If Wisconsin has a poet laureate, it would be the late Norbert Blei, a curmudgeonly pleasant wordsmith who worked in a former chicken coop. He wrote 17 books, mostly about Door County, but he is most famous for his 1992 article titled "Shut the Damn Door" decrying tourism in his beloved county.

### DESCRIPTION AND TRAVEL

Lyons, John J., ed. *Wisconsin: A Guide to the Badger State.* American Guide Series, Works Projects Administration, 1941. From the mother of all guidebook series, the Wisconsin edition, nearly seven decades old, is still the standard for anyone interested in the history, natural history, and culture of the state.

Ostergren, Robert C., and Thomas R. Vale, eds. *Wisconsin Land and Life.* Madison: University of Wisconsin Press, 1997. This heavy but eminently readable book is a perfect synthesis of natural history and cultural geography.

### OUTDOORS AND ENVIRONMENT

Leopold, Aldo. *A Sand County Almanac.* New York: Oxford University Press, 1949. A must-read for anyone who is attuned to the land. Also an education for those who think Wisconsin is a vast nothingness.

### HISTORY

McAnn, D. *The Wisconsin Story: 150 Years, 150 Stories.* Milwaukee: *Milwaukee Journal Sentinel,* 1998. Most articles are about historical minutiae most folks have never heard about but are fascinating addenda to general history. It's engaging and a good bet for an easy vacation read.

Nesbit, Robert. *Wisconsin: A History.* Madison: University of Wisconsin Press, 1989. A standard reading of the state's history.

### FOLKLORE

Leary, J. *Wisconsin Folklore.* Madison: University of Wisconsin Press, 1998. Linguistics, storytelling, music, song, dance, folk crafts, and material traditions. The chapter on Milwaukeeisms alone is worth the cost of the book. Even the Smithsonian has recognized the uniqueness of this volume.

### NATURAL HISTORY

Martin, Lawrence. *The Physical Geography of Wisconsin.* Madison: University of Wisconsin Press, 1965. The granddaddy of all Wisconsin geography books, first published in 1916 and updated in subsequent editions.

Reuss, Henry S. *On the Trail of the Ice Age.* Sheboygan, WI: Ice Age Park and Trail Foundation, 1990. A good compendium of the oddball geology of the state and the effort to establish the Ice Age National Scenic Trail.

## PEOPLE

The state historical society has produced brief booklets profiling every immigrant group in Wisconsin; they're available from the **Wisconsin Historical Society** (www. wisconsinhistory.org).

Bieder, Robert E. *Native American Communities in Wisconsin, 1600-1960*. Madison: University of Wisconsin Press, 1995. The first and, really, only comprehensive in-depth look at Native Americans in the state.

Maxwell, R. S. *La Follette and the Rise of the Progressives in Wisconsin*. Madison: State Historical Society, 1956. A fine account of Robert La Follette, the much-beloved Progressive Party politician of the late 1800s and early 1900s.

McBride, G. *On Wisconsin Women*. Madison: University of Wisconsin Press, 1993. An excellent book and one of few sources about many of the important women in the state's history.

Meine, C. *Aldo Leopold: His Life and Work*. Madison: University of Wisconsin Press, 1988. The best book on ecologist Aldo Leopold.

## LITERATURE

Boudreau, Richard, ed. *The Literary Heritage of Wisconsin: An Anthology of Wisconsin Literature from Beginnings to 1925*. La Crosse, WI: Juniper Press, 1986. This is a condensed version of the state's literary canon.

Perry, Michael. *Population: 485*. New York: Harper Perennial, 2002; *Truck: A Love Story*. New York: Harper Perennial, 2006; and *Coop*. New York: HarperCollins, 2009. Wisconsin has had a few luminaries of literature—Jane Hamilton, Kelly Cherry, Lorrie Moore—but Perry describes small-town Wisconsin in a wonderfully low-key, hilarious way.

Stephens, Jim, ed. *The Journey Home: The Literature of Wisconsin through Four Centuries*. Madison: North Country Press, 1989. A remarkable multivolume set of Wisconsin literature, tracing back as far as the trickster cycles of the first inhabitants.

## CUISINE

Recently more cookbooks have detailed Midwestern cuisine. Any bookstore will have selection on Midwestern regional cooking.

Allen, Terese, and Harva Hachten. *The Flavor of Wisconsin*. Madison: State Historical Society of Wisconsin, 2009. A dense volume cataloging all the ethnic groups of the state and their contributions to cuisine. Terese Allen is one of Wisconsin's most noted food writers, so look for her name; she updated Harva Hachten's legendary book.

# Internet Resources

## DOOR COUNTY
**Door County Wisconsin**
**www.doorcounty.com**
The official county tourism site; an excellent resource.

**Door County Navigator**
**www.doorcountynavigator.com**
As much a sounding board as a source of information, which means it's got lots of local ideas.

## SHOPPING
**Sconnie Nation**
**www.sconnie.com**
An online company that sells all sorts of apparel with "Sconnie" (meaning "Wisconsinite") written on it; there is a hilarious section on what it means to be a "Sconnie." You can spend hours perusing the videos submitted by proud Badgers, including a tractor square dance.

## TRAVEL
**Travel Wisconsin**
**www.travelwisconsin.com**
From the state's Department of Tourism, it's very useful and worth a look.

**Wisconsin Association of Convention and Visitors Bureaus (WACVB)**
**www.escapetowisconsin.com**
A good starting point for local information sources.

**Wisconsin Online**
**www.wisconline.com**
It doesn't have everything about the state, but it has a lot of it.

## STATE PARKS
**Wisconsin Department of Natural Resources**
**www.wiparks.net**

A good resource from the Department of Natural Resources; it also covers state trails.

## RECREATION
**Wisconsin Bicycling Federation**
**www.bfw.org**
An educational and advocacy group working strenuously for cyclist rights, more trails, and bike lanes in the cities. They have excellent cycling maps for sale.

**Wisconsin Off-Road Bicycling Association**
**www.worba.org**
Check out the expanding list of downloadable trail maps.

## ARTS AND CULTURE
**Portal Wisconsin**
**www.portalwisconsin.org**
A fantastic resource for all visual and performance arts in the state.

**Wisconsin Arts Board**
**www.arts.state.wi.us**
The website of the Wisconsin Arts Board has great sections on art fairs, galleries, and art museums.

## HISTORY
**State Historical Society of Wisconsin**
**www.wisconsinhistory.org**
The best starting place for learning about the state's history.

## ACCOMMODATIONS
**Wisconsin Bed-and-Breakfast Association**
**www.wbba.org**
Stay in small-scale lodgings to experience Wisconsin close up.

## Wisconsin Lodging
**www.wisconsinlodging.org**
The site has photos and information on lodging options around the state.

# FOOD
**Wisconsin Agricultural Marketing Board**
**www.eatwisconsincheese.com**
A great place to find resources on seeing, tasting, and buying cheese and other dairy products.

**Wisconsin Cooks**
**www.wisconsincooks.org**
A fun guide run by Wisconsin foodies, it has a good list of food-centric events and some recipes.

## Wisconsin Food Talk
**www.wisfoodtalk.com**
Foodies unite here and give their opinions and recipes and describe eateries in Wisconsin.

**Farm Fresh Atlas**
**www.farmfreshatlas.org**
Find out where you can purchase and eat Wisconsin-sourced products.

# TRANSPORTATION AND ROAD TRIPS
**Wisconsin Department of Transportation**
**www.dot.wisconsin.gov**
The state's Department of Transportation website has all the necessary information on construction, road conditions, and more. Check out its "Rustic Roads" section for fantastic country drives.

# Index

# List of Maps

# Photo Credits

# Also Available

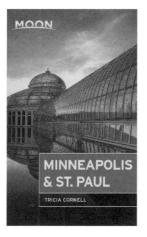

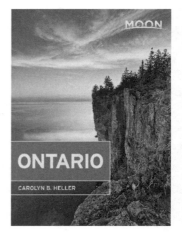

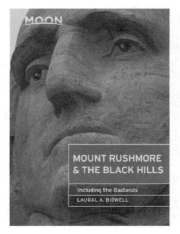

# MAP SYMBOLS

| | | | | | | | |
|---|---|---|---|---|---|---|---|
| ▦▦▦ | Expressway | ★ | Highlight | ✗ | Airfield | ⚲ | Golf Course |
| ▬▬▬ | Primary Road | ○ | City/Town | ✖ | Airport | P | Parking Area |
| ▬▬▬ | Secondary Road | ◉ | State Capital | ▲ | Mountain | ⬟ | Archaeological Site |
| ▪ ▪ ▪ ▪ | Unpaved Road | ⊛ | National Capital | ✛ | Unique Natural Feature | ⚱ | Church |
| - - - - | Trail | ★ | Point of Interest | | | ⛽ | Gas Station |
| ·········· | Ferry | ● | Accommodation | 〲 | Waterfall | ◌ | Glacier |
| ▬·▬·▬ | Railroad | ▼ | Restaurant/Bar | ▲ | Park | ▨ | Mangrove |
| ▦▦▦ | Pedestrian Walkway | ■ | Other Location | ⓣ | Trailhead | ▨ | Reef |
| ▥▥▥▥ | Stairs | ⋀ | Campground | ⛷ | Skiing Area | ▨ | Swamp |

# CONVERSION TABLES

°C = (°F - 32) / 1.8
°F = (°C x 1.8) + 32
1 inch = 2.54 centimeters (cm)
1 foot = 0.304 meters (m)
1 yard = 0.914 meters
1 mile = 1.6093 kilometers (km)
1 km = 0.6214 miles
1 fathom = 1.8288 m
1 chain = 20.1168 m
1 furlong = 201.168 m
1 acre = 0.4047 hectares
1 sq km = 100 hectares
1 sq mile = 2.59 square km
1 ounce = 28.35 grams
1 pound = 0.4536 kilograms
1 short ton = 0.90718 metric ton
1 short ton = 2,000 pounds
1 long ton = 1.016 metric tons
1 long ton = 2,240 pounds
1 metric ton = 1,000 kilograms
1 quart = 0.94635 liters
1 US gallon = 3.7854 liters
1 Imperial gallon = 4.5459 liters
1 nautical mile = 1.852 km

°FAHRENHEIT / °CELSIUS

| °FAHRENHEIT | °CELSIUS | |
|---|---|---|
| 230 | 110 | |
| 220 | 100 | WATER BOILS |
| 210 | | |
| 200 | 90 | |
| 190 | 80 | |
| 180 | | |
| 170 | 70 | |
| 160 | | |
| 150 | 60 | |
| 140 | | |
| 130 | 50 | |
| 120 | | |
| 110 | 40 | |
| 100 | | |
| 90 | 30 | |
| 80 | | |
| 70 | 20 | |
| 60 | | |
| 50 | 10 | |
| 40 | | |
| 30 | 0 | WATER FREEZES |
| 20 | | |
| 10 | -10 | |
| 0 | | |
| -10 | -20 | |
| -20 | -30 | |
| -30 | | |
| -40 | -40 | |

Clock:
12 / 24
11 / 23
10 / 22
9 / 21
8 / 20
7 / 19
6 / 18
5 / 17
4 / 16
3 / 15
2 / 14
1 / 13

INCH 0 1 2 3 4

CM 0 1 2 3 4 5 6 7 8 9 10

**MOON WISCONSIN'S DOOR COUNTY**
Avalon Travel
An imprint of Perseus Books
A Hachette Book Group company
1700 Fourth Street
Berkeley, CA 94710, USA
www.moon.com

Editor: Rachel Feldman
Series Manager: Kathryn Ettinger
Copy Editor: Christopher Church
Production Designer: Sarah Wildfang
Cover Design: Faceout Studios, Charles Brock
Interior Design: Domini Dragoone
Moon Logo: Tim McGrath
Map Editor: Kat Bennett
Cartographers: Stephanie Poulain, Brain Shotwell, and Kat Bennett
Indexer: Greg Jewett

ISBN-13: 978-1-63121-431-8
ISSN: 2332-0176

Printing History
1st Edition — 2014
2nd Edition — May 2017
5 4 3 2 1

Text © 2017 by Thomas Huhti.
Maps © 2017 by Avalon Travel.
All rights reserved.

Some photos and illustrations are used by permission and are the property of the original copyright owners.

Front cover photo: Chuck Eckert / Alamy Stock Photo
Back cover photo: © Jon Jarosh/ Door County Visitor Bureau

Printed in Canada by Friesens